VIOLENCE
& SOCIETY

LARRY RAY

VIOLENCE & SOCIETY

Los Angeles | London | New Delhi
Singapore | Washington DC

© Larry Ray 2011

First published 2011
Reprinted 2012

SAGE Publications Ltd
1 Oliver's Yard
55 City Road
London EC1Y 1SP

SAGE Publications Inc.
2455 Teller Road
Thousand Oaks, California 91320

SAGE Publications India Pvt Ltd
B 1/I 1 Mohan Cooperative Industrial Area
Mathura Road
New Delhi 110 044

SAGE Publications Asia-Pacific Pte Ltd
3 Church Street
#10-04 Samsung Hub
Singapore 049483

Library of Congress Control Number: 2010935084

British Library Cataloguing in Publication data

A catalogue record for this book is available from the British Library

ISBN 978-1-84787-035-3
ISBN 978-1-84787-036-0 (pbk)

Typeset by C&M Digitals (P) Ltd, Chennai, India
Printed by MPG Books Group, Bodmin, Cornwall
Printed on paper from sustainable resources

MIX
Paper from
responsible sources
FSC® C018575

For Emma

CONTENTS

LIST OF FIGURES

ABOUT THE AUTHOR

 Larry Ray has been Professor of Sociology at the University of Kent, UK, since 1998 and is Sub-Dean of the Faculty of Social Sciences. His research and publications extend across social theory, globalization, post-communism, ethnonational conflict, music and cultural memory, and the sociology of violence. Recent publications include *Theorizing Classical Sociology* (Open University Press, 1999), *Key Contemporary Social Theorists* (co-edited with Anthony Elliott, Blackwell, 2002), *Social Theory and Postcommunism* (with William Outhwaite, Blackwell, 2005), and *Globalization and Everyday Life* (Routledge, 2007). In addition he is currently working on social memory and Jewish cultural and musical revivals and is President Elect of the British Association of Jewish Studies. He is also a member of the Academy of Social Sciences.

ACKNOWLEDGEMENTS

The strands of research and teaching that led eventually to this book began through participation in the ESRC's Violence Research Programme (VRP) and in particular collaboration with David Smith on a project on Racial Violence in Greater Manchester. The several VRP symposia organized by Elizabeth Stanko stimulated broad reflection on the nature of violence and the participants in these have also influenced the analysis here. Thanks are further due to people who have commented on or in some way contributed to the development of this book – Susan Bachelor, John Brewer, Randall Collins, Martin Daly, Eric Dunning, Paul Iganski, Joanne Lawrence, Lynn Prince-Cooke, John Robb, David Schneider and Anthony Ward. Finally, thanks to Vikki for remembering.

INTRODUCTION

Only when you get into violence and its logic can you see the heart of darkness at the centre of ... civilization. (Gilligan 2000: 259)

This book develops a broad sociological and theoretical engagement with violence in different contexts, including violence perpetrated between individuals, by states and through unequal social structures. It further takes a long view of historical and contemporary violence in society and aims to offer an approach that crosses some traditional divisions in this area. My thinking about violence arose in part from working on post-communist transformations and particularly the ethno-nationalist civil wars in the former Yugoslavia. Whatever the multiple socioeconomic conditions for this violence, it was also apparent that these conflicts had profound roots in the ritual and local politics of memory that had the capacity to elicit often extreme violence. Alongside this work, I was co-researcher with David Smith on a project on racial violence, which was part of the ESRC's Violence Research Programme.[1] This project developed over the years into work on hate crime in the UK and elsewhere in Europe with several public bodies, especially the National Probation Service and (as it then was) the Race Relations Commission. During this time my thinking about violence was assisted by the regular meetings of researchers from across the Violence Research Programme organized by the programme coordinator, Elizabeth Stanko. These enabled us to consider many issues, including theorizing violence, power, gender and history from different points of view and intellectual traditions. The way in which racially motivated offenders talked about their communities and frustrations further pointed to the importance of Thomas Scheff's work on the shame/rage spiral, which also informs the analysis here.

Considering further the sociologically informed analysis of violence, it was apparent that while there are many thorough analyses of specific types of violence, these did not have central significance in sociological theory. There are two notable exceptions to this – the work of Norbert Elias and those working within his paradigm, if that is the appropriate term, and the rather different approach of Randall Collins, both of whose work is addressed in this book. There is an ongoing debate with Elias in these chapters, and in particular with

---

[1] 'Racial violence in Greater Manchester' (with David Smith and Liz Wastell, Lancaster University) funded under the ESRC's Violence Research Programme, 1998–2000.

his classical concept of the civilizing process. Although the analysis of violence was not his primary purpose, his thesis has become is an important attempt to place violence within an understanding of the historical emergence of modern social processes. However, this is not a book about Elias and will not address the full corpus of his work, much of which deals with other topics. Further, at various points I will formulate his theory somewhat more concretely than some of his adherents might approve. This is because if a theory is to guide our understanding of the social then it needs to be expressed clearly and define what it will and will not permit, which Elias did not always do. There are, of course, many other theoretical influences in this study, one of which is René Girard's concept of the sacrificial scapegoat mechanism, which while highly speculative, nonetheless opens up reflection on the significance of violence for the very constitution of the social. In order to survive in shared space, people have to find ways of containing destructive impulses and forging sustained bonds of solidarity. But Girard's theory, which places violence at the heart of the social, adds a profound warning to those who would make an overly simple distinction between peaceful sociality and violent destructiveness. Some of the epic stories of antiquity are tales of rape, jealousy, fratricide and torture, and it is telling that the next event in the Bible after the Fall from Eden is the murder of Abel by his brother Cain. Myths such as this are representations of the destructive passions of desire and humiliation. As Gilligan (2004) points out, 'the Bible makes it very clear why Cain kills Abel: "The Lord had respect unto Abel and to his offering: But unto Cain... he had not respect". In other words, God "dis'ed Cain!" who acted out his anger by killing'. The social conditions for shame-rage will be explored in the analyses here.

A fragmented view of violence that is broken down into specific sub-fields risks losing sight of the intimate connection between violence and the human condition, which this book attempts to address by providing a more integrated sociological approach. Not only has the study of violence been extensively fragmented into specific clusters, but it has also been generally absent from sociological theory as a topic of reflection (at least until recently) in its own right.[2] It appears in social theory of course but largely subsumed within a broader discussion – such as Weber's discussions of violence in relation to the state and legitimacy. On the whole, sociology seems to have assumed the existence of a pacified society in which violence appears in specific places and events – notably armed conflicts, civil disturbances and violent crime. By contrast, there is literature on specific types of violence that either treats these as discrete or generalizes to all types of violence. For example, domestic violence research has drawn attention to the presence of violence in the routine everyday

---

[2]It is possible this is changing with the recent work of Malešević (2010), Wieviorka (2009), Schinkel (2010) and Žižek (2008).

settings of the private sphere and the dynamics of power and patriarchy in intimate relations. Further, domestic violence illustrates how violence can permeate the everyday in a routine way, in extreme situations of civic conflict and in fantasies replayed through popular culture. It is a slippery concept that permeates the unstable divisions between public and private, legitimate and illegitimate, individual and collective. This book aims to address specific instances of violence while understanding the wider historical, cultural and political roles of violence in society.

Violence presents a paradox. Many writers, but particularly anthropologists (e.g., Abbink 2000: xi), note that violence is a human universal and interpersonal aggression, physical threat, assault, homicide and armed conflict seem to have existed in all known human societies. At the same time, and writing mostly from the standpoint of relatively peaceful social spaces, violence often appears as exceptional, external and threatening us from without. But it is not 'without' – it is embedded in the social fabric in manifold ways. This has been understood by epic writers and storytellers, and one can seek an understanding of the motivational dynamics of violence and desire through classics such as Homer, the Bible, Shakespeare and Dostoyevsky. Violence is in the public and intimate realms and is bound up with everyday lives in complex ways. Despite growing thresholds of repugnance towards violence that accompanied the development of modernity (as Elias persuasively argued), we also live in a universe of commercialized violent representations and voyeuristic violence through digital communication. Particularly in the two decades following Elias's death, a culture of reserve arguably gave way to a hedonistic culture of consumerism freed from restraints – so images of war, death and suffering are consumed as representations of everyday life, which Tom Wolfe (1976) described as 'pornoviolence'. How does the release from restraint through these visual fantasies interplay with 'real' violence? This will be discussed with reference to masculinities and violence in Chapter 5.

This is a study of violence from a sociological standpoint although it draws upon and aims to engage with a range of other disciplines. It is also informed by the growing influence of biosocial analysis, with which sociologists have generally avoided engagement. Such engagement, though, should not necessarily be the predictable riposte to non-social explanation, but could rather bring to bear on these debates the insights of sociological analysis. We should all be cautious about rejecting a priori the data and theories developed in other disciplines and might aim to pursue more constructive engagements. Fears that the expanding knowledge of the genome would lead to the replacement of social solutions by genetic engineering have by and large not been realized. Rather, according to Lemke (2004), the social power of genetic information 'lies less in the resurrection of genetic determinism and more in the construction of genetic risks'. Genetics he says seeks 'probabilities, possibilities and expectations, referring less to a model of determination than to the mode of dispositions'. This opens the field for more constructive engagement with sociological theories and imagination. I should say that this is not a central theme in this book, but my view that it is important to develop an interdisciplinary view of human aggression and violence explains certain choices made here. In particular the inclusion in Chapter 2 of an extensive discussion of debates about prehistoric violence which raises a host of biosocial, psychological and sociological issues. Debates about the extent of violence in human prehistory are linked to a centuries-old search for 'original' human nature. Many believe that studies of causes of premature death in the distant past might shed light on this debate. In a field traditionally and unsurprisingly dominated by paleo-archaeologists, there is an emerging debate that incorporates highly technical analysis of skeletal remains with broader sociological and historical questions about violence and culture (for example, in Robb 1997). This is again a debate with which sociologists could productively engage.

Further, as a study of violence this will engage with criminological literature, although its scope is broader than this. Most crimes are not violent (they are property crimes) and most violence is not necessarily criminal – for example, deaths from suicides, carelessness, warfare and structural violence. However, detailed and systematic use of criminological theories and data is a core aspiration of this work, especially since many sociological debates have proceeded without reference to it. Many criminological theories are not specifically theories of violence though, but of offending in general, and this will be highlighted in various discussions. It is also true that theories of illicit behaviour do not necessarily account for the violence performed by 'legitimate' actors such as agents of the state. Collins (2008) offers a situational approach to understanding violent incidents that intentionally plays down macrosocial dispositional factors (social class, social structure, ethnicity, inequality, etc.) in favour of understanding the interaction rituals that enable violent incidents to occur. The result is that he presents a highly focused study of the interpersonal dynamics of many different types of violence. But the analytical level adopted needs to be a response to the kinds of questions we ask. If we want to know how a violent confrontation occurs here, now, and not in some other place and time, then situational analysis is crucial. We need to know the precise chain of interactions and verbal and non-verbal cues that precipitate the tipping of a confrontation, argument, street robbery or whatever into violence. But violence, like any other social event, has distinct patterning in time and space. If one looks at the location of homicides in a city over time, for example, it is very likely that these will be concentrated in certain locations more than others over long periods of time. What is it about the social structuring of these localities that generates this pattern? Homicide rates further (I argue) demonstrate distinct patterning in relation to other social indicators – notably of inequality. The task is then to draw upon both sociological and criminological theories to develop theoretical accounts of the underlying processes that give rise to these phenomena.

The book is organized around a number of themes that are set out in the early chapters – the nature and 'causes' of violence (Chapter 1), cultural contexts for violence within human social evolution (Chapter 2), Elias's civilizational thesis (Chapter 3), the spatial distribution of violence and the relationships between space, social organization and vulnerability to violence (Chapter 4) and masculinities and gender (Chapters 5 and 6). The intersection of dynamics of shame, vulnerability and violence are developed within a view of dominant organizational trends in modern societies. Space is understood as an intersection of socioeconomic processes, architecture and behaviour that shape patterns of risk. The relationships between masculinity, power and violence are then explored through an examination of the domestic violence literature and debates, where I argue that the relationships between power and violence are complex and need to be understood thorough the dynamics of vulnerability and attachment. Themes of civilizational process, masculinity, space and the ways these interact with socioeconomic structures are then developed with reference to homicide and its explanations (Chapter 7). The discussion then moves to issues of race, collective violence and the debates about 'hate crime' (Chapter 8) which are again cast within a theory of the intersection of macro and interpersonal processes. This discussion leads into a final consideration of the Holocaust, genocide and state violence (Chapter 9). The capacity of the modern state for violence, and especially for genocide, constitutes a powerful challenge not only to the implicit optimism of Elias's civilizational thesis, but also to the claim that the modern controlled personality is less likely than those of earlier times to engage in violence. This discussion considers Bauman's argument that it is precisely the controlled and distanced personality that underlies the modern capacity to perpetrate genocide. However, the diversity and complexity of violence evades a single frame of reference and this book aims to weave together theories and perspectives that understand the relationship between violence and fundamental features of human sociality. Some key propositions are that violence is induced by shame, humiliation and cultures of masculine honour; the conditions for this are closely linked to socioeconomic inequalities in combination with a cultural ethos of informality and equalization; violence is spatially distributed in ways that coincide with the spatial structuring of global capital.

1

WHAT IS VIOLENCE?

The social context for both the performance and understanding of violence is of central importance. One often hears the term 'senseless violence', in cases where a serious violent incident was apparently unprovoked or has arisen from 'insignificant' insults or altercation. The notion of 'senseless' violence is, by implication, contrasted to some other 'reasonable' kind, or perhaps suggests that what we find repugnant needs to be placed beyond the bound of sense. Most people probably have a tacit conception of what constitutes a reasonable response to offence or provocation – so, for example, a fatal shooting following an altercation over a parking place appears inexplicable and senseless. Yet many acts of extreme violence occur in response to apparently minor incidents and violence nearly always has 'sense', that is, social meaning, to both perpetrators and victims. The targets of violence are rarely chosen randomly and victims and perpetrators are often already known to each other. In some cases the attribution 'senseless' refers to an assumed mental illness or other pathology that might account for otherwise incomprehensible behaviour. But these are themselves frames of meaning that are often invoked in order to deal with behaviour demonstrating extreme inhumanity. Even if some violent perpetrators act because of a pathology, the specific timing and nature of their actions will have meaning since even the 'most dangerous people are not doing anything violent' most of the time (Collins 2008: 3). Apparently inexplicable acts of extreme violence might be derived from past experiences of humiliation (Gilligan 2000). Moreover, violence often takes on ritual properties, is subject to cultural definitions and straddles the boundary between the physical and cultural (Robb 1997). It is intimately bound up with pain, security, transgression and concepts of the body and its placing in the social order.

Like many other critical issues in the social sciences, the field is marked by controversy. There is an extensive literature on the 'causes' of violence, although some criminologists and sociologists argue that posing causal questions is inappropriate and detracts from understanding the cultural, emotional and visceral dynamics of the act. The 'same' behaviour might be judged violent in some circumstances but not others – such as physical contact between players on the sports field as opposed to strangers on the street. Violence might be casual and perpetrated by individuals or be highly structured and politically organized. While violence is generally thought of as illegitimate and illegal, by contrast with the 'legitimate' *force* exercised by the state, the most destructive and extensive instances in recent history have been state organized and sanctioned. States have organized violence both as a means of punishment but also of entertainment and glorification of its power – as with the Ancient Roman 'games'. Further, violence is not only descriptive of a form of behaviour, but is always normative in that it evokes a negative evaluation such that attempts to legitimate violence will use terms such as 'force', 'defence', 'resistance', and so forth. 'To call something "violent"', says Bäck (2004: 223), 'is often to give at least a *prima facie* reason why it is morally wrong'. As Marvin and Ingle (1999: 312) point out, people rarely accept responsibility for violence – to own or enjoy it is taboo except for the most ritually circumscribed conditions. Moreover, since violence is intimately interconnected with the body, pain and vulnerability, its discussion evokes fundamental issues of security, embodiment, culture and power.

Concepts of violence

The question of violence has generated a large literature. This book is not centrally concerned with definitions or with the growing philosophy of violence (e.g., Schinkel 2010; Žižek 2008) but rather with developing sociological analyses of the multiple modalities of violence. However, it should be noted that there are trends and counter-trends, paradoxes and dilemmas that defy simple reductions. It might be true that 'violent acts are performances of power and domination offered up to various audiences as symbolic accomplishments' (Ferrell et al. 2008: 11), but it is difficult to arrive at more specific definitions. Elizabeth Stanko's often-cited definition is that violence is 'any form of behaviour by an individual that intentionally threatens to or does cause physical, sexual or psychological harm to others or themselves' (Stanko 2001: 316). This might be a reasonable working definition but violence need not be individual and is very often collective; the issue of intention is problematic (as we will see below); psychological harm is different from and more difficult to establish than physical and sexual harm; the notion of self-harm might often be appropriate but is sometimes contested; not all 'harm' arises from acts that would conventionally be regarded as 'violent' – they might arise from neglect or negligence, for example – and it is at least worth questioning whether a 'threat' is itself violence. Threats certainly trade on fear of violence by the threatened person, but there are probably far more threats made than actual violence (as physical harm). So we can ask under what circumstances threats and other forms of aggression are manifest as actual violence in this sense. I am raising these issues not because I have a perfect definition that escapes these difficulties but in order to highlight the problems entailed in specifying violence in an unambiguous way. We need to unpick these kinds of general claims and examine detailed dynamics of violence and aggression.

Bufacchi (2005) points out that there are two ways of thinking about violence – on the one hand, there is a narrow, 'minimalist conception' and on the other, a broader, 'comprehensive conception'. 'Minimalists' regard violence narrowly in terms of physical force and 'bodily response and harm' (Glasser 1998). However, narrow definitions are criticized as taking no account of the wider contexts of social relationships in which violence occurs, non-physical harms (especially psychological), and the possibility of violent outcomes that were not consciously intended. Further, violence does not always require physical force – poisoning or squeezing a trigger, for example, do not – while actions might be viol*ent* without being viol*ence*. Bufacchi (2005) gives the example of his slamming a door when alone (which might be violent but does not do violence to anyone) as opposed to slamming the door on your hand, which is an act of violence. Again, wrestling and boxing are violent but (at least as long as both participants enter the ring voluntarily and abide by the rules) might not be regarded as 'violence'. However, this example illustrates how definitions of 'violence' are subject to a social and political context that is both contested and subject to change. In the UK, for example, the British Medical Association (BMA) has for many years campaigned for stricter legal regulation of boxing and argued that it is an unacceptably violent sport because of the long-term damage often sustained (Brayne et al. 1998). While no court has decided on the legality of injury sustained in licensed boxing, there have been judgments on 'unlawful' though consensually entered into street fights, to the effect that 'a fight between two persons would be unlawful, whether in public or private, if it involved the infliction of at least actual bodily harm, or if actual bodily harm or worse was intended'.[1] Voluntary participation in an activity does not offer protection from prosecution for illegal acts of 'violence' – as in the case of the sixteen gay men in the UK who in December 1990 received prison sentences of up to four and a half years for engaging in consensual sadomasochistic activity (Green 2001). Another example of the way 'violence' is subject to socially and legally disputed definitions is the debate over physical punishment of children, where in 2004 in the UK the ability to use the defence of 'reasonable chastisement' was reduced.[2]

---

[1] Attorney-General's Reference (No. 6 of 1980) [1981] 2 All ER 1057.

[2] Section 58 of the Children Act 2004 removes the 'reasonable chastisement' defence where a parent or adult acting *in loco parentis* is charged with wounding, causing grievous bodily harm, assault occasioning actual bodily harm or cruelty to a child (CPS 2007a).

Proponents of the 'comprehensive conception' of violence avoid some of these difficulties by broadening the definition to include anything avoidable that impedes human realization, violates the rights or integrity of the person and is often judged in terms of outcomes rather than intentions. Jackman (2002) proposes a 'generic definition' – 'actions that inflict, threaten or cause injury. Actions may be corporal, written or verbal … psychological, material or social'. Felson (2009) describes violence as 'physical aggression, i.e., when people use physical methods to harm others'. However, he continues that 'The harm they produce is not necessarily physical… . It could be a social harm or a deprivation of resources'. The latter condition invokes Galtung's (1969) concept of 'structural violence', that is, physical and psychological harm that results from exploitive and unjust social, political and economic systems. This is not (necessarily) carried out by individuals but is hidden to a greater or lesser extent in structures that prevent people from realizing their potential. An example of this might be the injustices of the worldwide system for the trade in goods, which is correlated with infant mortality, infectious disease, and shortened life spans. Unemployment, job insecurity, cuts in public spending, destruction of institutions capable of defending social welfare, dispossession and violation of rights – these are social harms that could be encompassed within 'violence'. Žižek (2008) claims that when individual thresholds of sensibility to violence rise, objective violence in the forms of dispossession and poverty also increase. Thus, whenever people are denied access to resources, physical and psychological violence exists. This definition removes the necessity for any *intent* to harm for an outcome to be considered violent. Arguing for a broad definition of 'harm' in criminology, Tombs (2007) points to the exposure of workers to hazardous working conditions that result in death or injury which is not conventionally considered to be 'violent', either because the hazard level is within the law or because the motives of the corporation cannot be verified within legal notions of premeditated intent. The effects of these 'safety crimes', he says, 'far outweigh crimes of conventional violence' and 'there is no moral basis for treating one-on-one harm as criminal and indirect harm as merely regulatory'. This broadens the concept to that of harms, rather than limit it to individual offending. Conditions of hunger, sickness and destitution are then 'violence' and it is often from such structurally induced conditions that further violence emanates, as we will see in later chapters.

A further distinction is often made in the literature between instrumental and expressive violence (e.g., Wieviorka 2009: 35 and 88–9). Instrumental violence is oriented to a specific goal, such as obtaining money by threats or keeping competing dealers off one's territory, and will be used up to the point where the goal has been attained. Felson (2009) regards violence as always instrumental behaviour that is governed by rational choice in that it is always chosen and perpetrated for 'gain' of some kind, although he understands 'gain' broadly to include 'thrills', 'retribution' and 'produce compliance' in addition to monetary gain. Again, Englander (2007b: 3–4) writes of 'instrumental aggression' to achieve a goal as opposed to 'hostile aggression' that is enacted for its 'own sake' as a form of stimulus-seeking.

The latter is sometimes described as 'expressive violence' that is performed for intrinsic gratification and might express an underlying emotion such as hate, or gratifies a desire for a 'high' from violence. There is an extensive literature that points to the (learned?) pleasures of violence – an argument developed in Topalli (2006), whose interviews with violent offenders point to a sensual dynamic, gaining a high from the enactment of violence that he argues is not well understood by many existing criminological theories. According to the instrumental/expressive distinction, the latter is less limited to the attainment of specific goals and is therefore likely to be more severe. For example, McDevitt et al.'s (2002) famous typology of hate crime offenders distinguishes violence that is defensive (to 'protect neighbourhoods') and retaliatory (a response to an actual or rumoured incident) from more expressive violence motivated by 'thrill and 'mission' ('to rid the world of evil'). Similarly, Wieviorka (1995: 69–76) uses the instrumental/expressive dichotomy to differentiate modalities of racist violence. Racist violence might be instrumentally linked to preserving an entrenched system of social domination and will be limited to maintaining the inferior position of the racialized group, as was the case with antisemitic violence for several centuries. However, where the inclination is to communally exclude the group, violence may become unbounded mass terror and sadism, performed for the enjoyment of domination and cruelty in itself. Examples of this are seen in the Holocaust and other instances of genocide, but are manifest in many instances of violence including domestic violence (Dobash and Dobash 1992). It will be argued later that intimacy and breaching boundaries of the self are essential to interpersonal violence.

However, the instrumental/expressive distinction has been widely criticized since, in practice, the two are often combined. It can be argued that violence will always involve a heightened state of affective arousal even if it is aimed at instrumental gain. While robbery is done for gain, perpetrators might get a 'high' from the risk, and much violence is about asserting dominance over the victim (Levi and Maguire 2004: 811). Thus, describing all violence as 'instrumental' on the grounds that some kind of 'gain' is involved overlooks how even goal-directed violence provides gratification for perpetrators, not least the pleasure of exerting unchallenged power. Rational choice models of instrumental violence argue that actors will make decisions about the likely costs and benefits of using violence, which might sometimes be so. However, in many instances of homicide, for example, there is likely to have been no such calculation of cost and gain, especially where killing involves ritual and symbolic aspects. In what Katz (1988) calls 'Righteous Slaughter', people murder to defend what they believe is 'good', at least at the moment they act. These murders emerge quickly, most lack premeditation, are fiercely impassioned, are conducted with an indifference to legal consequences and are therefore unaffected by the risk of certain and severe punishment. Ritual aspects of such killing might involve degradation and defilement of the body which has no instrumental purpose. This is discussed further in Chapter 7. The ritual and non-instrumental dimensions of violence are also apparent in genocide and other forms of collective violence. This is discussed further in Chapter 9. Therefore, the analytical distinction between instrumental and expressive might prove useful and assist in making distinctions between patterns of violence and its resolution, even if the two are likely to be present in many instances of violence.

Violence and social theory

Violence has not been a topic of central concern to sociological theory. It has of course been a major topic of research, especially in relation to violent crime and social conflict. But theoretically it has tended to be regarded as residual to questions of social integration, the state, power and conflict. Delanty (2001) points out that sociology emerged in relatively peaceful times and was animated by a vision of social order within a world of internally pacified nation states. Violence is what happens when integrative institutions and values break down. Even Marx, despite his generally unsentimental references to the inevitability of violence as a 'cleansing force' in revolutionary change did not theorize violence *per se*, even less explore its potential as an agent of social formation. Subsequent Marxists spent a great deal of energy developing theories of social order and cohesion (ideology, hegemony, reified consciousness, etc.) rather than of violent struggle. Weber notably contrasted legitimate forms of domination to physical force and assumed that to persist for any time a social order would have to be based on legitimate (non-violent) domination. In such approaches the significance of violence (or its threat) in everyday life may have been neglected. The 'recourse to violence and war', Giddens commented, 'is an extraordinary blank spot in social theory' (1996: 22), although he proceeds to discuss military and not interpersonal violence.[3]

Durkheim is something of an exception here and developed an analysis of violence that in some ways points towards the significance of violent scapegoating in later writers such as Freud and Girard. Durkheim's (2001: 404ff) description of 'piacular rituals' (that deal with death and calamity) prefigures

---

[3]This is also largely the case in Malešević (2010) too although this is an important and systematic development of a sociology of war and collective violence.

Girard's concept of the mimetic dynamics of violence. Graham (2007) points out that in Durkheim's account of these rituals, sadness is exalted and amplified by its contagion from consciousness to consciousness, and is then expressed outwardly in the form of exuberant and violent movements. The result is something like a 'panic of sadness'. This panic turns to anger, and Durkheim says, 'one feels the need to break and destroy something, and this is taken out on oneself or on others' (Durkheim 2001: 297–8).[4] Participants imagine that outside are evil beings whose hostility can be appeased only by suffering – which can be directed against scapegoats. This insight suggests an idea that was to be central in Girard (e.g., 1977) that violence is not inimical to civilization but on the contrary lies at the core of social bonding. Collective killing, subsequently re-enacted through sacred rituals and myths establishes social unity, at least for a time, while emerging legal codes address that which must be prohibited to maintain that peace. However, the obligation to follow a law involves a radically different kind of social bond than the totemic ritual, a distinction that will be addressed here.

While attempting to place war and violence at the centre of social theory, Giddens (1996) discusses violence in terms of military power and the 'monopoly of violence' in the nation state. Following Elias, he focuses on the civic 'pacification' of the social spaces bounded by nation states and non-state-sanctioned violence (para-militaries, irregulars, civil conflict, domestic and other criminal violence) is mentioned only in passing (Giddens, 1985: 120–1). This is done partly on the grounds that secessionist civil wars still have the creation of a nation state as their objective, and are therefore part of the historical trend towards the national monopoly of violence. Nonetheless, not only does this ignore the extent of violent interactions within 'pacified' civil societies, but it avoids the question – what if the very processes of national remembrance and identity invokes and sustains potentially violent sociality? What if the idea of the nation is founded upon the sacrificial death of those who have fought in wars, as Marvin and Ingle (1999) argue, in which case violence lies at the heart of modern social collectivities?

Violence and power

A central theme in much theorization of violence is that it is intimately connected with power, as an instantiation of domination, especially of men over women. This has opened research into the violence of everyday life and its institutionalization in concepts of masculinity and the state. Violence does not arise in a vacuum; rather it generally occurs in a repeated and patterned way,

---

[4]Piacular rites (but not the link with Girard) are discussed by Mukherjee (2010).

often within entrenched social relations. But the relationship of violence to power is complex and nuanced, as is the concept of 'power' itself. Arendt (1970), whose view is evident in Habermas too, saw power as *empowerment* in the sense of popular sovereignty, as opposed to violence, which appears where power is in jeopardy. Arendt insists that violence can never generate power, from which it must be categorically distinguished. There is no continuity between obedience to command (the enactment of power) and obedience to law (as legitimate authority). Power is the capacity to act in concert (1970: 44) and can be an end in itself (1970: 51) while violence is instrumental and the 'hope of those who have no power' (Arendt 1970: 52). Similarly, Wieviorka argues that conflict represents a stable set of social relationships whereas violence appears when 'social ensembles are incoherent, fragmented and decadent' (2009: 165). But surely violence might also be a source of power – a resource that can be mobilized to enforce the compliance of others – and violence is clearly exercised by the powerful? In domestic violence, rape, racist violence and state violence, the perpetrators have privileged positions within systems of patriarchal, ethnic or political power. However, it is not the case that all manifestations of violence can be attributed simply to instantiating power. There is also violence that occurs on what Foucault calls 'the underside of power' (1979: 138), the violence of children against parents, women against men, black against white, clients against professionals, and the revolutionary violence of the colonized and oppressed. Similarly, Sartre celebrated violence as the motor of history. Oppression, he claimed, consists in 'a permanent and controlled taking of blood' and the violence of the oppressed is salutary such that 'one must kill: eliminating a European kills two birds with one stone, it gets rid simultaneously of an oppressor and of the oppressed' (Hoffman 2006). Then again there is the area of resigned acquiescence of the powerless, which may of course have 'pathological' manifestations of self-harm and self-abuse, such as alcoholism, which it was often claimed was the case in eastern European state-socialist societies despite many structural differences between them (e.g., Hankiss 1990: 45).

Power is furthermore encoded in systems of communication and normativity. Those who deploy power seek to be perceived as legitimate and for any exercise of violence to be regarded as just. Perpetrators of both 'legitimate' and illegal violence will appeal to normative justifications through culturally available languages of justification. According to Heitmeyer (1994), for example, racist violence may be expressive of a social situation of perceived powerlessness and estrangement. Anxiety from lack of jobs and housing combines with a sense of loss of traditions and abandonment, which, combined with fear of foreigners, justifies 'struggle'. This is manifest in a search for compensatory belonging in racial/national identity, rituals and value systems that promise 'strength' and integration into 'natural' hierarchies. This view draws on a wider sociological literature, which regards criminal behaviour as expressive of alienation, anomie and frustration. Further, the sense of trauma, loss and nostalgia for communities are powerful stimulants to oppositional identity formation. These are structured in terms of sectarian withdrawal and violent exteriorization, which authorize individuals to constitute themselves as actors in collective struggle to expel impurity from the community (Wieviorka 1995: 102ff). So the 'solution' to a conflict in these circumstances might be perceived as the destruction or expulsion of those defined as the enemy. Rather than a simple instantiation of power, violence might follow from perceived powerlessness, and as Gilligan put it, a 'blinding rage that speaks through the body' (2000: 55) and an attempt to achieve justice (2000: 11).

The availability of languages of justifiable violence, as revolutionary or self-defensive, offers perpetrators in general a view of themselves as powerless victims.[5] This is a theme developed in relation to psychoanalytic studies of sadomasochistic violence, in which perpetrators may view violence as a source of self-affirmation (Glasser 1998). Violence is a means of achieving status and respect for those who lack other forms of social power, such as money and education. Moreover, what is learned is not only how to do violence, but a desensitization to violence and rationalization for disengaging one's moral obligations to others (Topalli 2006). Further, learning to 'do' violence also involves acquiring normative languages of justification. Stewart and Strathern (2002: 35ff) develop Riches' triangle of violence (witness, victim and performer) where the perpetrator seeks legitimacy among witnesses. One strategy for this is for perpetrators to present themselves as victims. This occurs across a spectrum from interpersonal conflicts to extreme violence, such as the videos left by perpetrators of mass school killings and suicide bombers. Theorizing violence, then, will require examination of the discourses and practices that authorize the violent actor by providing a complex array of exculpatory resentments and imagined harms.

Causes of violence?

There is a wide range of theoretical explanations of violence which will be introduced in subsequent chapters in relation to specific topics. These range from biological/evolutionary theories through to psychological, sociological

---

[5]This can operate on both interpersonal and societal levels. The Nazis constructed the Jews as leagued in an international conspiracy against plain German folk that linked the Bolsheviks with finance capital (Wistrich 1992: 29ff). Many racist offenders interviewed for Ray et al. (2004) positioned themselves as powerless both in the circumstances of the act for which they had been convicted and in wider social life.

and criminological theories. Evolutionary and biological theories often regard aggression (which needs to be differentiated from violence) as an innate evolutionarily adaptive trait present in all people. Advocates of this view sometimes draw direct comparisons between primal and contemporary violence, for example between evidence of injuries from the Palaeolithic (Stone Age, between 2,000,000 and 10,000 years ago) and Saturday night admissions to hospital Accident and Emergency departments. Evolutionary theories at most explain a capacity for violence rather than its manifestation and incidence in particular times and places. These arguments are discussed in Chapter 2.

There is also a wide array of relevant criminological theories, although these are mostly theories of crime rather than aggression/violence *per se*. Some relevant criminological theories are briefly listed below, although readers will find them dealt with extensively elsewhere, e.g., Marsh et al. (2006: 91–133) and O'Brien and Yar (2008).

Differential Association is a social learning theory developed by Sutherland et al. (1939/1992) who claimed that criminal behaviour is transmitted through generations via learning. Since the law is made politically by the most powerful (a view that was around prior to the 1970s 'new deviancy theorists'), why do some obey and others offend? Criminal and non-criminal behaviour are both expressions of general needs and values – a person becomes delinquent because of an excess of definitions favourable to violation of law over definitions unfavourable to violations of law. Most learning of criminal behaviour occurs within intimate personal groups and this learning includes the often complicated techniques of committing the crime, and the specific direction of motives, drives, rationalizations and attitudes. Differential Associations may vary in frequency, duration, priority and intensity. This is a very general theory that simplifies the complexity of processes of normative learning and does not explain why there might be an excess of associations favourable to lawbreaking in certain social locations. Differential Association was addressed later in subcultural theories, such as Wolfgang and Ferracuti (1967) who claimed that there is a subcultural ethos where violent and physically aggressive responses are expected in some situations. Attitudes favourable to violence (most prominent among adolescent males) are learned through a process of Differential Association. However, a further difficulty with this is that Differential Association has an undeveloped theory of cognitive-moral learning. A more sophisticated theory was developed by Piaget and Kohlberg. In Kohlberg's (1981) final 'post-conventional' stage of moral development, moral judgement involves reasoning rooted in concepts of ethical fairness and laws are evaluated in terms of their coherence with basic principles of fairness rather than upheld simply because they exist. Thus, he argues, there is an understanding that elements of morality, such as regard for life and human welfare, transcend particular cultures and societies and are to be upheld irrespective of other conventions or normative obligations. According to this view, adherence to the law is linked to a judgement that it is reasonable and fair rather than a simple balance of 'associations' and moral action might in some circumstances involve breaking the law.

Strain and institutional anomie. Robert Merton's (1938) influential theory of crime identifies a potential 'strain' in modern societies where there is a disjuncture between collective cultural goals (such as financial success) and the institutional norms for their attainment. Legitimate means to attain success are education, thrift, deferral of gratification (this was the 1930s, prior to credit-fuelled consumer growth) and occupation. But inequalities structure access to legitimate means and the goal of financial success is not available to everyone, and this discrepancy causes 'strain'. Merton proposed a famous model of modes of adaptation:

- Conformity – achieving success through legitimate means (generates little or no crime).
- Ritualism – reject the socially approved goals or reduce expectations of success but gain pleasure from enacting the means, e.g., performing a job as an end in itself (again generates little or no crime).
- Retreatism – give up on both the goals and the means and find alternative lifestyles (might involve some crime, such as illicit drug use).
- Rebellion – reject both goals and means and replace them with new ones, as with new social movements, religious cults and militias where some crime will occur.
- Innovation – accept the goals but innovate means of attainment, as in organized crime, white-collar crime, insurance fraud, bribery, prostitution, etc. Most criminal activity will involve innovation.

This appears to explain property crime and many achievement-oriented forms of rule breaking, such as plagiarism, use of illicit substances in sport, bribing opponents, etc., although it does not necessarily account for non-property, especially 'expressive', crime. Nor does it explain why people who have access to the institutional means for attainment nonetheless break the rules, as with corporate and white-collar crime. Finally, this model does not provide a specific explanation of violence, although this is discussed further in Chapter 7 in relation to homicide.

Subcultural theories focus on processes of social learning within (especially) youth cultures where, according to one proponent, 'The process of becoming a delinquent is the same as the process of becoming a Boy Scout. The difference lies only in the cultural pattern with which the children associate' (Cohen 1955: 14). Cohen developed Merton's theory of social strain and argues that 'delinquency' is motivated less by material gain as opposed to expressive acts (such as vandalism and violence) through which working-class adolescents reject the dominant middle-class values. Cloward and Ohlin

(1960) suggested that there were three types of subcultures, each following Merton's categories, namely:

- Criminal: where adolescents pursue crime for material gain. This subculture is generally found in localities where there is an established pattern of adult crime providing an 'illegitimate opportunity structure' in which adolescents learn the 'tricks of the trade'.
- Conflict: where an illegitimate opportunity structure is not available, delinquents form conflicting gangs out of frustration and engage in expressive crime, including violence.
- Retreatist: the behaviour of those who cannot succeed in either of the other types of subculture who might be involved in drug use and hustling.

Standard criticisms of these theories (and one that we will meet often here) is that they over-predict criminality since the majority of young men (and even less women) do not join delinquent subcultures even though they might experience status frustration. The majority of those that do will cease offending during their twenties. The role of the wider social environment and the reactions of authorities are not addressed as determinants of youth subculture. Further, where identifiable groups do exist there can be dynamic movement between objectives. For example, in Northern Ireland many involved in paramilitary activity during the 1980s moved into organized crime in the 1990s and are now remerging as legitimate parliamentarians (Deane 2008). One of the most influential critiques of subcultural theory was Matza's (1964) drift theory. He claimed that rather than form permanent oppositional subcultures, individuals could be part of a 'subculture of delinquency' without taking part in offending behaviour. This will be significant in the analysis of racist offending in Chapter 8. Adolescents might act out delinquent roles from time to time – drift into these activities rather than adopt an alternative way of life – and nonetheless express adherence to dominant norms, including dominant notions of masculine behaviour. The latter is evident in their recourse to 'techniques of neutralization' through which offenders both attempt to deny intent and express commitment to conventional norms. These techniques are:

- Denial of responsibility and intent (e.g., 'It wasn't my fault').
- Denial of injury – did not cause any harm or damage (e.g., It wasn't a big deal; they could afford the loss').
- Denial of the victim – the victim deserved whatever action the offender committed (e.g., 'They had it coming').
- Condemnation of the condemners (e.g., 'You were just as bad in your day').
- Appeal to higher loyalties (e.g., 'My friends needed me, what was I going to do?').

The concept of neutralization techniques has been highly influential and has been applied to violent offenders (e.g., Ray et al. 2004). However, Topalli (2004) argues that the theory does not explain the behaviour of 'nonconventionally oriented individuals' such as 'hardcore' street offenders who do not discount responsibility through neutralization but affirm their crimes as unavoidable or enjoyable. Rather than point back towards subcultural theory, Topalli's analysis develops Schinkel's concept of autotelic violence.

Control theories shift the focus of attention from the question of why people commit crime to why most people do not? Working in the tradition of Durkheim, who regarded anomie as a state of weak normative regulation that allowed the release of potentially unlimited desires (Durkheim 1970: 253), control theories regard potential motives for deviance as ubiquitous, and focus on restraining or controlling factors, the absence of which lowers inhibitions to deviance. Gottfredson and Hirschi's (1990) social bond theory claims that attachments to family, school and peers keep people from committing crimes. Hirschi (1969) argues that people are kept from committing criminal acts by:

- Attachment (affection and sensitivity to others).
- Commitment (investment in conventional society).
- Involvement (keeping occupied which reduces opportunities).
- Beliefs (commitment to obeying the law).

All criminality can be explained with reference to the weakness of these bonds, which results in low self control (LSC) – a semi-permanent enduring personality characteristic that is present from early in life and remains 'reasonably constant over the life-course' (Gottfredson and Hirschi 1990: 151). This general theory sets out a simple universal causal process which 'pays no attention to possible variations in motivation for crime, disregards opportunity and other situational variables that may intensify or activate impulses for misbehaviour, does not tell how people become bonded in the first place, and implies that control has the same effect ... for all kinds of crime' (Tittle 2000: 85). Further, it offers no specific explanation of violent as opposed to non-violent offending. Although self-control is seen as a stable personality trait, the social bonds listed above are potentially contingent – beliefs and commitments that might be altered by changing circumstances and experiences – losing a job, home and family, for example, is likely to reduce bonding to conventional values and structures. Social control theory fits with many common-sense beliefs – that crime is the result of individual personality traits, low self control, impulsivity, insensitivity, and desire for immediate gratification. The theory is also criticized as tautological since LSC in early life predicts any kind of crime but evidence for LSC can be found only in lawbreaking behaviour. However, Hirschi and Gottfredson (2000) respond to this and other criticisms and the social control paradigm is present in other theories, such as Elias.

Conflict theories. While control theory does not analyse the dynamics of power, politics and inequalities, conflict theory, drawing on Marxism, rejected the idea that there is a consensus over core values and norms, and regards crime as a result of inequalities and conflicting values. Clearly social inequalities and conflicts are potential sources of violence, although the circumstances in which violence occurs are complex and often highly situationally specific. But radical criminology in the 1960s and 1970s developed a political analysis that regarded the law as determined by the powerful, who themselves often evade prosecution, and in labelling approaches there was a tendency to see the powerless offender as the victim in the process. Crime was sometimes celebrated as a mode of revolution, or at least transgression – as, for example, Eldridge Cleaver's view of his past rape of white women as an 'insurrectionary act' of revenge (1968: 26). However, as Rock (2002) points out, radical criminology was soon challenged by new victim politics – especially feminist insistence that the victimization of women through rape, sexual assault, child abuse and domestic violence be taken seriously (Rock 2002: 8). Taylor et al. (1975) modified conflict theory to combine structural explanations with analysis of immediate origins of the act – such as thrill and revenge. Drawing on Merton's social strain theory and challenging both 'right realist' and 'left idealist' theories of crime, Lea and Young's 'left realism' (1984) argued that consumer society encourages desire while alienating those who are excluded, some of whom turn to crime. However, the victims of crime are often themselves the most vulnerable and Lea and Young argue that 'Crime is one form of egoistic response to deprivation. Its roots are in justice but its growth often perpetrates injustice' (Lea and Young 1984: 72). Escalating violence is located within the 'square of crime' – a field of social relationships between the offender, victim, state agencies and the public. This is a non-deterministic theory since all actions involve reflexive moral choices – so while unemployment, for example, is likely to be accompanied by increased crime, this is not inevitable. Again in an echo of Merton, Young (2003) argues that choices involve adaptations where material circumstances block cultural aspirations that might make non-criminal alternatives less attractive. However, this is a theory of criminality in general rather than of violence in particular and the critical question for studying violence is to understand the circumstances in which both structural and transitory conflicts become violent.

Interactionist theories, such as Collins' (2008, 2009), address this by focusing on the micro dynamics of violent situations rather than individual behaviour, which is the focus of most of the theories mentioned above. The premise for Collins' analysis is that violence is difficult and risky and humans have developed deep commitments to reciprocal social solidarity which means that violent situations generate high levels of confrontational tension-fear. Violence can only occur, he argues, where there is a pathway round confrontational tension-fear which most often arises from dynamic interaction sequences – such as attacking the weak ('forward panic') in a state of high confrontational arousal;

audience-oriented conflicts such as duals and 'fair fights'; remote violence (where the victim cannot be seen); deception, for example when the killer avoids social contact with the victim often through establishing dominance in attention space; absorption in technique and routine – for example a hit-man regarding contract killing as 'just a job'. This account of violence can be combined with Scheff and Retzinger's (1991) theory of micro-interactional patterns that lead to violent confrontation. However, these focus on the role of 'unacknowledged shame' – that is, negative but largely repressed feelings of failure to have one's sense of self validated in interaction especially with significant others. The accumulated sense of shame is transformed into rage when parties get into a cycle of reciprocal shaming. Collins points out (2008: 344–5) that this cycle can also be understood in terms of a failed interaction ritual that breaks mutual solidarity and therefore lowers inhibitions to violence, although he also notes that most escalating quarrels break off at the brink of violence and we need to understand the paths that lead from verbal confrontation to violence.

Critique of causality. Causal explanations in the social sciences have always been controversial and contested by interpretative phenomenological approaches that aim to understand the quality of the act rather than place it within an external framework. Schinkel (2004) argues that in social science the 'causal path remains in the dark'. He draws partly on David Hume's critique of causality – that what is called 'cause' is merely observed regularity – but also argues that causal accounts lose focus on the meaning of violence and the nature of the phenomenon. In particular, it 'ignores the aesthetics of violence' – its intrinsic features pursued for 'its own sake'. In this context he cites the existence of websites devoted to extreme violence, the idea of 'hooliganism as fun' and the preoccupation of art with violence. However, his favourable reference to the 'ground-breaking work of Lorenz' (who is discussed in Chapter 2) reveals an implicit belief that violence is an innate human capacity. This ignores many issues about the differential occurrence of violent actions within and between societies and over time and its multiple styles. Even if everyone possesses the 'will to violence', it is still appropriate to question why it appears in some times and spaces more than others. He does not say quite what he regards as 'aesthetic violence' and his references to filmic violence seem to eclipse the difference between representations of violence and the real thing. The aesthetic metaphor is telling in that it assumes that the artistic creator and violent actor are both autonomous and cannot be explained with reference to anything outside themselves. Both of these assumptions, though, are questionable – violence might arise more from situations of interaction than from individuals and patterns of violence might be explicable in terms of broader social processes. However, while autotelic violence is not a sufficient explanation of patterns of violence, there are

circumstances in which violent spirals (such as tit-for-tat killings in Northern Ireland) create a kind of autonomous violence as a self-sustaining activity (Stewart and Strathern 2002: 41).

Violence is socially organized

A theme of this book is that violence needs to be understood not primarily as a problem of individual behaviour but embedded in social and cultural relationships. Moreover, levels and types of violence are not constant across societies and throughout history. On the contrary, there is considerable evidence that these change over time and are related to other complex changes in social organization. Norbert Elias (1897–1990) famously advanced the thesis of the 'civilizational process' that between the European Middle Ages and the modern period there was a transformation of social 'habitus' (lifestyles, norms and personality) first apparent in a growth of courtly etiquette around eating, sexual behaviour and the body that gradually established new norms of interpersonal conduct in wider society. Linked to increasing social interdependence and the growth of the state's monopoly of the means of violence, a modern personality emerged that was increasingly self-regulating, calculating, reserved and mannered in everyday (especially public) interactions. One consequence of this personality structure was a diminution of interpersonal aggressiveness and violence. Elias's thesis is dependent on a Freudian concept of social control over instinctual (especially sexual and aggressive) drives, although he 'historicizes' Freud's theory in that rather than regard it as a timeless conflict between civilization and instincts he views the relationships between the body and emotional performance as changing over time in response to wider social transformations.

Elias's thinking has been influential in sociological studies of violence. In a not dissimilar way, Cooney (2003) writes of a trend towards 'privatization of violence'. Over several hundreds of years manners and increased restraint around public aggression has resulted in a decline in public violence but at the same time a proportionate increase in intimate–familial violence, an issue not addressed by Elias. Other theorists too, notably Michel Foucault, from a very different theoretical standpoint, have identified a historical shift in modes of discipline with the birth of the prison along with new techniques of self-reflection. There is controversy of course about the historical support for these theses but in both approaches there is a focus on modernity as a process of enclosure within structured spaces. Not only social order but also violence is spatially organized. Sometimes the potential for violence is dramatized by visible markers such as the 'Peace Lines' separating communities in conflict and Protestant and Catholic communities in Belfast, Derry and elsewhere in

Northern Ireland. At other times urban divides are less visible and appear in crime reports, tacit knowledge of relevant agencies and of course everyday mapping of dangerousness in the city. These issues are discussed in Chapter 4.

The evolutionary context

Violence is complex and difficult to define and even if a comprehensive theory of violence were possible, this would need to be interdisciplinary (Glasser 1998). There are many levels at which violence could be studied: sociological, anthropological, psychological, physiological, genetic, etc. The focus of this book is sociological but the wider disciplinary context within which violence is researched cannot be ignored. Violence is affective behaviour that engages neurological processes – mostly people get aggressive when they are angry or aroused and particular areas of the brain and physiological systems that under-lie emotion are generally active. This does not mean that aggression is 'caused' by neurological events. Indeed, one study comparing children with aggressive conduct disorder (CD) with a control group found that only in the CD group certain brain areas (the amygdala and ventral striatum) were stimulated by witnessing deliberately caused pain, suggesting that they enjoyed watching pain (Decety et al. 2009). This suggests that some people might *learn* to derive gratification from pain (and aggression) rather than aggression being explicable in terms of brain function. However, the idea that human aggression has a bio-logical and evolutionary basis is long-standing and is currently becoming increasingly popular through the influence of evolutionary psychology. It is claimed, for example, that where universal forms of aggression can be identified – such as masculine defence of honour and status – there will be an evolutionary basis for these. Or at least that at some time these behaviours solved some adaptation problem. There is a large area of research that com-pares human behaviour to that of other primates and finds similarities – chimps hunt one another in packs, for example (although bonobos do not), orang-utans regularly rape, and gorillas kill unrelated infants. Even though few would now claim that these behaviours are somehow hard-wired into humans, evolution-ary psychologists claim that evolution works on genes and genes influence the development of individual physiology. Therefore, the argument goes, we must link evolution to particular genes (or combinations) and these to developmental processes, brain pathways and actual behaviour. For example, in most societies male status-seeking mechanisms and territory defence systems have developed, which leads to violence under some conditions. Is there some sort of genetic mechanism that accounts for the (near) universality of male status-seeking in the great apes? These kinds of backward comparisons can seem like 'just-so stories' and it is important to recognize that widespread behaviours, such as male status systems, are subject to cultural variation and political challenge. I argue that evolutionary explanations of contemporary domination, aggression and violence are flawed. Humans do share with great apes a capacity for violence, but humans have also developed complex systems of conflict resolution, moral regulation and the linguistic ability to call into question any received mode of conduct or moral norm. However, the importance of these issues warrants further discussion and this is the topic of the next chapter.

Humans have a history of violence and violence has a history. Violence has been ubiquitous in human history but like all other forms of human behaviour it has been socially and culturally organized and varies greatly in its nature and extent over time and between societies. In early human societies there is evidence that interpersonal violence was often restrained, although there is evidence of Palaeolithic warfare too. The emergence of state societies in the Ancient world, though, appears to have instigated practices of public theatres of violence and cruelty that continued at least through to the Middle Ages and early modernity. This indeed is where we will now begin.

2

ORIGINS OF VIOLENCE

It was noted in Chapter 1 that violence appears to be more or less ubiquitous in human societies, and this is often invoked to underpin evolutionary theories of innate human aggressiveness. Those advancing theories of innate human aggression often draw on arguments based on human evolution from pre-human primates where a capacity for violence is linked to primal hunting and defence of territory. Such arguments often refer to present-day 'hunter-gatherer' societies to derive evidence of innate human propensities. There is an argument that runs like this. Humans share around 98 per cent of their DNA with chimpanzees and around 3 million years ago had a common primate ancestor.[1] Chimpanzees are not the peaceable animals they were once thought to be, but rather display violence similar to humans – they are organized in male status hierarchies and males enact lethal coalitionary aggression, that is, they form parties to raid neighbouring settlements to capture females. Great apes make and use tools, form life-long social bonds, demonstrate grief, spontaneously adopt and care for infants, and show evidence of compassion. But they also wage war, rape, practise infanticide, and hunt other mammals for food. It is argued, then, that since human males likewise engage in violent conflict over territory, food, and females, primate studies illustrate that the (especially male) human propensity for violence has been 'hard wired' by evolution and will therefore prove difficult to overcome. Further, it can be argued that prehistoric human skeletons indicate that violent death was quite common, suggesting that this pattern of violence continued into early human societies.

However, there is considerable uncertainty and speculation about prehistoric human existence and the process of evolution from ape to human. Against theories of innate human aggressiveness there are many alternative accounts. Some writers stress the disjuncture between pre-human and human social organization and some claim that early pre-state human societies were largely egalitarian and peaceful prior to a cataclysmic change that occurred

---

[1]This often quoted figure refers to 'coding DNA' that is necessary for production of proteins while the differences in non-coding DNA seem to be larger and might be significant (Marquès-Boneta et al. 2004).

after the Neolithic period and the subsequent emergence of state societies. Others argue that comparisons between humans and the great apes (chimpanzees, gorillas, orang-utans and bonobos) show that among the latter aggression is largely limited and defensive. Human violence, by contrast, is extensive and intraspecific (enacted within our species) rather than being limited largely to competition with other species. Eric Fromm (1974), for example, claims that aggression among non-humans is largely 'benign' and defensive, whereas human violence is 'malignant' and pathological. Then again, there is an argument that will be developed in the following chapter to the effect that early human societies through to the European Middle Ages were marked by high levels of interpersonal violence but that there has over the past few hundred years been a 'civilizational process' in which interpersonal interactions have overall become more mannered, restrained and governed by self-control and forethought.

Trends in violence can be looked at over millennia, over centuries or compressed into decades. This chapter examines debates over the role of violence in human evolution and prehistory and their relevance to understanding contemporary patterns of violence. Modern humans (*Homo Sapiens Sapiens*) began to appear around 100,000 years ago in Africa and bordering areas of southwest Asia, although evidence of culture and social organization is more recent, with bone carving, tools, ornamentation (such as bead jewellery), drawn images and arrowheads from around 50,000 years ago. There has been much speculation about the life of humans during the greater part of their existence. Sociologists and criminologists generally focus on the contemporary historical period and rarely extend analysis into pre-modern let alone archaic times. The kind of historical analysis and understanding that informed classical sociologists such as Marx and Weber has become more rare in the past few decades – a development that Elias (1987) called 'the retreat of sociologists into the present' with excessive concentration on contemporary phenomena. Elias's own theory of the civilizational process takes a long-rage view of the relationships between social organization, interpersonal interactions and violence. This chapter will examine claims made in evolutionary psychology and archeo-paleontology about the ubiquity of aggression and violence in human societies. Such claims can be used as 'evidence' that violence and intergroup conflict are essential, if not inevitable, human characteristics. At the same time there are good grounds for being sceptical of evolutionary arguments for at least the following reason. As Habermas (1979) has argued, human communication has the distinctive feature of being normatively guided and justified with reference to values that are shared by particular communities. Human language offers the 'always already' potential to question the reasons for any action or norm. Whatever dispositions towards violence there might be in human neurological networks, action is mediated by norms and linguistic communication. These require us to provide ourselves and others with good reasons for actions, which separate action from initial motives and desires. Further, like any other form of human behaviour, violence derives its meaning from prevalent forms of social organization, culture and language and there might therefore be no grounds for supporting the idea of an uninterrupted evolutionary progression from ape to human.

State of nature – paradise or pain?

Many social and political theorists have sought to locate the origins of violence and aggression often by imagining an 'original' human condition from which a theory of 'essential' human nature could be derived. Thomas Hobbes (1588–1679) imagined a pre-social state of nature although he claimed neither that such a state had existed historically nor that it could exist in the future.[2] 'In the nature of man we find three principal causes of quarrell', he says – competition, diffidence and glory. The pursuit of each gives rise to violence. That is, violence is used to gain control over 'other men's persons, wives, children and cattell'; again violence is used in defence of these, and also arises over 'trifles and slights', which we might now call honour violence (Hobbes 1651/1994: 71). The 'state of nature' is a heuristic depiction of essential human tendencies that were an ever-present threat to social peace, which for Hobbes could be guaranteed only through contracting sovereign power to the Leviathan, or Sovereign State. In the state of nature there was 'No culture of the earth [agriculture]; no navigation ... no account of time; no arts; no letters; no society; and which is worst of all, continual fear, and danger of violent death; and the life of man, solitary, poor, nasty, brutish and short' (Hobbes 1651/1994: 71). This is because without a Common Power, or state, people live in a 'condition which is called Warre, ... as is every man against every man' (1651/1994: 71). Rationality and mutual self-interest, however, persuade people to combine to seek peace and be contented with only so much liberty as they would allow against themselves.

Hobbes' thesis, that the social order is fragile and continually threatened by violent disintegration, has been very influential but also frequently challenged. Although accepting that Hobbes correctly posed the problem of order, Parsons (1966: 93) argued that people do not adhere to social norms because of a utilitarian belief that it is in their individual interests to do so but because it is obligatory to do so. Further, once the social bond is conceived in terms of values of social solidarity, then violence needs to be understood with reference to

---

[2]However, the colonization of America and encounter with Native Americans led some seventeenth- and eighteenth-century theorists to believe that there were people still in a 'state of nature'. This was bad anthropology but was remarkably persistent, being repeated, for example, by Engels (1884/1968), and is still found in contemporary discussions of 'hunter-gatherer' societies.

social norms that may differentially sanction or condemn it. Nonetheless, in pointing to the state's claim to an exclusive right to punish ('an Evil inflicted by publique Authority', 1651/1994: 185), Hobbes addressed a key issue in subsequent debates about violence and the state that continued through subsequent theorists such as Weber, Elias and Foucault.

Debate about the 'original' condition of humanity continued through the following two centuries. Against Hobbes, John Locke (1632–1704) argued that the state of nature was not terrifying but naturally sociable, in which people enjoyed liberty and recognized one another's rights, and warned that it was the state that could make subjects slaves and destroy them when it had 'a fancy to it' (Locke 1980: 278). Rousseau and his followers argued that life in austere, simple societies was virtuous while Hobbes' competitive individuals were a product of 'civilization' (Rousseau 1968: 16). However, by the nineteenth century anthropological evidence was being assembled that aimed to provide indications of an original human condition. Marx and Engels, in common with several other Victorian social theorists, believed that original human societies were egalitarian and largely without conflict and violence. This underpinned the idea that since class division was the main source of violent conflict throughout history, a future classless society would be free from structural conflict and violence. Towards the end of his life Marx was working on Lewis Morgan's *Ancient Society* (1877/2000), and in 1884, the year following Marx's death, Engels published the classical Marxist analysis of the origins of the state, class and patriarchy (Engels 1884/1968). He argued that women's subordination in class society had an economic basis in property relationships, and that material relations included both senses of reproduction – economic production and bearing and rearing of children. The conditions for patriarchy were historical and not natural. Drawing on Marx's *Ethnological Notebooks* (1972), he claimed that pre-state societies were democratic with matrilineal descent and elder women powerful in deposing chiefs. The appearance of the state, structured division of labour, patrilinial descent and the enslavement of women as concubines were all part of the historical appearance of private property, from which, in turn, arose the violence of both the dominant and subordinate strata.

Durkheim's social theory speculated on the original nature of humanity, but treated violence as an outcome of the mode of moral regulation and integration. Like Engels, Durkheim began by accepting Morgan's thesis of primal equality. In early societies women were equal to men, 'mingle in political life … [and] accompany men to war'. In the past, woman 'was not at all the weak creature that she has become with the progress of morality' (Durkheim 1933: 57). In complex societies, however, we find institutions of marriage, fidelity and division of labour, differences Durkheim thought had become embodied in different male and female physiological dispositions. However, in later work he came to the opposing view that primitive society was not the site of archaic equality, but of extreme segregation and gender inequality. The taboos on endogamy, incest and blood symbolize male fear of women as 'dangerous magicians', and women's association with blood through menstruation reinforces men's fear of women as profane. Marriage and sexual rites are social institutions that aim to avert consequences arising from the proximity of unequals (Durkheim 1969). By contrast, modern societies develop greater reciprocity and formal equality between different groups whose successful interaction can be guided by moral norms and institutional constraints. But Durkheim appreciated that there are two sides to the risk of violence. With weakening ritual bonding, suicide and homicide rates rise in modern societies that allow desires and competitive rivalries to be unleashed. However, violence can also result from close ritual bonds of solidarity such as the piacular rites noted above (p. 11–12). This is a sociological theory of the ambivalent consequences of moral regulation where ritual practices might either inhibit or prompt violence.

The idea of innate aggressiveness returns in Freud's influential speculative theories of primal violence. In *Totem and Taboo* (1913/1950), he argues that the law 'only forbids men to do what their instincts incline them to do … crimes forbidden by law are crimes which many men have a natural propensity to commit' (1913/1950: 123). Having initially regarded aggressiveness arising from frustration of libidinal desires – for example, from the infant male's failed Oedipal love for his mother – later Freud reluctantly came to regard aggressiveness as an innate instinct alongside libido. In *Civilization and its Discontents* (1930/1961), civilization *is* aggression turned inwards to construct the super-ego, which with the ego-ideal censures desires and behaviour. Further, assuming that people originally lived in small communities dominated by elder males (a view now known as the 'male coalitionary' theory), Freud depicted an act of primal violence and cannibalism, the consequences of which continue to exert a hold over contemporary life:

> One day the brothers … killed and devoured their father. … Cannibals … as they were, it goes without saying that they devoured their victim as well as killing him. … The totem meal, which is perhaps mankind's earliest festival, would thus be a repetition and commemoration of this memorable and criminal deed, which was the beginning of so many things – of social organization, of moral restrictions and of religion. (1913/1950: 141)

The dead father, however, proved stronger than the living and the deed was symbolically revoked in prohibitions on the killing of the totem, which served as the substitute for the father. Since, for Freud, repression of the memory of a desire is never successful but gives rise to a compulsion to repeat – the desire to commit the crime of parricide – is repeated symbolically in the ritual sacrifice of the totem animal, which is an occasion for reaffirmation of collective bonds. The sacrificial feast was an 'occasion on which individuals rose joyously above their own interests and stressed the ritual dependence existing between one another' (1913/1950: 134). Noting the significance of sacrifice in religious rituals, he further saw religion as an extended and collective form of guilt and ambivalence about the 'memory' of killing the father figure.

This vision of the primal horde – a patrilocal band of male foragers acting out primal aggressiveness – is not now seen as consistent with evidence of early human societies since these were neither essentially virilocal (living in a single locality) nor patrilocal (living with the male head) but highly fluid (Knauft 1991). However, the influential ethologist Konrad Lorenz[3] went considerably further in attempting to subsume human behaviour within instinctual animal behaviour. He claimed that when humans 'reached the stage of having weapons, clothing and social organization, so overcoming the dangers of starving, freezing and being eaten by wild animals ... an evil intraspecific selection must have set in. The factor influencing selection was now the wars waged between hostile neighbouring tribes' (Lorenz 1963: 34). No selection pressure arose in human prehistory, he claimed, to breed inhibitory mechanisms preventing killing cospe-cifics until 'artificial weapons upset the equilibrium' (1963: 207). He claims that it was weapons that prompted cultural restraints on violence although 'man' is still a 'jeopardized creature' because of his nature (1963: 204). It will be seen shortly that many contemporary writers challenge his claim that there were no early inhibitory mechanisms against violence. However, the central issue in the instinctivist theory is that we are doomed by nature to be destructive since human aggressiveness is an instinct fed by energy and not just a reaction to stimuli, as behaviourist psychologists supposed. For Lorenz, aggressiveness is 'appetitive behaviour' and people search for outlets for aggressiveness in socially available channels, for example in political movements. Although the spontaneity of this instinct has furthered survival of humans by favouring the selection of the better fighter, it is also dangerous and needs to be transformed into symbolic and ritual behaviour.

In a detailed critique of instinctivist theories, Eric Fromm (1974: 69) argued that they live 'in the past of the species' and see 'man' as 'a machine that can only produce inherited patterns of the past'. He argues that Lorenz's argument is tautologous, like Hobbes, in claiming that humans *are* aggressive because they *were* aggressive and *were* aggressive because they *are* aggressive (Fromm 1974: 19). Indeed the genetic reasoning here is open to question since even if there was widespread warfare in the Late Palaeolithic, the death toll would have been more likely to select more aggressive individuals *out* of the evolutionary

---

[3]Lorenz joined the Nazi Party in 1938 claiming that his 'whole scientific work' was devoted to the ideas of National Socialism, although he later apologized for his former Nazi sympathies. In 1973 he won the Nobel Prize for medicine. See www.spiritus-temporis. com/konrad-lorenz/. In the 1980s he supported the Austrian Green Party.

process. On the contrary, Fromm quotes Niko Tinbergen (who shared the Nobel Prize with Lorenz) that 'Man is the only species that is a mass murderer and feels satisfaction in doing so' (Fromm 1974: 19). Nonetheless, Fromm argues that people aim to *avoid* conflict and experience intense forces that find cruel behaviour intolerable. Inhibitors are evident in people's sense of empathy, identity and affective bonds but where these are cut destructiveness assumes a different quality (Fromm 1974: 120). Similarly, Collins argues that humans are 'hard-wired' for solidarity and 'interactional entrainment', which makes violence difficult because it 'directly contravenes the tendency for entrainment in each other's emotions when there is a common focus of attention' (Collins 2008: 27). By 'entrainment' he means the rhythmic synchronization of interaction through which emotional states become contagious among actors. 'We have evolved', he says, 'in such a way that fighting encounters a deep interactional obstacle. ... Confrontational tension/fear is the evolutionary price we pay for civilization' (2008: 27). Therefore in Collins' (and Fromm's) view 'violence is not primordial and civilization does not tame it'.[4]

However, whereas Collins assumes this evolutionary basis for his subsequent thesis, Fromm attempted to demonstrate his claim by assembling evidence from primate studies and archaeology. He argues that chimpanzees in the wild have low levels of aggression and violence is rare. Following Sahlins (1974), Fromm depicts the Stone Age as one of abundance, absence of property and hierarchy, where quarrels were adjudicated, primitive warfare was infrequent, not aimed at mass killing and neither centrally organized nor led by chiefs (Fromm 1974: 146). See Figure 2.1 for a schematic outline of human prehistory. The Neolithic Revolution involved the cultivation of wheat and barley, animal breeding (sheep and cattle-raising) and a settled economy along with the development of chemical processes evident in pottery and ceramics. Excavations of Gatal Hüyük (in Anatolia) from around 6,500 years ago found evidence of worship of a matriarchal mother-goddesses, mirrors and ceremonial daggers but little evidence of hierarchy and skeletons that showed few signs of violence. A similar picture of the Neolithic is presented by Sanderson (1995), of societies without private property or stratification, although he suggests that with the appearance of larger and more permanent villages, social ranking and stratification developed along with knowledge about plants and animals. It was with the subsequent rise of state societies (which for Hobbes was the guarantor of social peace) that stratification and warfare began (Sanderson 1995: 21ff). Again, for Fromm it was the urban revolution at around 4000–3000

---

[4]Collins and Fromm are, however, arguing differently. Fromm infers the cooperative nature of humans from primate and early human behaviour, while Collins infers a hard-wiring for solidarity from the ubiquitous presence of confrontation/tension and humans' poor fighting competence.

Paleolithic (c 2,000,000 – c 10,000 BCE) **Old Stone Age**	Began around two million years ago with the first evidence of tool making and ending with the last Ice Age. Is subdivided into: • Lower Paleolithic (2m – 100,000 BCE). • Middle Paleolithic (100,000 – 30,000 BCE). • Upper Paleolithic (30,000 – 10,000 BCE). *Homo Sapiens Sapiens* evolved in Africa somewhat prior to 130k and then gradually dispersed out of Africa displacing earlier forms of Homo over the next 100k years. Language developed with recursive property that enabled critical reflection and cultural development.
Mesolithic (c 10,000 – c 5500 BCE) **Middle Stone Age**	Period from last Ice Age until introduction of farming in the 'Neolithic Revolution' around 5500 years ago. The introduction of pastoral agriculture took place over several thousand years and the epoch overlaps with the Neolithic.
Neolithic (c 5500 – c 2500 BCE) **New Stone Age**	Onset of farming until metal tools in widespread use although this again appeared at different times in different places. Around the Mediterranean and Asia metal tools began around 6000 BCE. End of the Neolithic was marked by the appearance of the state, warriors, hierarchical status divisions, the growth of cities and increased skeletal evidence of interpersonal violence.

Figure 2.1 Human Prehistory

BCE[5] that brought complex social organization, authoritarianism, central power, specialized labour, divisions between owners and slaves and war as an instrument of state strategy. This was also the beginning of sadism and destructiveness, which he characterizes in terms of 'non-adaptive malignant aggression' that is no longer limited to defence (Fromm 1974: 337ff). One manifestation of this is nationalism (group narcissism), where aggression is directed against non-members, while the worship of technique and power-centred megamachines embodies a 'passion for destruction'. In this 'fatal web of circumstances' (Fromm 1974: 436), war and violence become central aspects of human life.

Disputes over prehistoric violence

Since Fromm's work in the 1970s subsequent studies of primates and evidence from paleo-archaeology call into question this pacific picture of primal exist-ence. Guilaine and Zammit (2001) claim that there was periodic fluctuation of hostility and docility in prehistoric societies but that war was ubiquitous. They further claim that there is a strong link between lethal aggression among closest

---

[5]'Before Common Era', a non-religious alternative to the use of BC.

primates and humans (2001: 17). While primate aggressiveness towards other species is related primarily to predation, among humans the development of weapons might have been linked to intraspecific (within species) violence in response to ecological crises and struggles for dominance (2001: 17–18). Human violence can then be understood as a result of evolutionary inertia – that is, a form of behaviour that no longer serves a useful purpose but persists from a time when it was adaptive. David Schneider (2005) argues that the relationship between genes and environment is complex but if something is universal (such as male aggression to defend honour and status), then we ought to be looking for some evolutionary bases to explain it. There are also likely to be some analogues in the behaviour of primates with which humans shared their evolutionary development. This favours chimpanzees as comparators since the environment for much of human development was more like theirs than other great apes. Bonobos ('pigmy chimpanzees' that branched from the chimpanzee line around 3 million years ago) evolved in a different area with different environmental opportunities. This was rich in food, did not encourage the creation of territorial boundaries and allowed females carrying infants to keep up with the males and to bond with other females. This might explain the relative lack of violence among bonobos compared with chimpanzees and humans.[6]

Evolutionary inertia?

Violence and aggressiveness can be viewed as a result of 'evolutionary inertia', a claim that will be briefly considered. In support of this claim it is argued that there are similarities in intercommunity aggression in chimpanzees and primitive warfare in humans. Boesch et al. (2008) document fatal violence in the course of an attack by 'South Group' on 'Middle Group' chimpanzees in Taï National Park (Cote d'Ivoire). They argue that although lethal violence varies dramatically between chimpanzee groups, intergroup conflicts are frequent and involve both sexes. Roscoe (2007) describes coalitional killing among chimpanzees but also notes that they have an aversion to violence that can (as with humans) be overridden by higher cognitive functions. Similar claims are made by Wrangham and Peterson (1996:14), who claim that male chimpanzees are an 'amazingly good model for the ancestor of hominids' and are 'ferocious defenders of community territory'. This they regard this as the precursor of ethnic violence among humans (1996: 24). Clastres (1994) claims that 'primitive societies' enjoy war, which, as for Hobbes, is a natural state. Whereas for Lévi-Strauss (1969) exchange is at the heart of human interaction, for

---

[6]David Schneider, personal communication 25/11/08.

Clastres there was a primal thirst for war to which exchange was a less attractive substitute. Exclusivity in use of territory and the existence of the Other meant that the possibility of war was inscribed in the being of 'primitive society' (Clastres 1994: 156) and was crucial for the formation of boundaries and identities (Bowman 2001: 30). However, one cannot constantly be enemy to all, so alliance and exchange are also necessary, albeit temporarily, but this condition of permanent war (as for Hobbes) ends only with the appearance of social division and the state, which are the 'death of primitive society' (Clastres 1994: 165).

Evidence of aggression in terms of the archaeological record is difficult to prove unambiguously for very early *Homo Sapiens* and for Neanderthals. Primarily reliant on very limited skeletal data, only evidence of aggression that causes damage to bones will survive and there is always the possibility of deliberate or accidental post-mortem treatment of the bone, and decompositional processes over time. Aggression causing damage to soft-tissue or aggression that is essentially psychological will be invisible in the record for early populations, although there is some 'art-historical' evidence of between 30–20,000 years ago of humans being pierced by projectiles. More abundant and unambiguous evidence for aggression in terms of an archaeological record is present, at least, in Europe from the early post-glacial period, from around 10,000 years ago. This has been a rich source of myths that humanity 'fell' from an earlier state of perfection, and, more recently, anthropological speculation driven by the probably false assumption that looking back in time approaches an authentic or essential human social state.

However, the 'romantic conception of the past does not accord well with osteological and archaeological data' (Martin and Frayer 1997: xiii). War is 'almost ubiquitous in the ethnographic record ... and the frequency distribution is skewed sharply toward the high end' (Ember and Ember 1997: 5). It has 'become apparent that many pre-state societies do not conform to their peaceful "harmless people" stereotype'. Clearly violence leading to homicide is an ordinary occurrence in most '*present* hunter-gatherer and horticultural groups' (Frayer 1997). Keeley (1997) claims that the search for an earlier, less violent way to organize our social affairs has been fruitless – peaceful societies are rare and warfare extremely frequent in non-state societies (1997: 25) and wherever modern human beings appear there is homicidal violence (1997: 37). Skeletons from the Late Palaeolithic (12–14,000 years ago) indicate that warfare was common and brutal. This was possibly because continued peace is costly and warfare brings benefits of spoil from vanquished opponents (1997: 158). All the evidence suggests that peaceful periods have always been punctuated by episodes of warfare and violence. Similarly, Kelly (2005) claims that intergroup violence in the Palaeolithic originated from coalitionary killing and there was an intrinsic development from defence of territory to war around 12–14,000 years ago.

McCall and Shields (2007) argue that there is an evolutionary basis for violence and aggression and their analysis moves between paleo-archaeology and modern studies of violence. They find significant evidence for some evolutionary basis for violence given its ubiquity in both the present and the deep archaeological past. They propose a synthetic model (a 'general aggression model') that combines evolutionary theory and interactionist perspectives of the inputs leading to aggression and violence in human social groups. The 'general aggression model' weighs 'inputs' from biological, environmental and psychological features, combined with personality, to map routes to aggressive or non-aggressive behaviour. There is 'clear evidence', they say, 'for a universal biological basis for aggression' which is stronger in males than in females and is evident in both hunter-gatherer societies and North American cities. Even so, the homicide rate in New Guinea is 568 per 100,000 of the population, which is 100 times that of the USA in 2004. Similarly, Knauft (1991) argues that evidence points towards a 'universal biological basis for aggression' but there was a 'dramatic increase' at the end of the Pleistocene, around 10,000 years ago.

Through comparison of warfare in modern and prehistoric societies, from modern European states to the Plains Indians of North America, Keeley (1997) claims to demonstrate that prehistoric warfare was in fact more deadly, more frequent, and more ruthless than modern war. There is evidence of cruelty and murderous urges from australopithecine as brain enlargement enhanced possibilities for cooperation and killing (Keeley 1997). One frequently cited example of prehistoric brutality is the evidence of a massacre that was uncovered in 1908 by archaeologists excavating Ofnet cave in Bavaria. Dated from around 8,000 years ago, the cave revealed 'trophy sculls like eggs in a basket' in two pits containing 38 decapitated skulls, of which 20 had been children. Many of these skulls show bevelled fractures at the back of the head that strongly suggest perimortem bludgeoning. This is used to suggest that organized homicide predated the development of sedentary agricultural communities. Similarly, Walker (2001) argues that 'Mesolithic huntergatherers, like their modern counterparts … sometimes lived in societies where fear of becoming a homicide victim was a fact of everyday life'. Further, he argues, bioarchaeological research indicates that throughout human history interpersonal violence (and cannibalism) have been prevalent and the 'roots of interpersonal violence lie deep in evolutionary history'.

Discontinuity in human development

The Hobbesean view of the state of nature as nasty, brutish and short is reflected in many of the above arguments. However, the idea that violence and aggression are consequences of evolutionary inertia is flawed in several respects.

Jürgen Habermas (1979: 135) argues that 'humans broke the social structure' of pre-humans, which was a 'one-dimensional rank ordering in which every animal was … assigned one and only one status'. The reproduction of *human* life began, he suggests, when the economy of the hunt was supplemented by a familial social structure and social role systems based on mutual recognition of normative expectations (1979: 136). According to this view, acquiring knowledge of motives for action, which presupposes language, transforms the conditions for human behaviour and makes any suggestion of a simple continuity between pre-human and human action problematic. Linguistic communication creates entirely new bases for action based on forethought and in particular means that (a) participants can assume the perspective of other participants; (b) action is situated within temporal horizons of past and future and consideration of its possible consequences; and (c) action is connected to systems of sanctions and norms and behaviour is guided by anticipated judgements of others.

Sussman (1999) argues that comparisons between humans and chimpanzees are flawed because chimps have been evolving as long as humans and there is no reason to assume an unchanged and shared pattern of environmental and genetic influences over their behaviour. Bonobos are even more closely related to chimpanzees than humans but are peaceful and non-hierarchical. In any event, he suggests that intraspecific chimpanzee killing is much rarer than studies such as Wrangham and Peterson (1997) suggest, and might be affected by human interference – for example, providing food that is then fought over. Sussman further argues that there are variations in the degree of violence in different human (and chimpanzee) communities, which suggests that neither genes nor evolution are determinant. Observations derived from the putative evolutionary process are therefore of limited significance and can be 'just so' stories into which evidence is selectively inserted. He illustrates this by claiming that it would be possible to assemble evidence for 'man the dancer' as much as 'man the hunter'. Many typical human characteristics, such as face-to-face sex, bipedalism and moving into open spaces, could be cited as evidence for a desire to dance as much as to hunt!

Paleo-archeological research generates lots of skeletal data but more micro-sociological evidence is needed on the situations in which violence is enacted. Further, extrapolating the data to modern societies is highly problematic. For example, the fact that young males of reproductive age commit most violence does not fit only with evolutionary theory, but also with cultural theories of masculinity, subcultural theories and social structural explanations, to mention a few. Anyway, most young men of that age are *not* violent and only a minority are, which suggests the pervasiveness of social solidarity and that the needs for conflict avoidance are stronger than any biological, psychological or social pressures to be violent.

Further, there is evidence that Neolithic societies in the Danube Basin (for example) were relatively peaceful and cooperative until the predatory invasions in the Upper Palaeolithic around 10,000 years ago (Bacciagaluppi 2004). His explanation of this is essentially materialist. The meeting of 'hungry nomads' and 'sedentary horticulturalists' who had accumulated a food surplus perhaps led to predatory behaviour on the part of the nomads, and this behaviour then became culturally inscribed into subsequent human development. 'In the course of prehistory', Bacciagaluppi (2004) argues, 'there seems to have been a turning point from peaceful cooperative human groups to hierarchical groups led by aggressive males'. The emergence of war and intraspecific violence, then, was not necessarily a carry-over from a pre-human form of life but, according to Bacciagaluppi, was a novel development that required 'pseudospeciation', that is regarding other human groups as belonging to a different species, against whom violence was legitimate.

Similarly, Knauft (1991) argues that in the Late Palaeolithic, primal hierarchies were replaced by stable, egalitarian, and reliable relations of obligations. This divergence of simple societies from other primate communities means that there was no uninterrupted evolutionary progression from primates to human 'tribal' and much less state societies (Knauft 1991). In the evolution of *Homo Sapiens Sapiens*, 'it is likely ... that coercion and violence as systematic means of organizational constraint developed especially with the increasing socio-economic complexity and potential for political hierarchy afforded by substantial stored food surplus and food production' (Knauft 1991). Like Habermas, Knauft argues that elaborate symbolic communication was highly developed among *Homo Erectus*, for whom there is evidence of culture in beads, animal bone pendants, crayons, and use of red ochre powder. The rapid spread and socioeconomic adaptation of *Homo Sapiens* further suggests the development of linguistic facility. This in turn means that through socialization and symbolic communication, behavioural traits were learned faster than the process of biogenetic selection and point to the distinctive impact of cultural rules in human behaviour.

According to Knauft, then, one cannot draw conclusions about an essential tendency to violence from early human evolution. Further, Robb (1997) argues that violence is a cultural style or reflex of political economic conflict and cannot be explained with reference to innate aggressiveness. Meanings of violence change through history. Evidence of trauma becomes more common as time passes and from hierarchical societies in the Iron Age there is extensive evidence of violence among men, which Robb suggests is linked to defence of honour. Violent acts define and reinforce the identities of categories of people and the role of violence depends on its place within the symbolic character of relations between groups. Robb (1997) argues that we need then to map out its historical and social context.

However, implicit in this discussion is a significant ambiguity to which we will return later. Despite the thesis that violence and hierarchy increased in the Late Palaeolithic, Robb (1997) also suggests that interpersonal violence is *less* frequent in societies with male status hierarchies, as does Knauft (1991). One explanation of this is that there are clearer boundaries of status and spatial distance than in more diffuse societies. His point is that the effects of status hierarchies on violent behaviour is not straightforward but depends on the symbolic order within which they are situated. However, there are two hypotheses implied here:

1 Egalitarianism is accompanied by low levels of violence, particularly if there if there are few surplus resources to contest (cf. Marx and Engels). A corollary of this is that violence increases with hierarchy and inequality. Systems of honour and rigid stratification increase victimization of people of lower standing.
2 Egalitarian societies have higher levels of interpersonal violence than hierarchically ordered societies because the latter establish structured entitlements to resources and increased social distance between members of the communities. A corollary of this might be that violence in hierarchical societies is more collective and organized while increased social distance reduces interpersonal confrontation and conflict.

However, this is complicated further by the way violence can appear in private and public settings. In the Ancient World and Medieval Europe there were many spectacles of publicly organized violence. The body became a 'theatre for engagement' of violence entering the most intimate areas (Appadurai 1998). Indeed, the state emerges around the spectacle of violence (Aijmer 2000: 16) in public executions and violent contests as forms of public sacrifice to honour the political authorities. Ancient Rome was exceptional in the extent and intensity of state organized violence throughout its existence and 'killed on an enormous scale, with efficiency, ingenuity and delectation' (Kayle 1998: 2). The Arena was a space in which power, leadership and empire were symbolized through ritualized killings, often followed by ceremonies. In AD 107, for example, Emperor Trajan held 23 days of games in which 11,000 animals were killed and 10,000 gladiators fought. These were spectacles of death and cruelty that were enthusiastically attended by hundreds of people (Kayle 1998: 35). Similarly, Collins (1974) writes of 'preemptory executions, torture and mutilation [as] ... characteristics of iron age (agrarian) societies which are highly stratified around a patrimonial form of government'. Further, 'torture and mutilation ... are distinctively human acts; they are indeed advanced human acts' rather than emanations of primal rage. The patterns of state-organized violence need to be understood with reference to their place within hierarchical and military social structures rather than rooted in the distant past of the human species. 'Ferociousness', Collins (1974), says 'is most institutionalised where ritual boundaries are structured within an autonomous state'.

Symbolic context of violence

One of the weaknesses of the literature on prehistoric violence is its emphasis on osteological data and neglect of consideration of the cultural meanings of violence. Indeed, Ferrell et al. argue that 'all interpersonal violence involves drama, presentation and performance', it carries communicative power and pain involves both physical and symbolic public degradation as well as physical domination (Ferrell et al. 2008: 8). The importance of this can be illustrated with reference to debates about cannibalism, a Freudian motif that has been the focus of considerable controversy. Evidence of cannibalism in the human fossil record is rare but it is now becoming apparent that the practice can be found in human history. There are different types of cannibalism – survival cannibalism (driven by starvation), ritual cannibalism (for example, as part of funerary rites) and that which attracts most attention, gustatory cannibalism (the culturally encouraged consumption of human flesh). Claims for the existence of the latter are controversial and accounts often relate cases of cannibalism among cultures that are already despised, feared, or are little known. For centuries, attributions of cannibalism to 'savage' peoples were part of the often racist othering of non-western cultures under colonial rule. This practice provoked the counter-reaction that regarded claims of cannibalism as 'pure travellers' myths' (Arens 1979: 139). Noting that most documentation of ritualized cannibalism was second-hand and there was an absence of credible witnesses, Arens further pointed out that many explorers' descriptions of cannibalism are inherently unreliable, because the Spanish royal proclamation of 1503 specifically permitted the use of cannibals – and only cannibals – for slaves. Nowadays the methodological requirements for establishing evidence of cannibalism are quite specific – including human and animal remains found in the same spatial relationships, with similar patterns of bone modification (e.g., chop marks), evidence of cooking (Knüsel and Outram 2006) and possibly also evidence of human proteins in fecal remains (Walker 2001).

However, Robb (1997) points out that many studies of cannibalism and prehistoric violence are marked by descriptive empiricism, such as detailed osteological data and simplistic theories of ecological crisis prompting (survival) cannibalism. Robb argues that violence is always symbolically constructed behaviour involving semantics of the body. It is also a performative act of masculinity in many societies. Knüsel and Outram (2006) suggest that cannibalism was part of feasting rites and was done to 'capture the essence of the personal strength of the individual consumed', although it can also be seen as 'an act of supreme denigration and disempowerment' of those who are eaten (2006: 256). Many anthropologists identify sacred meanings in cannibalism, for example Goldman (1999: 16–17) says:

> One school of thought is that anthropophagites [cannibals] are ingesting posi-
> tively valued qualities in either exo- or endocannibalism. ... Cannibalism is a
> means of processing life-generating substances often linked to ideas about femi-
> nine reproductivity especially among the Gimi (Papua New Guinea). ... Flesh
> eating may be a way of reconverting immorality of witches into sociocentred
> exchange behaviour of the kin group.

A second argument is that exocannibalism is an expression of hostility, violence and domination, which is discussed by Kantner (1999) in relation to the Anzsazi.[7] He argues that most research has focussed on identifying whether or not actual acts of cannibalism occurred. Rather, he suggests that two or more behaviours could be responsible for evidence that is spatiotemporally clustered and is linked to lines of power in the political system. There is evidence that in changing environmental and socio-political contexts around AD 900–1100 sedentary Anzsazi communities protected land and power through use of violence and intimidation. 'Extraordinary violence' can be exemplary – 'it does not just kill but also disgraces the deceased and shames surviving relatives and compatriots while enhancing the credibility of threats in future interactions' (Kantner 1999:95). He continues that powerful individuals in later Anasazi communities 'could have used threats of torture, corpse mutilation and cannibalism to intimidate opponents' (1999:96), thus deterring potential competitors and maintaining the status quo. Further, when the system of social divisions weakened he found that the evidence of skeletal trauma pointed towards warfare but not cannibalism.

That cannibalism was embedded in the social beliefs and ritual practices of various societies illustrates the importance of understanding the cultural meanings of violence.

Violence and the social bond

A major problem encountered by evolutionary–instinctivist theories is in some ways Hobbes' problem – how was it that warring people developed sufficiently stable social bonds and cooperation to organize for survival? But it might be that the solution to this problem is at the same time the source of a specifically human form of violence. Turner (2007) argues that most ape species became extinct in the past 16 million years and those with the best survival chances in predator-ridden savannah were species that had the ability to form complex social organization.

---

[7]The Anasazi region goes across the southern Colorado Plateau and the upper Rio Grande, spanning northeastern Arizona, northwestern New Mexico, southeastern Utah and southwestern Colorado.

This in turn required enhanced emotionality, something developed particularly in humans, who have the widest palate of emotions of any animal, in terms of the number and intensity of emotional states they can experience. Further drawing on symbolic interactionism, Turner argues that humans developed the capacity for self-evaluation through internalizing the expectations and judgements of others. This 'looking glass self' is in a constant state of explicit and implicit emotional arousal and is evaluating the self from the perspective of others. The combination of enhanced emotionality and self-reflection created increased capacities for social bonding, particularly through the emergence of shame, guilt and alienation, as second-order elaborations of the primary emotions of happiness, anger, fear and sadness. The significance of these secondary emotions is that they enhance the potential for social solidarity by making people more self-aware and motivated to monitor their own behaviour and interactions with others. Shame is particularly powerful since it signifies a breach in social relations and expectations that is painful for the self. However, 'one of the ironical consequences of a large-brained, emotional animal that can see [its]self as an object is the ability to repress and distort the very emotions that lead to interpersonal attunement and solidarity' (Turner 2007). Shame is a negative emotion that threatens the self and will often be repressed from conscious awareness. Turner suggests that 'shame will often erupt as anger and disrupt social relations and … lead to high-intensity violence' (2007). In other words, if this analysis is correct, the wide palate of emotions that facilitated complex social bonds and increased survival abilities might also be the source of human violence where shame is repressed and then attributed to external objects. Whereas positive emotions are attributed to the self and reinforced in interaction rituals, negative emotions will tend to be repressed and attributed to external objects. For example, street gangs whose members dropped out of schools often do not vent their anger at the schools but at other gangs (Turner 2007). Shame and its associated emotions are thus two-sided – on the one hand they work to ferment social bonds, while on the other hand repressed shame will often erupt as anger and can violently disrupt social relations.

Thomas Scheff (1997: 9) similarly sees shame as 'the master emotion in that it is an actual part of, or more frequently, it is anticipated in virtually all human contact', and again argues that repressed shame is a 'signal of threat to social bond'. In modern societies, he suggests, shame has not decreased but 'gone underground' and become 'unacknowledged', although nonetheless operative in social interactions. While conflict is functional if it repairs the social bond, it is dysfunctional to the extent that it creates further alienation. Where there are interminable conflicts (whether within families or between nation states) all participants have contributed more or less equally to the discord. Scheff indeed claims that all violence is based on these two conditions – that parties to a conflict are alienated from each other and are in a state of shame and that their states of shame and alienation go unacknowledged (Scheff and Retzinger 2001: xvii).

Emotions cannot, however, be regarded as historically constant within and between societies. While Turner's and Scheff's emphasis on the dynamics of shame might be valid, there is also evidence, which will be considered in the next chapter, that human emotional configurations have emerged historically. By contrast to violent emotions, compassion, the active moral demand to address others' suffering, is a further social emotion, although one that according to Sznaider (2000) has emerged historically within certain sociological conditions. He argues that although modern society is often thought of as having eroded morality, on the contrary, compassion as a social emotion has risen since the eighteenth century and has its roots in the Latitudinarian Anglican divines[8] between 1660 and 1725. They aimed to combat Hobbesian notions of egoism and elevated universal benevolence as a religious virtue (Sznaider 2000: 13). Through the following two centuries, compassion grew in significance and was linked to the growth of the market, civil society and middle-class concepts of privacy and domesticity. The nineteenth-century campaign against cruelty to children, he suggests, reflected a new morality of the home (as a place of refuge and safety), the critique of industrial working conditions, the emerging generational space of 'childhood' and a universalist morality that extended responsibility to anyone suffering (2000: 45ff). In other words, social conceptions of both cruelty and compassion have emerged historically, as have other social emotions, and are crucially influenced by wider social changes and emergence.

Further, evolutionary psychology operates at mostly non-linguistic levels of emotional response. But moral codes are central to human societies and these are articulated in mores, traditions and laws that are enacted and re-affirmed through rituals. Neoevolutionary theory does not give serious attention to the autonomous significance of normativity in social evolution. After all, in Neolithic societies collective identity was based on social roles and kinship as shared origin. But as Habermas pointed out (1979: 119), the very concept of 'kinship' already presupposes the existence of norms – that one has obligation to members of the kinship group. Power and normativity remain crucially linked in state societies where tribal identities are replaced by more abstract identity based in territory and loyalty to the sovereign. Here the spectacle of violence appears as a means of demonstrating dominance of the sovereign over public space. Later, in the modern constitutional state, autonomous legal subjects pursue interests in a public sphere that is governed by universal norms of legality, equity and universalism. Violation of these norms – for example, through the conflict between official values of equality and the realities of structures of inequality – can itself give rise to feelings of estrangement, injustice and shame that can be a stimulus

---

[8]These were theologians such as the Cambridge Platonists, who rejected the dogmatism of the Puritans and materialist philosophies such as Cartesianism and advocated the application of reason to understanding scripture.

to violence. Even if there were evolutionarily adaptive forms of aggression in human development, the key to understanding violence will still rest in understanding the interplay of norms and structures within the social order.

Conclusion

Violence is apparently ubiquitous and lies deep in human history. This has prompted many theorists over many centuries to suggest that there is something innately violent or at least aggressive in the human condition. Hobbes formulated the view that in a natural state life was nasty, brutish and short while other philosophers, such as Locke, have viewed humans as more social and solidaristic. This is a debate that has continued into contemporary social sciences. Some archaeological anthropologists and evolutionary psychologists argue that a predilection for violence has been selected into human social development and has its origins in hunting and the survival needs of pre-human hominids. The conclusion drawn from this is not that we should be complacent about aggression and violence in modern social life, but that we need to recognize its deep roots in the human constitution. On the other hand, there are studies that also draw upon evidence from human evolution that develop a different view. While not denying that evidence of violence lies deep in the paleological record, they emphasise evidence for the disjuncture between pre-human uses of violence and its emergence within more recent post-Neolithic and state societies. According to this view, evidence of violence in the human fossil record increases considerably with the historical shift from relatively egalitarian non-state societies to complex hierarchically organized social systems, as incidentally, Marx and Engels suggested. Further, arguments for a continuous evolutionary link between pre-human and human life do not pay sufficient attention to the importance of symbolic communication, multiple role taking and the complex role of emotions in systems of human social organization. Like all other human behaviour, violence takes place within systems of power and meaning in which the body is symbolically represented. To see violence as the product of neural capacity inherited through evolutionary development ignores the social and cultural meanings and significance of violence that expresses complex forms of social organization, power and communication. Rather than see violence as the outlet of some primal desire or instinct, it is better understood as innovative behaviour in which the capacities for human development of ritual cruelty (such as the Roman Arena) reflect a particularly human capacity for innovation. Paradoxically, the very emotions that ferment social bonds might also underpin violent behaviour because of the complex mediations between social rules and the constructions of meanings around the body. This suggests that any links that there might have been between pre-human and human social developments were highly attenuated and no simple lines of continuity can be drawn.

3

VIOLENCE, BODIES AND CIVILIZATION

Few social theorists have placed violence at the centre of their theories but most have dealt with at least some aspects of violence, especially in relation to political power and the state. However, Norbert Elias has exercised a significant influence over the understanding of these problems in sociology. Elias argued that there is a long-term trend towards the pacification of civil society that is linked to the emergence of state control of the means of violence and the widening of the scope of civil society as opposed to the military or warrior elite. Elias's theory of the civilizing process is in some ways comparable to Foucault's theory of the transition from the spectacle of punishment to the panoptic carceral institution, and this will be briefly discussed. The chapter concludes by identifying some limitations of Elias's approach that will set the scene for subsequent discussions.

The last chapter showed how violence in human societies has complex relationships with patterns of social organization and how the state both contains but also concentrates the means of violence. This will now be developed further. Many commentators note that modern societies have seen increased thresholds of repugnance to public theatres of cruelty that were once commonplace. Nowadays 'we drink coffee and engage in leisurely activities' in European heritage city squares that are silent on their earlier role as sites of 'the scaffold and gibbet', where 'the condemned were hung while the flames devoured their mortal remains and citizens gathered to observe and be amused' (Basson 2006). Carnivals of cruelty were public festivals and 'holidays' from habitual prohibitions. For example, according to James Fraser, 'In the midsummer fires formerly kindled on the Place de Grève in Paris it was the custom to burn a basket, barrel, or sack full of live cats, which was hung from a tall mast in the midst of the bonfire; sometimes a fox was burned. The people collected the embers and ashes of the fire and took them home, believing that they brought good luck'. Similar festivals occurred in the Vosges, Alsace and in the Ardennes cats were flung into the bonfires kindled on the first Sunday in Lent (Fraser 2000:, ch 64, para 8).

These events were also sites of potential disorder. As Foucault noted, in addition to public 'executions, which ought to have shown only the terrifying power of the prince, there was [also] … carnival in which the roles were inverted, the powerful mocked and criminals transformed into heroes' (Foucault 1976: 63). The end of these spectacles was in part a reflection of changing sensibilities but also signalled new modes of control. Similarly, when public cruelty to animals was criminalized in the UK, the 1911 Cruelty to Animals Act was 'passed in part to place tighter controls on the actions of the lower classes … [and] "welfare" reasons were only in the background', only to develop much later in the twentieth century (McCormack 2008: 201). The prohibition here is largely against the visibility of violence. Until the later twentieth century in Europe and some other countries, capital punishment did not end but was removed from public gaze into closed institutions. Violence has been enclosed and removed so far as possible from public spaces rather than eradicated. There is now widespread sensitivity towards gazing on violence and death. So, for example, animal slaughter is hidden from view in abattoirs and meat is neatly packaged in cuts that have little in their appearance to resemble living animals, and there are rules governing TV broadcasting of both actual and fantasy violence.

Nonetheless this is an ambiguous process. The claim that there has been a decline in violence in the modern period is contested by the view that modernity brought social disorganization and alienation and therefore rising levels of crime and violence. The twentieth century can be seen as an age of exceptional violence – with millions of deaths in two world wars, genocides,[1] the Soviet Gulag and the development of weapons of mass destruction. Critical theorists such as Adorno and Horkheimer have claimed that the consequences of western modernity and the Enlightenment have been ambivalent and that the separation of technology from ethics, which was part of an instrumental rationalized culture, has unleashed unprecedented destructiveness. So 'mankind, instead of entering into a truly human condition, is sinking into a new kind of barbarism' (Adorno and Horkheimer 1973: xi). This view also informs Bauman's (1989) claim that the Holocaust was not a deviation from rational modernity but, on the contrary, 'it was the spirit of instrumental rationality, and its modern, bureaucratic form of institutionalization, which had made the Holocaust-style solutions not only possible, but eminently 'reasonable'– and

---

[1]The twentieth century opened with the genocide of Hereros in German South-West Africa (now Namibia) between 1904 and 1907, which was followed by that of Armenians in Turkey (1915–22), the Stalin-engineered Ukrainian famine and mass deportations of 1933–35, of Chinese under Japanese occupation in Nanking (1937), the Holocaust (1940–45), Cambodian urban dwellers, Buddhists and ethnic minorities under Pol Pot (1975–78), of Mayans in Guatemala (1982–86), of Tutsis by Hutus in Rwanda (1994), and of Bosnians by Serbian nationalist militias in 1995. See www.ppu.org.uk/genocide/g_genocide_intro.html.

increased the probability of their choice' (1989: 18). On the other hand, it can be argued that, compared with past societies, the present is one of the *least* violent periods in human history. Steven Pinker claims that there is a historical 'decline of violence' which is 'visible at the scale of millennia, centuries, decades, and years. It applies over several orders of magnitude of violence, from genocide to war to rioting to homicide to the treatment of children and animals. And it appears to be a worldwide trend, though not a homogeneous one' (Pinker 2007). Indeed, until the later twentieth century this was a widely held view expressed in ideas of 'civilization' and 'progress' from earlier 'barbarism' – ideas that now appear naïve. However, the idea that there is long-term trend towards reduced violence and cruelty is also central to Elias's thesis, which is significant in that it theorizes violence in relation to historical relationships between the body and its boundaries, emotions and cultural meanings.

Civilizational process and privatization

There appears to be a wide agreement among sociologists (such as Beck, Giddens and Bauman) that contemporary societies are marked by individualization, reflexivity and flexibility. Indeed, individuality in the sense of a self-governing self that has no choice but to make choices might have become 'compulsory' (Moran and Skeggs 2004: 11–12). However, as Durkheim argued, greater individuality weakened social integration and risked rising crime, anomie and social disorganization. Elias describes this as the 'I–We' relation – secure social bonds require balance between excessive isolation (the 'I') and engulfment of the self by society ('We'). His theory of the civilizing process attempted to show how modern societies secure a balance through individualization combined with new types of emotion fostering social solidarity. It was noted in the last chapter that a number of theorists have stressed the importance of emotion, and in particular shame, in relation to violence, in opposition to the dominant cognitive focus in the human sciences (e.g., Scheff and Retzinger 2001). Scheff argues that 'Elias's study suggests a way of understanding the social transmission of a *taboo* on shame' (Scheff 2000a). However, it was also noted that Scheff sees shame as double-edged – a means of social bonding, but also a signal of threat to the social bond, of failing to conform to external normative expectations. It is 'unacknowledged shame' in particular that is a potential source of aggression.

Elias famously proposed the thesis of a 'civilizing' (or 'civilizational') process – that during the transition from European medieval to modern societies, complex social, cultural and psychological changes occurred that resulted in a reduction in interpersonal violence. This was because as the modern state secured a monopoly on the means of violence and pacified territories under its control, commerce, urbanization, wealth and taxation developed. Taxation facilitated larger armies and administration, but also the development of interdependence and legal systems in which conflicts could be settled in non-violent ways. As more people began to live in pacified areas, the division of labour became more complex and interdependent and control increasingly shifted from external control by others to self-control. These increasingly complex and interdependent social networks engendered changes in personality – broadly speaking, from high volatility to self-control, a growing sense of time and forethought and ethos of calculation and self-regulation. These changes were evidenced first in the growth of manners among court circles that then diffused into wider circles of society, increasing shame around the body and a sense of privacy linked to the emergence of the division between public and private. Interdependence was not only lateral but also horizontal – the upper classes were becoming more dependent on classes below them while rising classes (the urban bourgeoisie) began to copy the manners of the court aristocracy. In due course, the bourgeoisie began to enunciate ascetic morality and feelings that differentiated them from both the 'unfeeling mob' and the 'arrogant and exclusive aristocracy' (Vaughan 2000).

Elias's use of the term 'civilizing' can be misleading since it carries connotations of colonialism and western beliefs in their superiority to other peoples – views that Elias rejected. Civilization generally has the connotation of restraining violence and of 'civil' as opposed to military society – *civilian*ization is a process of reducing the power and status of warriors relative to civil society. It further refers to the legal process in which grievances are carried into civil rather than criminal courts. For Elias, a crucial aspect was the growth of self-control over impulses and emotions. In identifying a civilizational process in western modernity, Elias tried to avoid Eurocentrism – all societies he argued have to socialize members and address how to satisfy elementary needs without 'destroying, frustrating, demeaning or in other ways harming each other' (Elias 1996: 31), and all societies undergo civilizing processes that are 'never completed and always endangered' (1996: 173). Indeed, he speculated that future historians may come to judge even the most 'advanced' present-day western societies as having formed part of an 'extended Middle Ages' (Elias 2001: 436ff) and their members as 'late barbarians' (Elias 1991: 146–7). He insisted that there was no 'zero point' in the civilizing process – that is, no point at which humans are uncivilized and begin to be civilized (Linklater 2004).

However, he did aim to reverse the view that industrialization and urbanization are inseparable from rising violence. Elias claimed that the growth of increasingly mannered social interaction was accompanied by increased public intolerance of violence and cruelty. Repugnance towards physical violence further increased with advancing thresholds of shame and embarrassment surrounding the body – acts once performed publicly, such as defecation and sexual intercourse, become private. At the same time, most people would regard carnivals of cruelty and violence with repugnance. Underlying this cultural and psychological shift there are deepening and widening interdependencies between people, which Elias calls 'figurations'. These are networks of interdependence between a 'plurality of reciprocally oriented individuals' (1994: 250) that are continually in flux and have a dynamic of their own – like the interdependence of people on a dance floor. Figurations frequently mutate into new forms, as did the system of social relations within states in the transition to modernity. Here the development of the monopoly of force, creation of civil pacified spaces, urbanization and complex interdependencies generated a new habitus.

The first volume of *The Civilizing Process* (*History of Manners*) provides an historical account of the period from the European Middle Ages to modernity, arguing that there was a transformation in the European 'social habitus' – the personality characteristics that people share with other members of their group. Elias claimed that in the transition from medieval to modern societies, initially in courtly circles, conventions governing acceptable displays of violence, sexual behaviour, bodily functions, table manners and forms of speech were gradually transformed by increasing thresholds of shame and repugnance. This, in particular, required the internalization of 'self-restraint' required by increasing social complexity and interdependence, which involved the strengthening of what Freud called the 'super-ego'. In the second volume, *State Formation and Civilization*, Elias developed a theory of the origins of these processes, particularly in the formation of an increasingly centralized state and increasingly differentiated and interdependent networks of modern societies. Like Weber, Elias sees as crucial to state formation the monopoly of legitimate violence within territorial boundaries.

In medieval society, Elias suggests, war is the normal state and pleasure is derived from cruelty, destruction and torment, evidenced, for example, in the mutilation of prisoners of war, burning heretics, public torture and executions, as noted above. However, in modern societies there is a concentration of the means of violence in the state and as the power of central authority grows people are forced to live at peace with a gradual corresponding change in emotional behaviour (Elias 1994: 201). Elias argued that with the centralization of state power there was a growth in personal restraint and mannered conduct, initially in court society, gradually spreading more widely along with the expansion of trade, urban life, a more complex division of labour, and the formation of 'civil society'. The longer and denser were networks of interdependence, the more people were obliged to attune their action to those of others and the less their interactions were marked by overt violence. Elias (1994: 368) suggests an example of these changes, in the difference between a medieval and modern journey. A medieval journey was a difficult and dangerous undertaking, along muddy roads on which there were few other travellers and risk of collision was low. However, the medieval traveller had to be alert to dangers posed by animals, other travellers and bandits. This state of alertness required a volatile temperament and eager readiness to fight and a personality that would be impulsive and resort quickly to violence. On the other hand, on modern roads the danger of physical attack is low but the risk of collision high. In this context (typical of the interconnected and complex nature of modern society), the development of control systems based on self-regulation, constant vigilance, foresight and self-control is crucial. These require personalities that are not impulsive but rational, calculating and technically competent.

However, in modern society people still feel the need for excitement, which is provided by institutionalized and regulated activities such as sport in which rules reduce the risk of injury but gratify the need for excitement. Sport institutionalizes calculated violence without loss of self-control, while spectators have the opportunity to vicariously enjoy the excitement of contest without the actual violence of earlier spectacles such as gladiatorial struggle. Thus, 'we no longer regard it as a Sunday entertainment to see people hanged, quartered, broken in the wheel. We watch football, not gladiatorial contests' (Elias 1986: 2). This analysis does raise the issue, though, of how to explain actual violence among rival spectators, which has become a major topic of research pursued particularly by followers of Elias, such as Dunning et al. (1987), and which is considered in Chapter 5. Elias describes the formation of a personality structure governed by self-control and foresight combined with feelings of shame, repugnance and embarrassment towards our own and others' behaviour. The pressures of surviving within highly interdependent social networks lead us to treat others and ourselves as a 'danger zone' – we feel anxiety about our vulnerability to others' behaviour and to our own inner drives (Elias 1994: 445). The experience of these tensions has two consequences in particular. First, modern human beings draw tight boundaries between themselves and whatever is 'outside', to the point of doubting the 'reality' of our perceptions of the outside world. Second, there is therefore a tendency to see ourselves as free and unique sovereign individuals (that Elias called *homo clauses*). Greater individualization, privatization of social life, instilled shame and self-control lead people to experience themselves as isolated individuals although this actually obscures the extent of modern interdependencies (Elias 2001: 28). Privatization is itself a social relation within complexly differentiated societies.

This is not simple though. In addition to privatization, the civilizing process also entails informalization, as social distance, status rituals and hierarchies weaken, people consequently have increased empathy with one another and will be less inclined to display aggressiveness. Informalization refers to the loosening of the hierarchical character of social relationships and the breakdown of formal social codes regulating behaviour. Since the First World War in particular (Elias 1994: 119), this began to apply not only among people occupying similar social positions, but between super- and subordinates as well. Elias illustrated this with the example of changes in courtship rituals and sexual relations among German university students. He contrasted rituals prior to the First World War, when contact was ruled by well-established, strictly formalized codes such as bowing, kissing a hand, use of the formal '*Sie*' and '*Gnädiges Fräulein*' [gracious young lady], to those of the late twentieth century, when individuals have to negotiate social relationships for themselves but within a more sexually 'permissive' context (Elias 1996: 35–7). Thus, in the twentieth century there was a gradual reduction of distance between social strata that was associated in part with increasing material security and complex role differentiations. The latter means that we engage in multiple role performances and move between situations bounded by different levels of formality and hierarchy in social relations of say, a parent, lover, public official, teacher, friend or colleague. Sociologists such as Simmel and Goffman have shown how competent social interaction requires management of, as Goffman says, different 'presentations of self' for different audiences. However, as Misztal (2000: 44) argues, the less is the gradient between formality and informality the more we come to behave similarly in all situations. In particular, since the 1960s manners have become less stiff and attitudes more 'permissive' than in earlier times such that 'many things forbidden earlier are now permitted' (Mennell 1992: 242).[2] Forms of address between people of different social status become more informal with relaxed codes of dress and the widespread use of 'du' and 'tu' and first names rather than family names. Children are raised in a less authoritarian way than in the past – literature on upbringing has, since the early twentieth century, condemned corporal punishment, scolding, fear-inducing fairy-tales, emotional distance and ostracism, and encouraged allowing autonomy and self-control, accommodating developmental needs, positive encouragement of approved behaviour and so on (Kitchens 2007). This has further consequences. More formal and stiff social interactions presuppose high risks of shame (if one falls short of expected modes of conduct) and highly censoring super-egos, whereas more informal and less scripted social encounters presuppose a more rational and calculating mode of self-regulation. This also involves higher levels of reflexivity – life planning, self-creation and transformation of intimacy with less 'conventional' and more experimental social relations. Informalization places greater stress, though, on self-restraint to make and maintain boundaries and creates greater insecurity since in the absence of formal rules much more has to be worked out by actors themselves.

---

[2]This is an inversion of Elias's quote from Caxton's fifteenth-century *Book of Curtesye*: 'Things that were once permitted are now forbidden' (Elias 1997: 235). The inversion illustrates how the civilizing process is many sided. What is permitted varies. In the nineteenth century urinating in public was permissible, but holding hands, kissing and displaying ringed navels was not (Siebel and Wehrhelm, 2006).

Elias argues (or at least this argument can be extracted from his thesis) that informalization and reduced hierarchy reduces interpersonal violence because a lessening of social distance and hierarchy requires more self-restraint and increases empathy between people in different social positions. Informalization, then, is an important element in the civilizing process. However, it might also contain an opposing tendency. Lack of external regulation might not produce planning, skilful reflexive actors but rather, as Lasch (1979) suggests narcissism, vague feelings of emptiness and avoidance of maturity. Kiliminster (2008) suggests that new pleasures might be derived from contemplating scenes of violence which people before would have found repugnant. Niche markets will cater for diverse tastes in a situation of high commercial penetration in everyday life and 'emancipation of emotions'. Wouters (2007: 216) similarly argues that with the reduction of formal hierarchy and apparent equalization there is a 'controlled decontrolling' in the realm of the imagination where superiority and inferiority are constructed in fantasy, such as films like *American Psycho, Natural Born Killers* and *Pulp Fiction*. Kiliminster (2008) argues that although informalization brings an expansion of permitted expression and pleasures, which could increase aggressiveness, in the end this process increases interdependencies and therefore ferments social bonding and reduces interpersonal violence. Further, Wilkinson (2005: 140ff) argues that exposure in the media may not desensitize audiences to suffering, but rather makes it more visible and cultivates a duty to care about strangers. While this will be true of certain media portrayals of suffering, the popular voyeurism of both fantasy and real extreme violence is more likely to have a decivilizing effect.

Further, it was noted in the last chapter that there is an argument that hierarchy and greater social distance *lessen* the likelihood of interpersonal violence, because they reduce status ambiguity. Increasing informalization then creates what Gould called a 'collision of wills'. 'I propose', said Gould (2003: 17), 'that much of human conflict occurs when relations involving rank are ambiguous or under challenge'. Struggles about dominance can be expressed in conflicts about symbolic matters and these are particularly likely in relations that are symmetrical or are undergoing instability (Gould 2003: 66). If this is so, then informalization might risk tipping over into increased interpersonal conflict. For example, reduced status differences and an egalitarian culture, where there is more uncertainty about social position, might allow conflicts over social status and shaming of the kind – 'Who do you think you are?', 'Do you think you're better than me?'. A society in which material and cultural differences remain, or indeed are widened, but where there is an appearance of equalization and informality, might actually see an increase in interpersonal violence and this is one of the core theses of this book.

Elias identified four key processes in the formation of modern societies and habits:

- State monopoly of the means of violence that ended medieval civil wars between local barons, which permitted a process of internal pacification and rule of law.
- Increasing interdependencies (figurations) such as market economies, which consolidated pacification and increased empathy with suffering.
- A rise in the repugnance threshold of witnessing or perpetrating violence, reflecting a new habitus of mannered self-control and greater forethought.
- Increasing taboos and shame surrounding the body and privacy, which are transmitted and stabilized through socialization.
- Enclosure of violence that occurs 'behind the scenes' rather than in public.

In summary, complex processes of pacification of civil spaces created by a state monopoly of violence allowed the growth of increased interdependencies across social space. These presupposed increased levels of internalized self-control, along with boundaries between the private and public that were focused on the body and a growing sense of body shame. Along with increased functional differentiation, there is democratization and a lessening of hierarchies – so informalization both necessitates increased social control and a greater empathy between people who are less divided by status, which in turn results in less readiness to act aggressively. This thesis does not necessarily predict that violence will diminish, even less that it will disappear, but it does predict lower levels of affective and impulsive aggressiveness in interpersonal interactions. This discussion has identified some ambiguity in the relationship between the civilizational process and informalization, to which the discussion will return.

Privatization of violence

Cooney (2003) develops further the theme of privatization of violence though modifying Elias's approach. Cooney argues that as intimate social ties weakened and the state strengthened, collective and non-legitimate forms of violence declined and violence became proportionately less public and more private. Like Elias, he argues that prior to modernization violence was evenly distributed through ranks in society and was not generally subject to taboo. For example, aristocrats fought duels and violence was used by nobles and commoners alike to settle disputes. However, in modern societies violence came to be negatively correlated with social status and regarded as 'lower class' behaviour. Further, violence is now more individualized and offenders more likely to act alone. He cites figures that in thirteenth-century England only 6.5 per cent of homicide victims were killed by relatives, a percentage that had risen to 33 by the mid-twentieth century (Cooney 2003). However, for Cooney, this trend was not a result of increased social ties but, on the contrary, weakening ties of family and community and greater social distance resulted in a wider role for the law to resolve disputes rather than recourse to informal feuds and confrontations. The result was a reduction of public violence and a *relative* increase in violence in the private sphere, even though it might not have risen in absolute terms.[3] But recourse to the law, as opposed to settling scores personally, is also consistent with the civilizational thesis. Gould (2003) shows how a weak legal system fostered a culture of honour feuds in Corsica while 'the increasingly visible presence of the criminal justice system imported from the metropole lowered rates of violence overall (Gould 2003: 156). Cooney (2003), though, introduces a structural dimension to the theory, arguing that violence is more frequent in lower structural locations manifest along vertical (economic), horizontal (relational), corporate (organizational), symbolic (cultural) and normative (moral) lines. He further argues that violence is closely linked to social control and in the majority of cases is moralistic – it is about restoring honour in a conflict. The pacification of society does not then preclude the continued existence of less visible but habitual and routine violence. Braithwaite (1993) said: 'A ducking stool for the disciplining of nagging wives could not be installed in an English town in 1992. Because this would be shameful in the late twentieth century, brutal men discipline their wives secretly: away from the disapproving gaze of others.' While Elias acknowledged this, he has been criticized for ignoring the extent to which much violence is hidden, 'private' and endured in silence, and most is kept away from the criminal justice system. This notably applies to intimate (private) violence that Cooney argues is proportionally greater with the process of privatization.

Decivilizing process

The civilizing process was a gradual, partial and unplanned long-term process of pacification. In later work, Elias (1996) introduced the idea of a 'decivilizing process' with which he explained the Nazi period and its regression from civilization into barbarism. Although he does not present an explicit theory of a decivilizing process, Fletcher (1997: 176–84) argues that there are three theses:

- A shift in the balance between self-restraint and constraint by others towards the latter.
- Change in social standards of behaviour and feeling that allowed for a desensitization towards violence and reduced differentiation of habitus.
- A reduction in mutual identification between groups.

---

[3]Cooney also points out that if in the past, as now, homicide perpetrators were mostly young males, then with a shorter life span among the general population, homicide would have been higher per head of the population than it is in most modern societies.

The introduction of the concept of 'decivilization' emphasizes the contingent and reversible nature of the process, although it does also protect the theory from any apparent counter-evidence. Faced with evidence of counter-trends (such as rising homicide rates in the later twentieth century), the thesis can always be defended with reference to the appearance of a 'decivilizing process'. There is a possibility of tautology in this concept – the conditions in which violence occurs are also those of the decay of empathy and self-control so they will always be 'decivilizing'. In order to be an explanatory theory it needs to specify the conditions in which each process (civilizing and decivilizing) occur. Further, while Elias introduces the 'decivilizing process' partly to account for the genocidal Third Reich, there would be further problems if it could be shown that the Holocaust presupposed not so much a decivilizing process but the very attributes of civilized habitus – planning, forethought, technical sophistication and a state monopoly over the means of violence. This is discussed below and in detail in Chapter 9.

Elias and Foucault

Some commentators, such as Smith (1999) and Spierenburg (2004), argue that Elias's thesis parallels Foucault's work on similar themes, though it is worth noting Adorno's warning here. He quotes from Nietzsche that 'He who seeks to mediate between two bold thinkers ... has not the eyes to see uniqueness: to perceive resemblances everywhere ... is a sign of weak eyesight' (Adorno 1974: 74). Even so, it is true that Foucault's archaeology of modern systems of control and discipline, like Elias, pays attention to high levels of public violence in pre-modern societies (by contrast with later periods), where public execution, corporal punishment and mutilation of offenders was normal and symbolized the sovereign power of monarchical law over the people. Both Elias and Foucault identified enclosure as a significant means of modern control and attached importance to the way the self and bodily functions were transformed and repressed. For both theorists, ascetic techniques, which in later work Foucault (1988: 18) called 'technologies the self', aimed at controlling spontaneous, unchecked activities of the body, were crucial for the development of modernity.[4] This idea echoes a core theme in classical sociology, notably Weber's concept of Protestant asceticism, where by contrast with traditional life, the highest form of moral obligation was methodical self-discipline and fulfilling one's duty in worldly affairs (Weber 1974). Even so, while Elias identifies an

---

[4]Foucault regards these as methods which permit individuals to effect by their own means or with the help of others a certain number of operations on their own bodies and souls, thoughts, conduct, and way of being, so as to transform themselves in order to attain a certain state of happiness, purity, wisdom, perfection, or immortality (1988: 18).

increase in sensibility to cruelty, Foucault sees only an exercise in ubiquitous deadening discipline (Miller 1990).

It is well known that Foucault's *Discipline and Punish* begins with the description of the public torture and death in 1757 of Damiens, the attempted 'regicide' who had scratched Louis XV with a knife. The spectacle of public torture and execution by drawing and quartering was a public ritual which repaired the injured sovereignty of the monarch (Foucault 1976: 3). In the event, the mutilation and torture of Damiens was chaotic. The horses were unable to tear his body apart, after repeated attempts, so his limbs were hacked off and his torso was thrown on to the fire, possibly still alive. This was not just about punishing the individual, but was also the playing out of a ceremonial in which the king's justice had to be seen to be done in public in a display of royal power over a dissenting individual's body. The ritual element of this killing is similar to Katz's (1988) 'righteous slaughter', where the violence exercised on the body continues beyond death as symbolic desecration and 'sacrificial marking' of the victim, exceeding any 'instrumental' purpose. However, what Foucault did not note was that Damiens was the last person to be executed in France by drawing and quartering, and the public spectacle provoked revulsion from some spectators.[5] Foucault was not attentive to the way the transformation documented in *Discipline and Punish* could also be seen as being driven by increasing compassion and violence-repugnance in the manner described by Elias.

At the same time, Foucault was highly attentive to the ways in which state power became embedded in institutional disciplinary practices. The consequence of this was not that violence ended, but that it was enclosed within walls and removed from the public gaze (Vaughan 2000). Foucault contrasts the spectacle of Damiens' death with the inscription of a 'micro-physics' of power in the disciplined routine of the prison, exemplified by the House Rules of Paris Maison des Jeunes Détenus 1838 that described in detail at what time the prisoners will rise, dress, make their beds, proceed to the chapel, wash, eat and work (Foucault 1976: 6ff). Central to the new disciplinary regime was the principle of surveillance embodied in Jeremy Bentham's concept of the Panopticon – an architecture that incorporated the individualization of prisoners in isolated cells, combined with the possibility of continual observation by an unseen observer from a central tower. But there is a further shift here in the concept of victimhood. The mutilation of Damiens was a public spectacle that 'repaired' the symbolic damage to the sovereign. So the hand in which Damiens held the knife is

---

[5]In his Memoires, Jacques Casanova records revulsion at the execution of Damiens, whom he regarded as a 'victim of the Jesuits' since he had been influenced by their doctrine of 'tyrannicide': 'I was several times obliged to turn away my face and to stop my ears as I heard his piercing shrieks'. See www.nalanda.nitc.ac.in/resources/english/etext-project/Biography/casanova/chapter59.html.

covered in sulphur and the degeneration of his physical body repairs the insult to the body politic. However, in modern society it is the subject not the state who is the victim (Wieviorka 2009: 54), and protection and compensation is less about the collective order and more about the integrity of individuals. In due course, by the later twentieth century, victimology, the study of victims, would become central to both policing and criminology and a more explicit part of the criminal justice system (CJS) in the form of victim statements.

For Elias, increased self-control was facilitated through the state monopoly of force (which reduced 'private' conflicts), expanded interdependencies and an increased sense of privacy and shame. Along with these went increased repugnance at bodily functions and greater management of feelings (Smith 1999). This was a movement of *longue durée*, in which the state centralizes social life and undergoes 'functional democratization', that is a broad process of democratic egalitarianism and informalization. By contrast, Foucault's attention is on disciplinary practices that abruptly change between around 1760 and 1840. Spierenburg (2004) notes that the changes in punishment and the prison did pre-date the 1750s and continued long after 1840, so a concept of gradual reforms is more plausible than a rapid discursive shift from public spectacle to carceral institution. Foucault (1991: 336) himself said: 'I know that this reading is schematic: things did not really unfold so neatly, and there were many obscurities and hesitancies along the way.'

However, Foucault's notion of power is rather one-dimensional when one considers how power is bound up with notions of compliance, justice and norms. Just as Foucault was inattentive to growing compassion in eighteenth-century upper-class norms, he similarly did not acknowledge that power requires compliance. Even in the Panopticon, observation alone would not be sufficient to secure order; rather, the system presupposed actors who internalized carceral discipline and acted in the required regimented way, although the system still would not be able to distinguish between internalized and pretended conformity (Simon 2005). Further, punishment is intimately bound up with norms of justice. Part of the penal revolution Foucault described was not only about more finely calibrating punishments and offences, but also creating punishment that was to be just. However, the more justice becomes a core value of the system, the more that which is perceived as unjust by its recipients (however others regard it) becomes a focus for resentment and shame-rage. Indeed, punishment generally has the effects, Gilligan (2000) and Thome (2001) argue, of decreasing guilt and increasing shame, which is a potential condition for further violence. Prisons were then producing less disciplined and more chaotic bodies than Foucault suggested since the institutional regime and multiple acts of resistance to it occurred within a field of constraints and violent emotions. Emotionality, and especially shame, is key to understanding the dynamics of violence and punishment.

Beyond the civilizational thesis

There is a problem with evaluating Elias, though, as Scheff (1997: 50) notes, in that it is 'difficult to argue with [his] findings or even to state with precision exactly what they are'. The civilizational thesis is partial – privatization and individualization might diminish public and interpersonal violence but might also be the source of further violence, especially that exercised through impersonal means. One of the most vigorous critics of Elias's thesis is Hans-Peter Duerr (1988), who argues that the civilizational process is a myth. He challenges Elias's concept of 'civilization' on the grounds that although Elias set out to *analyse* the self-perception of Western European civilization, he actually accepted that self-perception which coincides with colonial ideology of the west as 'more civilized' than the rest of the world (van Kreiken 2005). Further, Duerr claims that human sexual relations are always socially regulated and subjected to some patterned set of rules and norms, which will universally produce a division between public and private bodily domains, with the private domain being the focus of social regulation. For Duerr, the kind of lack of restraint of impulses Elias seems to observe in the Middle Ages is simply impossible, because the family relations which existed at the time required some regulation of sexual conduct (van Krieken 1998: 116). Elias is accused of exaggerating the novelty of 'modern' phenomena such as bodyshame. In the past 40,000 years, he says, 'there have been neither wild nor primitive peoples, neither uncivilized nor natural peoples … it is part of the *essence* of humans to be ashamed of their nakedness' (Duerr 1988: 12, quoted van Krieken 2005). Similarly, as Katz (1996) argues in an analysis of the Adam and Eve myth, body shame (a fearful sense of isolation and embarrassment) might be a foundation of the social order. Clothing, he suggests, constructs a sensibility of being observed and reveals shameful privacy in relation to what 'others are kept from observing'. Duerr provides a list of non-state societies in which people exhibited 'civilized' personality traits, and rather than see social control increasing in complex societies, he regards impersonality as bringing freedom from the constraints and 'village eye' of small communities. On the other hand, Fletcher (1997: 37) points out that Elias repeatedly said that there was no society in which drive-impulse control were absent. He was interested in how these were configured within different types of social process and his interest in interdependent state societies was to demonstrate that impulse control was more stable there than in non-state societies.

Turner (2003) argues that Elias's theory was primarily a secular history of manners, whereby crude, vulgar and rustic behaviour was converted into courtly dispositions, but (surprisingly, in view of the influence of Weber in Elias) he paid little attention to the role of religion in regulating and shaping violence. In feudalism, religion provided an institutional check on violence by integrating the warrior into society, and Chaucer's chivalrous Knight was an idealized example of the warrior civilized by Christendom who 'loved chivalrye/ Trouthe, and honour, freedom and curteisye'. As well as inhibiting violence, Turner suggests, religion also controls and sustains it. He examines the evolution of military violence and charisma among American Plains Indians, especially the Cheyenne, and suggests that their mode of warfare is a form of spiritual violence, in which military interaction was highly ritualized. Cheyenne warriors, Turner suggests, had ritually prepared themselves for death prior to going into battle and their indifference to death both humiliated and terrorized their opponents. Violence and the sacred are further intertwined in religious rituals such as self-flagellation at the Shi'a festival of Muharram, and Girard notes that there is nothing quite as socially cathartic as controlled and righteous violence, especially when it is unanimous (Girard 1977: 78–81). The question for Elias, then, is whether civilization overcomes violent passions or whether they metamorphose into more calculated forms. The sociologist-theologian Jacques Ellul argued that 'The more complex and refined civilization becomes the greater is the "interiorizing" of determinations. These become less and less visible, external, constricting and offensive. They are instead invisible, interior, benevolent, and insidious' (Ellul 1976: 41).

Turner contrasts this 'warrior charisma' with the western routinization of military charisma and instrumental calculated killing. Following Bauman (1989) and Arendt (1963), he argues that the civilizing process involves the spread of norms of self-control and bureaucratic calculation combined with the state's monopoly of violence, which means that modern societies have the capacity for dispassionate mass killing. In the Holocaust, 'It was because the guards were civilized in Elias's sense that they had to be protected from the stress of killing' and the gas chambers provided a means of remote mass murder (Turner 2003). This view is critically assessed in Chapter 9.

Crucial to Elias's thesis is the claim that over several hundred years there developed increased sensitivity and repugnance towards violence. Is there any evidence for this? As we saw in the last chapter, some archaeological anthropologists argue that in prehistoric societies violence was more deadly, more frequent and more ruthless than in recent periods. It was also noted in the last chapter that there is considerable dispute over such claims and attempts to compare prehistoric with contemporary levels of violence are fraught with difficulties of interpreting and comparing sparse data. Pinker (2007) claims that:

> pre-state societies were far more violent than our own. It is true that raids and battles killed a tiny percentage of the numbers that die in modern warfare. But, in tribal violence, the clashes are more frequent, the percentage of men in the population who fight is greater, and the rates of death per battle are higher. ... If the wars of the twentieth century had killed the same proportion of the population that die in the wars of a typical tribal society, there would have been two billion deaths, not 100 million.

He further cites figures from the Human Security Brief (2006: 6) to suggest that with the decline in interstate wars in the later twentieth century, average battle deaths per armed conflict fell from 50–70,000 in the mid-twentieth century to under 5000 during 1990s and 2000s, making this the *least* violent period in human history.

However, the long-range comparisons are based on questionable extrapolations from prehistoric societies to the present, taking a single and simple measure – battlefield deaths in relation to total population. It was noted in Chapter 2 that the historical pattern of violence is more like a U-curve: low among hunters-gatherers, much more common among horticulturalists (which are the groups from which his examples came), peaking in agrarian societies and then beginning a gradual, though bloody and uneven decline in modern societies. Further, calculating the percentage of death per population in modern times does not deal with the significance of state-induced killings of civilian populations. The death toll is not limited to those directly killed in battle since major consequences of modern warfare are the displaced and refugees and civilian populations generally. In the Iraq conflict, for example, there are no verified records of civilian deaths but these are frequently estimated in hundreds of thousands. In all, as Mennell (2009) says, the process of state formation is 'Janus-faced: as larger territories became *internally* pacified, the wars *between* territories came to be fought on a steadily larger scale'.

There is some evidence, though, that over several centuries (and despite a post-1960 increase in western societies) there has been a long-term decline in interpersonal and especially lethal violence. Gurr (1981) argued that this was a result of growing sensitization to violence and the development of increased internal and external controls on aggressive behaviour. Similarly Eisner (2001) argues for a steeply declining rate of homicide between the thirteenth and twentieth centuries (shown in Figure 3.1). These data should again be interpreted with caution, however, because of the inadequacy of records over much of this period, changes in key juridical concepts, such as *mens rea*, changing rules of evidence, and so on. However, Garland (1991: 233) argues that there is a 'substantial body of historical evidence which would support' the civilizing process, although this could also be a problem in that the thesis is not differentiating enough and in particular cannot distinguish between long- and shorter-term trends in violent behaviour.

Thome (2001) also argues that there was a steady decline in violent crime from the seventeenth to the mid-twentieth century, after which it began to rise again. This latter change, he argues, is a result of a rise of individualism and erosion of collectivism. That is, the forms of social solidarity created by social democratization and the growth of welfare states in the mid-twentieth century have been eroded. He cites post-industrial changes in occupational structure, lifestyle changes and the legitimation crisis of the late 1960s, leading to the transformation

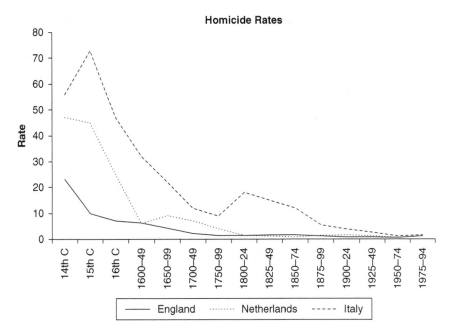

Figure 3.1 Long Term Trends in Homicide Rates
Source: Adapted from Eisner (2001)

of family structures, and, in particular, globalization and the rising inequality and marginalization of certain groups, as factors that have undermined the ability of nation states to maintain their taxation base and monopoly of violence. Wieviorka (2009) similarly relates the increase in political and organized violence in the later twentieth century to weakening social bonds in globalized, post-industrial societies, where the state's territorial integrity is weakened. The latter were important conditions for Elias's civilizational thesis and their erosion (if this argument is valid) could explain rising levels of violent crime in the later twentieth century. This is discussed further in relation to homicide trends in Chapter 7.

Elias has, then, provided a theoretical framework for understanding a tendency in the modernization process towards reduced interpersonal violence, although there are shorter-run counter-cycles, where interpersonal violence increases. Before ending this chapter, two issues are worth noting. First, let us look again at privatization and internalization. For Elias, mannered interaction is based on a habitus of body shame and the private self. But the public/private dichotomy that was important for Elias has arguably been eroded by media and communication technologies as private suffering, grief and death appear in the news reports while mundane 'private' lives become public through self-surveillance on digital networking sites. Wouters (2007: 175) refers to the breakdown of taboos on what can be discussed in public such as intimate sexual experiences, detailed descriptions of violence and 'every kind of emotion'. Again, Duerr (1988) says 'late modernity' involved a frontal assault on shame as nakedness, sex, violence and rage are turned into consumer items which have weakened thresholds of shame (quoted in Braithwaite 1993). It was noted above that the civilizational process involved prohibition on the visibility of violence, but a culture of voyeuristic violence re-enters a virtual public realm through digital communication and games. The early modern Puritan ideal of ascetic denial of pleasure has given way to a hedonistic culture of consumerism freed from restraints, so images of war, death and suffering are consumed as representations of everyday life. This 'pornoviolence' (Wolfe 1976) retains the audience's attention with the promise of disclosing gruesome details, thus degenerating to the level of sadistic sensationalism.

The significance of this is unclear since it could also be argued that the reception of images on screen is a truncated spectacle in which the visceral experience of real-life violence is absent. The commercial dispersal of communication technologies creates complex relationships between the public and private and violence. There are ways in which communication technologies might contribute to increases (or new modes of) violence:

- They encourage the distribution of images that can be instantaneously viewed all over the world, increasing the market for 'transgressive' images.
- Web blogging and posting private selves on networking sites that many people can access anonymously might increase susceptibility to stalking and 'cyber-bullying'.
- The many-to-many transmission of visual data might normalize 'happy slapping' and other violent forms of 'entertainment' while indicating lowered thresholds of repugnance.
- Mass school shootings such as Columbine in 1999 and suicide bombings are often preceded by video or digital dairies that dramatize the crime and address a potential audience of millions.

However, there is no simple relationship between media imagery and extreme violence. As Jenkins (1999) says in his congressional testimony following the Columbine killings:

> Cultural artifacts are not simple chemical agents like carcinogens that produce predictable results upon those who consume them. They are complex bundles of often contradictory meanings that can yield an enormous range of different responses from the people who consume them. … Cultural studies research tells us we need to make meaningful distinctions between different ways of representing violence, different kinds of stories about violence, and different kinds of relationships to violent imagery.

In response to claims about the role of violent fantasy videos in the motives of the Columbine killers (Harris and Klebold), Oliver James (1999) says that 'the problem of male aggression goes deeper than gory videos, as does the problem of male failure in the English syllabus'. Yet he continues, Harris and Klebold had not simply imitated mainstream masculine role models, but were alienated members of a 'Trenchcoat mafia' that had evolved in response to dominant footballing 'jocks' who regularly abused and attacked them. Shame at a failure to perform the masculine role will be a significant source of extreme violence (Gilligan 2000: 80).

A second issue is the relationship between civilization, shame and infor-malization. For Elias, the transition to modernity was accompanied by rising shame levels which increase social bonding by establishing boundaries around the body and increasing impulse controls. Scheff takes this argument further and argues that not only have shame thresholds decreased, but shame has 'gone underground' in that we are now ashamed of being ashamed. Elias noted that as courtesy became routine, no justifications needed to be offered for social conventions – the socialization of children automatically both inculcated and repressed shame in order to instil 'modesty'. Scheff (1997) develops the con-cept of unacknowledged shame which can take two forms. First, 'undifferenti-ated' shame that is overt and associated with silence, withdrawal and resignation (this is close to the everyday meaning of 'shame'), and second, 'bypassed shame' that is associated with anger and rage.[6] With the latter, rage is a response to feelings of helplessness, passivity, humiliation which in turn lead to further shame which is in turn repressed. This is a state that, depending in part on the responses of others, can last for a few minutes, hours, days or a lifetime of hatred and resentment. Scheff (1997: 233–5) provides elaborate accounts of links between unacknowledged shame and violence, including verbal, paralin-guistic and visual markers for shame, with which we will all be familiar – silences, stammering, raid speech, mumbling and hesitation. Based on analysis of verbal interactions and texts (such as telegraphic communications between the European powers prior to the First World War), Scheff (2000b: 83ff) argues that violence at both collective and interpersonal levels can be explained with reference to spirals of unacknowledged shame.

If this view is correct, then the relationship between shame and violence is more two-edged than Elias suggested. Culture and violence are not necessarily opposed and as well as constraining; culture can also embody violence. Elias draws a contrast between impulse control and self-restraint but what if the process of social bonding itself is founded on both repression of shame and violent exclusion through which collective identities are maintained (Bowman 2001)? It could be that social peace is secured through modern institutions

---

[6]However, Scheff is not as clear as he might be as to when shame results in aggression as opposed to depression, saying that 'an act of violence represents an attempt to re-establish control, to escape from shame into a state of pride', but also that 'shame and lack of community cause depression' (Scheff 2001).

such as the legal system, functional democratization and increased empathy with suffering. But these might be weakened by media commercialization that sees profit in a wholesale erosion of constraints. It was noted above that the process of informalization that is in some respects part of the civilizing process might tip over into unrestrained 'emancipation of emotions' and become decivilizing. Braithwaite (1993) claimed that Elias was 'inattentive to the fact that' shame has diminished as a means of control which was increasingly based on a rational exchange of infraction and punishment. Popular culture has for several decades promoted the transgression of shame boundaries and the breaking of taboos – epitomized perhaps in 'reality TV' shows that create a new public spectacle of voyeurism and humiliation – a process of voting that presents itself as 'democratic' in that it 'deploys the promise of access, participation via interaction ... [and] accountability' but is actually a medium of surveillance and provides producers with demographic data about voters (Andrejevic 2003: 161). In sum, then, informalization combined with commercialized public spectacles might contribute to a decivilizing process, especially, as we will now see, in social spaces of inequality and exclusion.

4

SPACES OF VIOLENCE

You cannot cheat with the law of conservation of violence: all violence is paid for, and ... the structural violence exerted by the financial markets, in the form of layoffs, loss of security, etc., is matched sooner or later in the form of suicides, crime and major everyday acts of violence. (Bourdieu 1998: 39–40)

This is in many ways a core chapter since it makes the link between macrosocial structures and cultures of everyday life. The process of enclosure was central, in different ways, to both Elias's and Foucault's theories of modernity. The space of the modern city is increasingly enclosed through internal security, CCTV, regulations on behaviour (e.g., controls on alcohol consumption and dress codes), architectures of control that manage visibility and regulated movement of bodies through urban spaces, and 'defensible spaces' for crime prevention. However, enclosure has multiple meanings and consequences, and can, like the 'enclosures' of land from the eighteenth century onwards, involve violent processes of dispossession. Further, the spatial organization of the city is structured by wider global socioeconomic processes which in turn structure patterns of violence. As Lefebvre (1991: 73) argues, as well as producing goods and services, economies also produce spaces. This 'abstract space' is carved into parcels to facilitate the power of capital or the state, which he contrasts with space that is 'lived' and can be contested and reclaimed. The long-term decline of violence noted by Elias, for which there is some evidence at a macro-historical level, needs to be set against the spatial and particularly urban unevenness in the risk and frequency of violence, which is the topic of this chapter.

The risk of violence is distributed through geographical space. Basic everyday knowledge of urban life tells us that some areas are 'safer' than others – we will move through some localities more confidently than others and some we will try to avoid altogether. Ward-level crime is higher in some places than others. Exposure to crime and victimization varies widely and the threat of finding oneself 'out of place' frequently appears as a literary trope. The city is the focus of social and cultural transformations and in the Victorian novel it was often the site of squalor and crime – in the rookeries depicted by Dickens, Zola and

Gissing. This theme was developed by Louis Wirth, for whom the city creates a 'substitution of secondary for primary contacts, the weakening of bonds of kinship, and the declining social significance of the family, the disappearance of the neighborhood, and the undermining of the traditional basis of social solidarity'. The results of these are 'personal disorganization, mental breakdown, suicide, delinquency, crime, corruption, and disorder' (Wirth 1938). The city embodies in its social organization the complex forces structuring the development of contemporary societies and this has profound impacts on issues of crime, security, policing and violence. Further, urban spatial divides map the intersecting divisions of class and race. A crucial issue here is the reordering of urban space in developed (and, in different ways, developing) societies during the last quarter of the twentieth century, associated with neoliberal, post-Fordist restructuring, creating what Soja calls new 'islands of enclosure' (2000: 299). In economically abandoned areas of cities, the rate of recorded violence quadrupled between 1960 and 2000 (Rosen 2003: 33) and Castells (1998: 138) argues that there is a systematic relationship between the structural transformations of capital, the growing dereliction of the ghetto and the emergence of a global, yet decentralized criminal economy.

A note on crime rates

Since this chapter will refer to local criminal statistics on violence, a brief note on these is in order. The limitations of official statistics on crime are well known and these are affected by many, often incalculable, issues including: the extent of crime that goes unreported; the media's generation of fear of crime, which in turn influences police strategic priorities; the categorization of incidents and offenders by police, prosecution services, and the criminal justice system; and changing reporting and accounting practices.[1] Some of the possible processes involved in generating crime statistics are shown diagrammatically in Figure 4.1. Between an event occurring, being reported as a crime and an eventual prosecution, decisions and classifications are made by various agencies in the criminal justice system (CJS) and the final published figures are a reflection of these. There are many reasons why people might not cross the first threshold of reporting a crime (most of which are quite predictable),

---

[1]For example, the Home Office (2004: 1) reports that 'A count of reports conducted by ASBU [Anti-Social Behaviour Unit] in England and Wales in September 2003 found that over 66,000 reports of anti-social behaviour were made to agencies on one day'. Prior to the Crime and Disorder Act 1998, of course, this would not have been possible because there was no category of anti-social behaviour, the ASBU did not exist, and nor did the strategic police priority of cracking down on ASB.

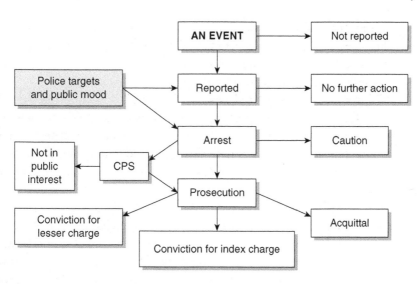

Figure 4.1 Production of Official Statistics

such as fear of recriminations, they regard what happened as a 'private matter', they do not feel any loss was suffered, fear of the consequences (such as family breakdown in the case of non-reported domestic violence), low expectations of the CJS, and embarrassment if they feel themselves partly responsible for their victimization. There is also evidence, for example, that while unemployment increases the risk of victimization, people who are unemployed are less likely to report crimes so the effects of particular social factors might be underestimated.

There are two main types of information on the crime rate – the crimes reported to the police and the results of crime surveys such as the British Crime Survey (BCS) and the US Criminal Victimization Survey. Police crime reports and victim surveys often generate quite different trends and pictures of the extent of crime, as we will see below. Any rate is simply one number divided by another and crime rates express the number of crimes reported per 1,000 (or 10,000, etc.) persons in the relevant locality. So if there are five violent crimes in an area where 1000 people live, the crime rate will be five per 1000. However, this is an inadequate measure since it takes no account of the population at risk. For example, it does not make a lot of sense to calculate the rate of automobile theft by dividing reported thefts by the number of people resident in a community since not all of them will have automobiles and some will have more than one. There are also different ways of calculating the rate – as Sherman notes, crime rates reflect the number of active offenders times the number of crimes each offender commits, but are reduced by the number of co-offenders involved with each crime. The reported rate will also be affected by the number of victims and separate offences involved in each event (Sherman, 1995). Some reported incidents will involve several offences but only one offender, and often police forces use discretion as to which charges are entered into the reported figures.

The BCS is an annually-updated cross-section of all households in the UK (with about 40,000 respondents) plus periodic booster samples – such as the ethnic booster sample in 2000 (of 4000 people) that focused on ethnic minorities' victimization and experiences with the police and criminal justice system. Whereas police crime figures record the location of the offence, the BCS crime count is based on the home location of the victim irrespective of where in England and Wales the crime actually took place. The BCS has a 'non-victim questionnaire' that gathers data on a range of issues, including fear of crime, views and perceptions of local crime, experiences of the police and attitudes to the CJS. The second victim form lists up to six different incidents, including the nature and circumstances of the incident, details of offenders, security measures, costs, emotional reactions, contact with the CJS and outcomes where known.[2] While the BCS has come to be seen as an alternative to official crime statistics, Walklate (2007: 105) suggest that it has itself become 'an institution' and part of the official presentation of crime data. 'All it actually does', she says, 'is to report findings of the survey' in descriptive fashion rather than offer analysis, so, for example, 'you cannot tell if the reason for high victimization of young men is because they are also in the low socioeconomic groups'.[3] Various descriptive data is presented in annual BCS reports, estimating the risk of victimization for demographic factors such as gender, age, marital status, residential status (e.g., homeowner or tenant), and whether respondents live in a 'disordered' area. It does not weight these factors or present more complex analytical models to assess their differential impact on risks of victimization. Most reports have indicated that the highest risk of becoming a victim of violent crime is associated with being male (in particular between 16 and 24 years old), living in an area with high levels of perceived anti-social behaviour, being unemployed, a tenant, visiting pubs (more than three times a week) and being single (e.g., Home Office 2009: 47ff). One can easily imagine how these characteristics and behaviour might interact with each other and be linked to wider issues of locality, socioeconomic status and lifestyle.

The two measures of crime generate different and sometimes conflicting trends. During 1960s and 1970s recorded crime was rising and this entered public perception that the problem was getting worse (Garland 2001: 107).

---

[2]More information on the sample and construction of the BCS can be found at www.esds.ac.uk/findingData/snDescription.asp?sn=6066.

[3]For a technical discussion of problems of sample bias in the BCS, see Elliott and Ellingworth (1997) and FitzGerald (2010).

This is supported by crime report figures – Figure 4.2 shows the pattern of violent crime recorded by police from 1995 to 2008, which shows a steep increase in 1998/99 followed by a steady rise through to 2005/06. This kind of trend (along with high-profile reporting of knife crime) generated the view in the media that violent crime in the UK was out of control. For example:

> VIOLENT CRIME FIGURES RISE BY 12% (*BBC News Online*, 22/7/04)
> VIOLENT OFFENCES TOP MILLION MARK (*BBC News Online*, 21/7/05)
> 14% RISE IN CRIME (The *Sun*, 19/10/07)
> VIOLENCE RISING AS CONFIDENCE FALLS IN FIGHT AGAINST CRIME (*The Times*, 19/10/07)
> GUN CRIME UP AS SMITH SAYS UK SAFER THAN EVER (*Daily Telegraph*, 24/1/08)

The last headline refers to Jacqui Smith (the then UK Home Secretary), whose claim that the UK is 'safer than ever' was based on the contrary trend shown in BCS data that all crime, including violent crime, was falling. This is shown in Figures 4.3 and 4.4. This consistent fall in violent crime reported through the BCS is in line with a general international decline in crime during this period. Further, the rise in numbers of crimes reported to the police in England and Wales shown in Figure 4.2 is largely a result of changes in recording practices, especially in relation to minor offences. Under the rules of the National Crime Recording Standard (NCRS), certain 'yobbish' behaviours, such as minor scuffles, have been reclassified as violent crimes and counted according to the

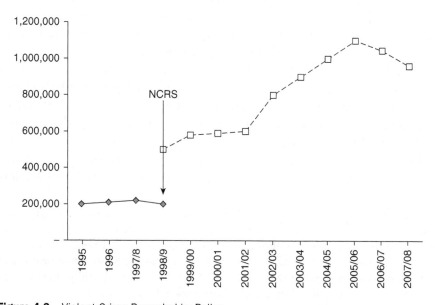

Figure 4.2 Violent Crime Recorded by Police

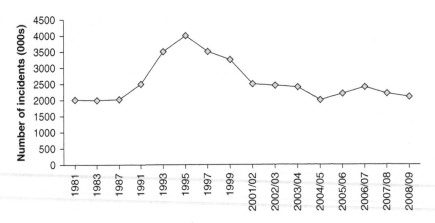

Figure 4.3 BCS Trends in Violent Crime 1981–2009

number of victims, so an incident with three victims is now recorded as three crimes. The numbers of recorded crimes continued to rise as the new recording rules became embedded in police recording practice.[4] Even so, although an apparent rise in violent crime might be explained in terms of these category changes, it is still worth noting that the total number of crimes extrapolated from the BCS data is larger than crimes reported to the police by a factor of around 10, which suggests that the prevalence of violence in everyday life is considerably greater than it might appear to be from police figures.

In view of the above problems, one could reject the use of crime data altogether but this would be neither practical nor desirable. Such rejection, says Jock Young (1975: 72), 'absurdly disqualifies' the criminologist 'from contributing to the topical, and politically consequential, debate as to the significance of the crime-rate' as well as 'closing off questions of comparison over time and across cultures'. Discussing reasons for the growth in recorded crime between 1955 and 1994 in most developed countries (except Japan), Garland (2001: 90) says that although criminologists have pointed to the pitfalls of official crime statistics, this growth is 'a massive and incontestable fact' that requires explanation. Crime data, like any other information, needs to be critically evaluated and interpreted, and arguments developed with reference to many different sources. The Home Office (2006: 8) report on official statistics points

---

[4]The NCRS was introduced across England and Wales in 2002 although some police forces adopted it earlier. It was a response to the criticism that police records under-recorded crime (Home Office 2006: 4). The reporting rules for violent crime were changed again in 2008 when 'most serious violence against the person' disappeared and was split into 'violence against the person', either 'with' or 'without' injury, thus creating such general categories that FitzGerald (2010) concludes that 'it is now impossible to track subsequent trends' in serious violent crime.

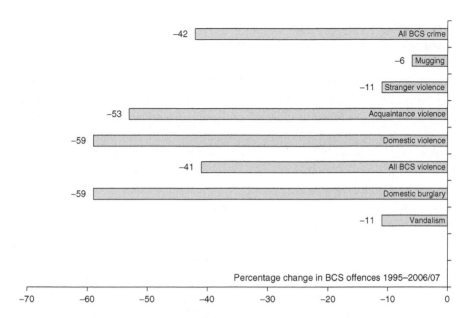

Figure 4.4 Breakdown by Type of Violent Crime

out that despite many advantages over police-recorded crime, the BCS only covers a limited range of crimes and victims and cannot be used to measure crime at the local neighbourhood level.

Finally, the figures from the BCS and the US Victimization Survey suggest that although violent crime has been falling since the mid-1990s in both countries, there are localized areas of high crime. The Home Office (2006: 21) reports that:

> Crime is often a localised phenomenon. Crime rates can and do vary between neighbourhoods and sometimes even from street to street. This means that the larger the geographic unit on which information is provided the less relevant it is likely to be for the person who wants to understand their own personal or family risks. The ideal, therefore, is information that is as localised as possible.

There has been a great deal of attention in criminological research to geographies of crime and understanding crime patterns on a local level. This method will be examined with reference to sociological approaches to violence.

Geographies of crime

Crime is geographically concentrated and the national rates might not reflect local experiences and risks. In Chicago in the 1920s, Shaw and McKay (1969) noted that some neighbourhoods had high levels of juvenile delinquency, year in and year out, decade after decade, regardless of who lived in the areas. They drew maps of delinquency in Chicago over three periods – 1900–06, 1917–23, and 1927–33 – a method influenced by Robert Park and Ernest Burgess's *Concentric Zone Model*, which identified five concentric zones of population movement and residence in Chicago and other American cities in the 1920s. Developing an approach that influenced crime theories throughout the rest of the twentieth century, Shaw and McKay used social disorganization theory to argue that delinquency rates varied with economic conditions, ethnic hetero-geneity and population mobility. Specifically, four urban conditions of 'disor-ganization' generated high rates of delinquency: the collapse of institutional controls, the disorganization of community-based institutions (often as a result of rapid industrialization), the economic dominance of the business sector over property values, and the development of criminal values and traditions that are self-perpetuating. Shaw and McKay argued that crime was a response to the social, structural and cultural characteristics of a locality and that this explained how deviant behaviour was produced among lower-class, urban males.[5]

Subsequent to the Chicago model of ecological zones, many explanations for differences in neighbourhood crime levels have been proposed. Many of these focus on the ability of local residents to control deviancy (Eck et al. 2005: 8). In particular, this 'second wave' of ecological studies (Hayward 2004: 98) has involved identifying 'hot spots', that is, areas that have a 'greater than average number of criminal or disorder events, or an area where people have a higher than average risk of victimization' (Eck et al. 2005: 2). This might be an address, street corner, store, house, or any other small location, most of which can be seen by a person standing at its centre. According to this approach, places have unique characteristics that affect the distribution of criminal activity over space and time (Sherman et al. 1989).

This literature often uses routine activities theory, which claims that victims and offenders converge in time and space in the absence of social controls. It identifies three crucial elements: a motivated offender, an accessible target and the absence of a 'capable guardian' such as Neighbourhood Watch schemes, door staff, police patrols, vigilant staff and co-workers, and CCTV (Cohen and Felson 1979). Thus, routine activities theory links in with social disorganization since disordered areas are less likely to have capable guardians acting as deter-rents to offending. Sherman (1995) describes crime 'hot spots' as a new approach that pinpoints small places in which the occurrence of crime is so

---

[5]This theory is subject to two limitations noted in relation to other theories of crime and delinquency – it over-predicts crime in certain localities and does not explain why most people in 'socially disorganized' areas do not commit crimes. It is also a general theory of offending, rather than of violence *per se*.

predictable that we should think in terms of criminal careers of *places* rather than individuals. For example, in Minneapolis in 1986, 5 per cent of locals produced 100 per cent of calls to police for violent and serious offences. Violent crime might be more concentrated than crime in general – in Seattle 78 per cent of districts had experienced some crime over a 14-year period (1989–2002 inclusive) but only 33 per cent had experienced violent crime (Weisburd et al., 2004: 32).

How might these patterns be explained? Using a range of statistical measures of local crime, Zhang and Peterson (2007) argue that social stress is a key variable. This includes factors such as racial and ethnic segregation, the proportion of female-headed households, poverty, low education, numbers of vacant properties, and unemployment. On the other hand, control factors include residential stability, home ownership and higher income. However, as Hipp et al. (2009) argue, neighbourhoods are not self-contained insular units and social processes can spill over into adjacent neighbourhoods and have independent effects on the focal neighbourhood. It is possible for violence between gangs to occur not across adjacent turfs, but through networks across space, while they also found that the frequency of *intra*group violence within neighbourhoods could be higher than intergroup violence. The latter they see as an indication of a breakdown in norms, which leads to higher levels of violence in all forms where poverty has the strongest correlation with locally recorded violence (Tita 2008).

It is generally possible to map areas of deprivation in cities on to levels of reported crime. In London the rate of recorded assaults in the most deprived tenth of wards is, at 30 per 1000 of the population, twice the average and five times the rate in the least deprived tenth, although burglary is less confined to high deprivation (Home Office 2009). Similarly, it is possible to map the known organization of gangs in London on to areas of highest deprivation and the greatest number are in the most deprived areas of Hackney, Tower Hamlets, and Newham, while there are no gangs present in the least deprived areas.[6] A further relevant factor here might be levels of deprivation combined with the visible and proximate inequalities of wealth and lifestyle. For example, the northwest English borough of Oldham (scene of inter-ethnic violence in 2001) contains both some of the most deprived areas in the UK – Coldhurst, St Mary's and Werneth contain Super Output Areas that rank among the 1 per cent most deprived in England – yet areas such as Saddleworth North and South are among the most affluent (Oldham Primary Care Trust 2008)[7]. The

---

[6]See http://gangsinlondon.piczo.com/londongangareas?cr=2&linkvar=000044.

[7]Super Output Areas are geography designed units for the collection and publication of small area statistics in the UK. Compared with wards, they give an improved basis for comparison across the country because the units are more similar in size of population.

demographic profile of Coldhurst, for example, indicates high social atomization and deprivation:

- Four in ten households are one-person households and over 60 per cent experience 'income deprivation' (against an Oldham average of 23.1 per cent) which rises to 70 per cent for children under 16 years.
- It has the lowest economic activity rate (50 per cent) in Oldham (average 65 per cent) and the highest unemployment – 13 per cent against 4.5 per cent for the city.

This concentration of poverty is racialized since ethnic minority groups make up nearly 60 per cent of the population. Coldhurst has the highest recorded crime rate in the borough, with rates of 147.4 per 1,000 as opposed to a 67.8 average for Oldham, and 20 per cent of residents 'feel unsafe walking alone in their neighbourhood' during the day (Oldham Primary Care Trust 2008). By contrast, the largely rural ward of Saddleworth North has the highest economic activity rate (72.3 per cent), unemployment of 1.4 per cent, the least social housing, and the lowest recorded crime rate of 32.8 per 1,000 (Oldham Council 2008).

This approach is open to question, however. Crime mapping, now widely used by a large number of public and private agencies in addition to police forces (including estate agents), is criticized for removing spatial distribution of violence from its wider socioeconomic context. Hayward (2004: 87) criticizes a criminology in which urban crime is 'torn free from its physical context – the city', thereby losing the potential for understanding the relationship between urban space and urban crime. In the idea of the 'mappable crime environment', he says the offender is lost to mainstream criminology (2004: 87). This administrative criminology, he says, is devoted to situational crime prevention aimed at blocking opportunities for crime. It envisages 'hollowed out urban space' through scatter diagrams, GPS and 'crime moments', while occluding the ways in which crime is very complex social-cultural phenomena (2004: 110). Outside the 'scanscape' is an increasingly violent social world in which interpersonal violence is a 'major currency in the schools, shops, parks and housing projects' of the poor neighbourhoods of major cities (2004: 120).

Further, routine activities theory assumes a control model in which the 'motivated offender' is taken for granted, rather than develop a motivational theory. Hayward (2004: 5) questions the simple association between crime and deprivation, claiming that 'crime is not a desperate act of poverty nor a defiant gesture against the system' but an act of 'transgressive identity construction' which involves the 'existential pursuit of passion and excitement' (2004: 9). Similarly, Ferrell et al. (2008: 4) ask 'what makes delinquency attractive in the first place?', to which they answer 'thrills', the pursuit of which is shared with the dominant culture. The appeal of transgression is the hollow cultural dominance of style against which crime represents an attempt to 'take responsibility for one's own destiny' (Hayward 2004: 157). The dominance of a culture promoting the right to consume (as Samsung put it 'Impatience is a Virtue'[8]), in which transgression is a weapon in the advertiser's arsenal, stimulates an insatiable demand for more which becomes focal for youth delinquency.

There are two different layers of analysis here. First, there is the phenomeno-logical approach introduced in Chapter 1, that emphasizes the sensual attractions of offending. Hayward is writing about crime in general but if this claim is applied specifically to violence, this kind of 'high' could be a manifestation of the emotions that Collins calls 'confrontational tension-fear'. However, Collins (2008: 66) also suggests that the joy of combat is rare and most evident as pre-battle elation – the delight of being 'up against it', which could be the case equally in street violence. But this suggests that the passion and excitement might appear more in *talk* about violent events than in their actuality. Hayward suggests this when referring to football hooliganism prolonging 'the emotional high by removing spontaneity from football violence' by extending the anticipation (Hayward 2004: 140). It is again possible that the joy of transgression arises from 'forward panic' – a hot rush of aggressive energy with strong entrainment that has 'gone down a tunnel and cannot stop its momentum' (Collins 2008: 94). But thrill-seeking is a limited explanation of violence in that other (legitimate) activities might also involve an emotional rush (such as extreme sports) and since crime and violence are spatially distributed we need specific explanations of these distributions. A second layer is the emphasis on spaces of crime, especially those polarized between safe zones and dangerous no-go areas, which suggests a more the structural and political economy approach that is taken here.

The cultural dimension of the analysis is nonetheless important and deprivation needs to be combined with other factors to develop explanations. Deprivation shows a strong association with violence, but other factors might mediate or intensify its effects so it is necessary to look at the spatial distribution of violence holistically and in a wider socioeconomic context. Community cohesion and 'collective efficacy' ('the willingness of local residents to intervene for the common good') might be more significant than deprivation alone (Sampson and Raudenbush 1999). Sampson and Raudenbush argue that collective efficacy is associated with lower rates of violence regardless of socio-demographic composition. The 'active ingredients' in high crime rates seem to be structural disadvantage and attenuated collective efficacy. In her classic critique of modernist planning, *The Death and Life of Great American Cities* (1961), Jane Jacobs (2002: 354) pointed to the immense variations in the degree of 'civilization and safety' in city spaces in proximity to one another. Similar to the idea of 'capable guardians', Jacobs wrote about 'eyes on the

---

[8]This was the slogan of the 2009 Samsung Jet commercial, www.youtube.com/watch?v=s8tWLEsLpxs.

street' and that safer environments are more active streets where people have developed ways of transcending the anonymity of the modern city. Safer places are those where people use the streets, where there are a substantial number of stores and other public places, enterprises are used evening and night and where there are many different kinds of enterprises so that people often cross paths. Wilcox et al. (2004) examine the relationship between violence and land use, beginning with the hypothesis that the greater are the tracts of public land, the less effective social control will be, while higher social disorder combined with less 'neighbouring' generates more crime. What they conclude, however, is that the effects of land use (public/private, isolated/busy) on violent crime is mediated by social structure – that is by the extent of deprivation and inequality. Even so, and not surprisingly, they conclude that some forms of land use do have an effect on violent crime and busy places reduce risks while empty public land might create dangerous 'hang outs'. There is, however, a broader issue here of the design, maintenance and visibility of urban public space that will now be examined in the context of global social changes.

Spatial relations in the neoliberal city

The approaches discussed above focus on specific matrices of spatial variables that might generate patterns of violent behaviour and they assume some version of a social disorganization-control theory. This regards offending as manifest in localities where controls and guardianship are weak. The key variables in spatial crime studies are collective efficacy, economic activity, population turnover and mobility – but these are shaped by wider socioeconomic and cultural processes. There is also the question of the influence of the particular character of spaces – such as interstitial spaces of dislocation and relocation across margins and borderlands. Further, it is necessary to attempt to account for particular patterns of offending, especially those that run against the overall trends in violent crime. This section will place deprivation in the wider global context of spatial restructuring and will attempt to identify the processes that generate violence in particular urban spaces.

The spatial distribution of violence in the city is a product of the major shift in the global economy during the last quarter of the twentieth century. These include post-Fordist flexibilization, labour market restructuring, deindustrialization, global production chains and the rise of service rather than producer economies.[9] As manufacturing declines, often with devastating consequences

---

[9]Flexibilization refers to the changing work practices whereby firms no longer use internal labour markets or offer employees job security, but rather seek flexible employment contracts (and outsourcing sub-contracts) that permit them to increase or decrease their workforce, which must itself be flexibly skilled and redeployed with ease.

for local economies, service industries become a new source of employment dependent on large numbers of casual workers. Highly mobile global economic flows require embedding in specific territorial places so that while the economy operates on a global scale, social reproduction takes place within definable territorial units – the household, cities, regions and the nation state (Perrons 2004: 239). Post-Fordist economic restructuring in western societies has created new dynamics of inclusion and exclusion that are mapped on to spatial zones corresponding with restructured labour markets, property values and social infrastructures. There is a kind of reversal here of the process described by Shaw and McKay (1969), which was driven by rapid industrialization, in that the rapid departure of industrial capital during the early years of the 1980s generated wastelands that in turn became associated with high levels of social disorganization and violence. However, the resultant spatial patterning of this is complex since, according to Soja (2000: 265), the 'older polarities have not disappeared, but a much more polymorphous and fractured social geometry has taken shape' (Soja 2000: 265). There is what Hayward (2004: 139–40) calls 'parafunctional space', a kind of in-between that resists habitation as anyone passing through it is already conceptually on the other side of the space in a kind of void. Hayward writes of city spaces that have 'given up' the struggle of shaping time and space and in which the refuse of an earlier mode of production accumulates. But there are also interstitial spaces structured by architecture, borders and function, where violence occurs.

Neoliberal restructuring had major impacts on urban space in at least two phases – the initial destructive phase in which many previously industrial areas were abandoned, and a subsequent phase of gentrification of former industrial inner-city locales and the generation of new spatial polarization. Sassen (2002) argues that globalization generates contradictory spaces of contestation – disparities between urban glamour zones and war zones. Walks (2001) documents this increasing social polarization. Many cities become global administration centres, with a reduction in skilled, organized, manual manufacturing labour and the growth of inexpensive migrant workers into new zones of transition. The break-up of welfare systems, state retrenchment and the growth of economies of flexible accumulation have generated a new grid of social spaces marked by the following:

- A decline in affordable housing as the inner-city growth of the FIRE (finance, insurance and real estate) sector creates a pool of gentrifiers who out-compete the poor for space in housing markets.
- Disinvestment in ageing industry downgrades older industrial districts both in inner cities and older suburbs, which generates high levels of social inequality.
- New 'edge city' patterns of employment create increased polarization in terms of income differences, but also between older settled and migrant minority groups and differential access to work (full-time, part-time and informal).

- Mature suburbs then appear to be the new 'zone of transition', containing some of the poorest and wealthiest tracts.

These are global processes that have profound impact on crime rates.[10] Parker (2008) describes the shift in local economies in the USA between 1998 and 2006, in which most expansion in employment (95 per cent) was in the service sector, which she argues had differential impact on urban space and ethnicity (2008: 3). At the same time, patterns of violence changed significantly in urban areas between 1980 and 2000, which she explains with reference to the stratification of the local economy. Parker emphasizes the uneven nature of the trend in urban violence: while national rates in the USA (and the same is true of the UK) have declined since the mid-1990s, there are localities in which the rates have remained high or have followed a different trajectory. Parker links high local rates of violence to the restructuring of local economies following deindustrialization during the 1980s and subsequent economic change between 1990 and 2000. The closure of large manufacturing plants in many areas generated growing concentrations of poverty but also had a differentiated impact on race and gender relations. Numbers of low-skilled manufacturing jobs receded, but African Americans were less able to move to new employers in out-of-town locations because of residential racial segregation and low wages (Parker 2008: 59ff). In central city areas, new service-based economies and administrative centres created a skills mismatch between employment opportunities and the local population. In the new economy, employability requires increased emphasis on flexible skills, but also on subjective personality attributes which may be based on white cultural perceptions (2008: 63).

Therefore, black workers lost out disproportionately and were highly represented in the areas of concentrations of poverty with low wages, declining schools, family dissolution and shortage of role models. Impoverished segregated communities experience breakdown in informal social controls (of the kind noted in the above section) and become more dependent on formal controls of policing and surveillance. In a context where legitimate employment avenues are limited, informal and illegal activities become more widespread and in the absence of formal avenues of conflict resolution, violence (including extreme exemplary violence) becomes a major currency of social interaction. By contrast, routines of work structure time and therefore contribute to crime desistance and reduced violence (Parker 2008: 85). So neighbourhoods of professionals are protective against violence and increased disposable income boosts employment opportunities and creates more diverse local labour markets which in turn reduces street crime.

---

[10]See Ray and Smith (2004) for an analysis of the relevance of this process in Oldham for the violent disturbances there in the spring and summer of 2001.

These local effects of global processes bear on the civilizational thesis, as Wacquant (2004) argues in relation to 'hyper-ghettoization'. For Elias, the civilizing process was dependent on the state's creation of institutions of governance and regulation of public space. In the later twentieth century, though this was weakened by the effects of neoliberal restructuring and the creation of areas where crime and the informal economy flourished. The erosion of public space and the 'retreat of the welfare state' undermined the infrastructure that had enabled public and private organizations to develop. Wacquant illustrates this with reference to Chicago, where there has been a highly racialized pattern of spatial exclusion and, within these areas, a collapse of structures of political representation, isolation from extended networks, and instead a rise of the informal economy and especially the drugs trade, sex work, itinerant hawkers, resellers of newspapers, parking attendants and day-labourers.

These conditions, he suggests, result in a de-pacification of local society and the growth of a 'culture of terror' – that is, regular displays of violence that are necessary in an underground economy. These socioeconomic structures are increasingly precarious, networks of interdependence are shortened and an unstable habitus is produced. This 'hyperghetto' is no longer a reservoir of disposable industrial labour – in the manner of the working-class districts of the industrial city – but 'a mere dumping ground for supernumery categories for which the surrounding society has no economic or political use' (Wacquant 2004: 113). These are, we might say, interstitial spaces of abandonment where, Wacquant says, social disinvestment facilitates the spread of a 'pandemic of violence and fuels an enveloping climate of fear'. Violence becomes the primary means of regulation of transactions in the street economy, where income levels are chronically insufficient and 'nearly all residents must hustle to get by' (Wacquant 1998). The organization of gangs on Chicago's South Side by 1990 created extreme dangerousness – between 40th and 59th Street going south there were 106 homicides per 100,000 of the population in 1990, and 849 homicides in Chicago, of which 602 were shootings where the typical victim was a black man under 30 years of age.[11] Wacquant (1998) emphasizes that one of his respondents, 'Ricky', was not a 'social anomaly' but a product of the 'exacerbation of the logic of economic and racial exclusion' in a social universe of pandemic violence and 'relentless precariousness'. In an economy of predation and day-to-day survival, there was no route back to conventional life in a closed circuit in which there was a kind of 'collective suicide'.

Auyero (2000) uses Wacquant's concept of hyper-ghettoization to analyse the social cost of neoliberalism in Buenos Aires, where he sees violence as

---

[11]This was, though, the peak recent period for homicide in Chicago, and by 1999 this had fallen to 705 and by 2004 to 448, but at 15.65 per 100,000 was still well above the US average of 5.5 (FBI 2009).

interconnected with manifestations of deeper socioeconomic and institutional changes in the previous two decades. In the Villa Paraíso shantytown, he argues, economic restructuring resulted in an unemployment rate of 62 per cent, with the switch from manufacturing to temporary flexible service sector working, rising income disparity, with 75 per cent below the poverty line, and the growth of the shantytown population by nearly four times between 1983 and 1995. Most homes are made of metal sheets; there are open sewers and no fresh water. He reports the destruction of social capital combined with state repressive violence and the structural violence of unemployment, with many kids out on the streets at night when gunfire is frequent, and there is widespread mistrust of the police as corrupt. He also suggests that a kind of shadow authority is exercised by the leaders of drug-dealing gangs. When three local teachers were mugged, the Principal 'talked to a person close the … top and told him that if they kept assaulting teachers, they would not want to come to the shantytown anymore. And they stopped.'

Explanations of spatial concentrations of violence should incorporate an understanding of agency and the emergence of affective responses to structural conditions. One cannot move automatically from objective analysis (of unemployment, etc.) to a subjective understanding of practices (Wieviorka 2009: 103). Crime theories that emphasize objective factors have an undeveloped theory of the subject, while social disorganization-routine activities approaches assume that violence will arise wherever controls are weak – which leaves unanswered the question of the motivational complexes that produce the desire for violence in the first place. It is not necessarily the existence of inequality in itself that stimulates crime and violence in deprived areas. While this is to some extent a result of exigencies of an extreme situation, as Wacquant and others suggest, exclusion from the formal economy stimulates informal hustling and illegalities in which violence is a means of exchange, power and enforcement of obligations. However, there is also evidence for the operation of a shame-rage cycle discussed above. The context described by Wacquant is one of loss of cohesion in which an identity of being the dangerous and excluded other is internalized, which leads to risk-taking and ordeals as modes of self-assertion. Wieviorka (2009: 103ff) argues that where the social bond is destroyed or impaired, people (such as rioters from the *banlieues*[12]) invert the stereotype that presents them as losers and violence allows them to compensate for the fact that they have no future and cannot assert themselves. Gilligan's analysis of extreme violence suggests that past shame from being despised (from, for

---

[12]Literally 'outskirts', this has also come to refer to estates with social exclusion, high crime and significant ethnic minority (especially North African) populations. There were violent clashes between hundreds of youths and French police in the Paris *banlieue* of Clichy-sous-Bois, which began on 27 October 2005 and continued for 17 nights.

example, poverty, racism, exclusion or rejection) leads to a raging desire to put an end to shame and thereby to the feeling of being mocked.

The concept of urban segregation can be misleading, though, if it suggests the existence of communities separated by physical barriers. Young (2003) points out that borders are regularly crossed and the 'excluded' are included in cultural aspirations for consumption though excluded from its realization. Exposure to mass media, mass education, the consumer market, labour market, welfare state and political system bind people in very different socioeconomic circumstances to common aspirations for the mass consumption 'good life'. Further, they frequently cross the tracks from marginal to affluent society through formal and informal labour, both on national and global scales, creating possibly unprecedented numbers of migrant workers. In a combination of Merton's theory of modes of adaptation to cultural goals and Katz's theory of the thrill of transgression, Young argues that discontent caused by the contradiction between (consumerist) legitimating ideas and the reality of structural inequalities generates ontological insecurity and rage. There is a consequent 'hardening of the self', such as machismo persona, that combats humiliation and exclusion which in turn promotes violence. Relative deprivation and crisis of identity combines with the use of violence as a means of settling problems, which acquires a transgressive edge driven by the energies of humiliation. This is not just instrumental but expressive violence – so guns are not just instruments for robberies, for example, but are carried with a swagger – a 'sensual retort to labour'.

While Young's analysis is plausible, he does not assemble much evidence to support it, and it is not obvious why humiliation shared by all residents of excluded areas manifests mainly in violence perpetrated by young men, largely against other local and equally disadvantaged residents. Further, the extent of traffic between marginalized and core spaces will vary considerably depending on the spatial organization of the local economy. The 'hardness' described by Young might also be a product of more micro processes. A South African study of violent criminal careers from within townships (where the majority of perpetrators were young men and victims were other local residents) argued that key influences were:

- The quality of relationships between parents and their children, levels of parental supervision, inconsistent or harsh discipline, family conflict and disruptions, and parental reinforcement of deviant behaviour and attitudes.
- The experience of humiliation of racist segregation under apartheid and relative deprivation (as described by Young and others) which was often accompanied by a desire for peer esteem – for example, 'If I steal your car and drive to a party with my girlfriend, everybody will go, "What a car he's driving and every girl will wish to be in love with me"'.
- Defiance, experimentation and the need to push boundaries in order to prove their manhood and independence, which cut across lines of material disadvantage – so boys from more affluent families would drift into violent crime to belong to their peer group.

- The absence of empathy, expressed in pride for extreme violence – for example, 'We sometimes kill each other. Say they [gang leaders] give you a duty and you don't perform it, they'll instruct one of the gang to kill you. It may be your friend it doesn't matter you should kill him. This one guy refused and his own brother was instructed to kill him and he did'. (CSIR 1998).

The report concludes that violent crime among young men in the township is a combination of resentment from multiple experiences of deprivation combined with a lack of investment in the routes through conventional society, exacerbated particularly by the experience of racism and an enjoyment of transgression. However, the crucial legacy of apartheid here indicates how the relationship between locales, crime and violence is further complicated by the wider political context.

Global spaces of violence

Violence in social space, then, is embedded within a complex sociality in which generational, local and global processes intersect. Further, it was noted in Chapter 1 that although violence is often conceived as intentional interpersonal action, structural violence is an outcome of unjust social arrangements and, as both Castells and Bourdieu suggest, the two are often closely connected. The international articulation of neoliberal strategies has generated a violent form of enclosure and dispossession. During the twentieth century there developed what might be one of the most significant social changes of recent times – the 'global growth of a vast informal proletariat … massively concentrated in a shanty-town world encircling the fortified enclaves of the urban rich' (Davis 2004). The global movement of people from rural to urban areas involved, as did the growth of urban capitalism in Europe, dispossession of rural labour and the rapid extension of commercial relations into the countryside (Ray 2007a). However, whereas the framework of national capitalism provided a territorial space for the organization of social movements and a gradual mitigation of its effects, the global dislocation of the countryside is both extremely rapid and largely unregulated. At the same time, since the 1980s the International Monetary Fund (IMF) and World Bank have required 'structural adjustment' as a condition of loans, which frequently involves reducing the size of the public sector, privatization of state enterprises, the promotion of flexibility changes to remove labour protection, increasing the wage gap between public and private employees and making social welfare cuts (Giroux 2005). The consequent deep penetration of commodity relations into the countryside left small owners of land exposed to the world market so that, for example, regions that had once produced surplus grain became deficit regions and in the developing world as a whole the ratio of food imports to food exports increased from 50 per cent in 1995–60 to 80 per cent in 1975 (Araghi 2000).

One manifestation of this is 'land grabbing' – essentially, the aggressive seizure of land but, specifically, here, where previously communal land is appropriated by global corporations. Cotula et al. (2009) found that land grabbing is fuelled by global food security concerns, particularly in investor countries in the face of global demand for non-food agricultural commodities and biofuels, combined with expectations of rising rates of return in agriculture and land values, and policy measures in home and host countries (2009: 100). A crucial consequence of this is that local people can lose access to the resources on which they depend for their food security (2009: 5–6). In particular, where there are 'insecure use rights on state-owned land, inaccessible registration procedures, vaguely defined productive use requirements, legislative gaps, and compensation limited to loss of improvements like crops and trees (thus excluding loss of land)' the position of local people can be undermined (2009: 7).

Land grabbing and violence are often directly connected. In the copper mining Rio Blanco region of Peru, a proposed mining concession to a Chinese consortium that will cover 6,473 hectares of deserts and cloud forests is opposed by local farmers. There are serious concerns about the environmental impact on fragile eco-systems and agricultural lands along with a legal battle over the mining company's entitlement to mine on the land. According to Oxfam America (2007):

> The social conflict reached its most critical moments in 2004 and 2005, when two demonstrations of thousands of community members coming from several miles around confronted police forces. Several peasants were injured in violent confrontations – some of them severely. Two died and more than 200 had lawsuits brought against them for taking part in the protests.

There were subsequent violent confrontations in October 2009 which resulted in one protestor being fatally shot and allegations that detained protestors were tortured (The Guardian, 19/10/09).

One consequence of encroachment on local means of subsistence is economic informalization. Kudva (2009) describes violence in Indian cities arising from inequality, socio-spatial segregation and lack of governance. Thick rings of poverty on urban peripheries house a 'vast informal proletariat lacking the strategic economic power' of socialized labour'. These informal residences include about half of Delhi's 13.8 million residents and feed factories of 1200 enterprises. Segmentation generates violence – for example, the closure of mills in Ahmadabad during the 1980s forced workers into the informal sector, which doubled in size by 1997. This also reduced interdependent networks since intercommunal institutions such as trade unions and representative political parties that had linked Hindus and Muslims collapsed. In 2002 there were communal riots in which 22 Muslims were burnt alive by Hindu mobs avenging an earlier attack on a train in which 58 Hindu activists died.

Conclusions

Chapter 3 presented a critical assessment of Elias's theory of the civilizing process. While there is some evidence for a long-term decline in interpersonal violence within pacified spaces of the modern state, this chapter has indicated that this is a highly uneven process. Although Elias has a concept of the spatial organization of cultural and economic interdependencies (figurations), this theory does not take account of the potentially decivilizational consequences of the spatial reorganization of capital. While most developed countries have seen declining rates of violent crime (measured by victim surveys), there have been spaces of much higher recorded crime that coincide with the spatial consequences of neoliberal restructuring. The statistically sophisticated analysis of crime 'hot spots' tracks the spatial manifestations of reported crimes but is limited in that it pays little attention either to the meanings of transgression for the actors or the wider socioeconomic context of spaces of violence. As Bourdieu (quoted at the beginning of this chapter) indicates, there is a relationship between structural violence and the manifestation of interpersonal violence on the street. The analysis here has suggested that certain spaces are constitutive of complex patterns of social relationships that persist over time, in which violence is more likely than elsewhere. While the relationship between deprivation and violent crime is well established in an extensive literature, we cannot simply read off the behaviour and meanings of actors from objective data such as unemployment and deprivation. The relationships between these factors are highly mediated by degrees of social cohesion (such as 'neighbouring') and the types of uses made of social space (as routine activities theory suggests), but this still does not really explain the particular motivational patterns of violent actors. A theory needs to understand the dynamics of shame and humiliation arising from class segmentation in a context where everyone has access to cultural ideals of a good life of high consumption. It further needs to understand the dynamics of shame-rage in relation to patterns of generation and masculinity. This will be the topic of the next chapter.

5

MASCULINITIES AND VIOLENCE

The claim that men commit most acts of physical violence is possibly the nearest that criminology has come to producing an indisputable fact. (Hall 2002)

Crime and masculinity

Crime, especially violent crime, is an overwhelmingly masculine activity. This gender pattern is not new – males have been over-represented in all major violent crime categories since the collection of crime statistics began and the same pattern is found in all countries. According to the UK National Statistics office in 2006, 1.42 million offenders were sentenced for criminal offences in England and Wales, the majority of whom (80 per cent) were male and of these 7 per cent were less than 18 years old. In the teenage years, the gap between girls and boys in delinquency, broadly defined, is relatively small, although the gap in more serious offending is considerably wider (Smith et al. 2001). Offending is highly gender and age-related.[1] Among males, the highest rate of offending for the most serious (indictable) criminal offences was among 17 year-olds, at 6116 offenders per 100,000 population of that age. The highest rate for females was among 15 year-olds (2,168 per 100,000 population). For male offenders in 2005, 15 year-olds received more cautions than any other age group, while 19 year-olds received the most convictions. Among female offenders, 14 and 15 year-olds received the most cautions and the most common age to be convicted was 16. The pattern of offending for both men and women falls away after about age 25, and in later life is negligible for both, which suggests a strong age as well as gender factor underlying offending behaviour.

---

[1]See www.statistics.gov.uk/cci/nugget.asp?id=1661 for a chart showing male and female offending in the UK by age.

It was noted in Chapter 4 that known violence is strongly correlated with socioeconomic inequalities and relative deprivation. However, if this were a sufficient explanation, then, as Alder (1991) notes, women should commit more violence than men since they are consistently, on average, in lower socio-economic positions than men. She suggests that masculinity involves an 'obsession' with social competition so that a minor affront to reputation, face, social status and enduring relationships can result in violence. However, such responses themselves are distributed by social location, class and age – so the relationship between masculinity and violence is complex. Masculine reputational violence may be most common among young, working-class men and street corner societies.

The masculine bias in offending should not mean that we ignore female violence. Motz (2001: 89) says that 'to deny female violence is to deny female agency' and reflects women's confinement to the private sphere. Further, she says that women's violence is treated as monstrous – like Lady Macbeth 'unsexing' herself to assist in the murder of Duncan – rather than understood as subject to particular emotional processes. There has recently been concern about rising levels of violence among girls that has featured in the UK media and crime prevention agencies.[2] There is a rising trend of convictions for women in the UK – between 2000 and 2006 violent offences committed by women doubled, from 7500 to 15,100 (Youth Justice Board 2009: 47), although these are figures for recorded *offences* not offenders. In the USA there is evidence for a trend towards in simple assault figures, although the gap remains large for more serious violence (Steffensmeier et al. 2005). This convergence could be a result of reduced differences in expectations of behaviour for young men and women. Or they could be a result of net-widening enforcement, broader definitions of youth violence and greater surveillance of girls that have increased arrest figures for girls relative to boys. This is discussed later in this chapter.

Explanations

While it is often taken for granted that (especially young) men do more crime than women, recent work has undertaken a more complex analysis of the nature of masculinity and its relationship with violent crime. A division has appeared between biosocial, evolutionary approaches, on the one hand, and sociological explanations on the other.

---

[2]For example, 'The Feral Sex: the terrifying rise of violent girl gangs' (*Daily Mail*, 16/5/08) and 'Laddettes blamed for rise in violent crime' (*ITN News*, 31/7/08) http://itn.co.uk/c28f0224a984378a5fb762f69767e9f2.html.

Evolutionary explanations

It was seen in Chapter 2 that there are evolutionary explanations of the human propensity for aggression that also attempt to explain the connection between masculinity and violence arising from hunting, competition and risk-taking that aided survival chances. The male age–crime curve suggests that offending is concentrated among men in the 11–25 age range. Evolutionary psychologists suggest that the bulk of offenders are 'young men displaying behaviour that evolved to increase their chances of finding a mate and having children' (Marsh et al. 2006: 29). Further, this is also the age where male testosterone peaks and young men are more aggressive and risk-taking.

Pavelka (1995: 28) argues that it is difficult to maintain that the connection between sex and aggression is purely learned and grounded in patriarchal human society when there is a strong connection between the two among primates. This is particularly the case, she claims, with male sexual violence against females, which is found among most primates (except bonobos). Schneider (2005) similarly argues that males (especially between the ages of 15 and 24) are more violent than women in all cultures, and while social and cultural issues (such as alienation, low income, weak social bonds, status differences and discrimination) are important, there is probably also a biological dimension. Even so, primal violence would have been balanced by the need to preserve the size of the group and cultural norms of reciprocity and reconciliation emerged to limit violence (Hatty 2000: 50). Further, Pavelka continues that 'no knowledgeable evolutionary theorist would argue that men (and women) are not responsible for their choices' (1995: 30). Steven Pinker (2004) claims that aggressiveness is largely genetically coded, although increased social complexity and learning have led to the long-term diminution of violence.

It was noted in Chapter 2 that evolutionary social theory pays little regard to the symbolic and culturally mediated forms that violence (for example, in rituals) and cannot easily explain why rates of violence vary among social locales, times and countries. If there is an underlying biological tendency towards masculine violence, this should manifest similarly in different cultures and places, which it does not. Violence, like sex, has been subject to cultural constraints throughout known human history, especially with reference to the killing of members of the in-group. Further, James (1995) takes issue with evolutionary theories of human aggression, arguing that family influences are critical. He claims that children born to violent parents but raised in peaceable households are no more likely to have violent criminal records than those born to non-violent parents. Further, these accounts cannot address the ways in which 'masculinity' and 'femininity' are multiply constructed through cultural and social processes and the complex ways in which violence and masculinity are interrelated.

Social learning

There are many social and cultural theories of violent behaviour, stressing social learning, youth subcultures, economic inequality (e.g., Newburn and Stanko 1995) and the potential thrill and enjoyment of violence (see Ferrell et al., 2008; Katz, 1988; and Presdee, 2000). Learning theorists argue that children are more likely to use violence as adults when they have witnessed violence in families among parents, siblings and other relatives, and where this is reinforced in childhood as a coping response to stress and conflict. However, men are more prone than women to familial influence. This is perhaps because men are more affected by additional influences of the reinforcement of aggressive attitudes in a macho culture while being less affected by mediating factors, which are discussed below. It has been claimed that 'young people exposed to family violence in multiple forms were twice as likely to be violent as those from non-violent families' (Youth Justice Board 2009: 27). However, social learning theories do not claim that exposure necessarily produces violent individuals, but that there is a complex process of learning and reinforcement.

An elaborated social learning theory is associated particularly with Albert Bandura, who argued that rather than being inherited, aggression is learned through a process of 'behaviour modelling' according to three principles (Bandura 1977: 204). First, how aggressive patterns of behaviour are developed; second, what provokes people to behave aggressively; and third, what determines whether they are going to continue to resort to an aggressive behaviour pattern on future occasions? Bandura is well known for the Bobo doll experiment where children would watch a video in which an adult role model would aggressively hit an inflatable doll '…pummel it on the head with a mallet, hurl it down, sit on it and punch it on the nose repeatedly, kick it across the room, fling it in the air, and bombard it with balls …' (Bandura 1977: 77). After watching the video, the children were placed in a room with attractive toys, which they were prohibited from touching and told they had been reserved for other children. Unsurprisingly perhaps, the children became angry and frustrated. Then they were led to another room where there were identical toys used in the Bobo video and Bandura found that 88 per cent of the children imitated the aggressive behaviour. Eight months later, 40 per cent of the same children displayed the violent behaviour observed in the Bobo doll experiment.[3] However, despite the influence enjoyed by his work, Bandura's results were inconclusive and were subject to a number of limitations, in particular that of observer effect – the children may have punched and kicked

---

[3]Many critics believe that the experiment conducted was unethical because the children were trained to be aggressive.

dolls because they thought that the study was a 'game', and that this was what Bandura wanted them to do, rather than because they had previously watched an adult punching and kicking the dolls. Moreover, since the dolls were designed to bounce back when knocked over, this 'violence' lacked realism.[4]

Further, learning takes place in a wider social context that creates a large number of mediating factors. Mihalic and Elliott (1997) suggest that the effects childhood exposure to violence will lessen where the child has the love and support of one parent, a supportive relationship as an adult, fewer stressful events in adult life, and self-reflective acknowledgement of childhood abuse and a determination not to repeat it. The latter is particularly important since there is also evidence that where violence is depicted and understood as justified, acceptable behaviour, it is more likely to be imitated in later life. For example, Messerschmidt (2007) reports the case of 17 year-old Kelly, who at the time of her interview was on probation for assaulting several boys at school.

> When I asked Kelly whether it bothered her that her stepfather physically abused her mother, she responded that her mother 'had it comin', 'cause she always hassled my stepfather, you know. She got what she deserved.' Kelly defined her mother as a 'hassle' to her stepfather because she 'just got drunk all the time, give him shit, not do anything around the house, just lazy, you know.' In contrast, Kelly looked up to her stepfather because 'He taught me all kinds of things and he didn't take no shit from my mom. So that had a lot of influence on me, you know. My mom didn't really care about me, you know, but my stepfather did'. (Messerschmidt 2007)

These mediating conditions indicate that the genesis of violence is complex. In particular, the normative acceptance of violence as a legitimate response to stressful situations means that violence is not simply a conditioned reflex (whether this is evolutionary or learned) but occurs within a language of normative justification. Further, the idea of a moral as well as a cognitive learning process links with the thesis that violence (especially extreme violence) is 'moralistic' behaviour born of righteous rage-shame.

Hegemonic masculinities

One of the problems with biological and evolutionary theories is their assumption that masculine (and presumably) feminine personality characteristics are

---

[4]There are other criticisms of social learning theories of adult aggressiveness – samples are often small since it is hard to know who was subject to violence and abuse, the samples might not be representative, interviews are retrospective and involve long recall periods, and little is known of the effects on women if they are not among violent offenders.

given and fixed at least on the level of underlying predispositions. But as MacInnes (1998) says, 'masculinity does not exist as the property, character trait or aspect of identity of individuals' and no one is born knowing how to be 'male' or 'female'. Interactionist sociology has made the techniques by which social roles are enacted and presented in interaction contexts central to social analysis. Connell (1987 and 1995) and then Messerschmidt (1993 and 1997) developed a performative analysis to understanding gender dynamics, violence and masculinity. Their central claim is that one does not 'possess' gender but it is rather something *done* and enacted especially on and through the body. It is possible that through violence men may attempt to affirm a positive self-concept, enhance self-esteem and reclaim personal power, while women, on the other hand, may see violence as a failure of self-control. Drawing on psychoanalysis, they argue that the adult personality is under tension and develops from a range of possibilities in gender development. Justifications for violence are learned speech acts that prepare the ground for violence and deploy wider available narratives in society.

In these terms, excess male violence reflects patterns of socialization in which the male role involves greater readiness to use violence as a means of control and assertion of power. In Connell's and Messerschmidt's theory, 'hegemonic masculinity' is viewed as a crucial point of intersection of different sources and forms of power, stratification, desire and identity. Hegemonic masculinity refers to cultural representations of dominant cultural ideals of masculinity that reinforce the subordination of women and marginal masculinities, such as gay and racialized minorities (Connell 1995: 77ff).[5] Unlike socialization-learning theories, Connell and Messerschmidt emphasize performance and choice rather than passively learnt behaviour. Violent behaviour is *chosen* while calling upon dominant discourses of masculinity for support and legitimation. Connell thus sees crime as a way of 'doing gender', which manifests differently in social situations structured by the influences of race, class and age. Violence is a resource that men can call upon, based on prevailing idealized cultural conceptions involving the dominance of women, heterosexuality, the pursuit of sexual gratification and independence.

Patriarchy is not a static but a fluid process, embedded within culture, presentation of self and bodies, in which there are struggles for hegemony. 'In our daily interactions', says Messerschmidt (2008: 83), 'we continually make sex assignments and attributions with a complete lack of information about

---

[5]The Gramscian term 'hegemony' was current at the time Connell developed the thesis with reference to masculinities, although Connell and Messerschmitt (2005) subsequently say this 'risked significant misunderstanding' given Gramsci's stress on historical class mobilization.

others' genitals. ... Our recognition of another's sex, then, is dependent upon the presentation of such visible bodily characteristics as hair, clothing, physical appearance, and other aspects of personal front (including behavior).' Thus, he continues, embodied gender is an interactive process involving both 'sex (body)/gender' presentation and a reading of that presentation by those who are party to the interaction. 'Hegemonic' masculinities are not necessarily statistically normal (they might be enacted only by a minority of men), but they are normative and represent the most honoured way of being a man while legitimating the subordination of women and non-hegemonic – notably effeminate, gay and some racialized – masculinities. Sports, especially at school, represent an 'endlessly renewed symbol of masculinity', and men who participate in sports that most exemplify the qualities of hegemonic masculinity are reconstructed as embodiments of the ideal (Connell and Messerschmidt 2005).[6]

Criminal behaviour is seen here as a resource for 'masculine validation'. For example, white, middle-class boys can achieve masculinity through moderate academic success, sports, and preparation for a career. But schools are repressive and authoritarian, so these boys will deviate outside school through, for example, vandalism, drinking and petty theft. This is 'opposition masculinity' that demonstrates to peers dominance, control and aggressiveness. White, working-class boys, on the other hand, tend to demonstrate opposition masculinity outside school, but also in school, through fighting, vandalism, and so on. They do still have opportunities in the labour market, however, whereas disadvantaged (racial minority and lower-class) boys have even fewer conventional opportunities to accomplish gender (they perceive no future in schooling or good job prospects in the real world), and are more likely to use illegal means, such as robbery and crimes of violence, to demonstrate their masculinity. They are more likely, then, to engage in serious crime in and out of school. This somewhat generalized claim is similar to institutional anomie theory – men who are unable to 'achieve' cultural goals of normative masculinity validate masculine identity through non-legitimate means, or perform non-hegemonic forms of subordinated masculinities.

How useful is the concept of hegemonic masculinity for explaining the predominance of men in violent crime figures? This approach has the advantage of avoiding the reification of 'masculine' and 'feminine' traits and emphasizing the active process of 'doing gender'. One limitation is that it does not explain the meaning of crime perpetrated by women, while at the same time 'over-predicting' male criminality (see Miller 2002). There are problems with specifying what performance of masculinity is hegemonic since these will vary by class, ethnicity

---

[6]I appreciate that Messerschmitt and Connell initially developed different versions of the thesis, but their joint work develops a common position.

and generation (Demetriou 2001). While a willingness to fight is seen as an attribute of the hegemonic masculine identity, this needs to be balanced by the point, following Elias, that physical fighting contradicts societal and individual aspirations to civility and is not therefore a hegemonic norm. Demetriou says the concept of hegemonic masculinity constructs a closed and binary opposition between hegemonic and non-hegemonic forms that appear to be alternatives. But these might actually be hybrids that are continually negotiated. In modern societies, he suggests that there has been a gradual ascendancy of 'feminized' masculinity, in which gay identity has become more visible within a commodity culture. So Sylvester Stallone, whom Connell sees as the epitome of hetero-sexual masculinity, subsequently acquired a new masquerade (in *Lock Up* and *Tango*) with homoerotic male bonding that may partially subvert traditional concepts and power relationships (Demetriou 2001). Further, cultures of mas-culinity vary by class, race and generation and many men in power do not embody idealized masculine attributes, while normative models provided by the mass media change over time – Leonardo DiCaprio rather than John Wayne might represent the aspirational face of contemporary masculinity. Masculinity involves multiple meanings among which men can move.

MacInnes (1998: 57ff) regards the concept as misleading since it assumes that only men 'possess' masculinity and yet provides no empirical description of hegemonic masculinity. He regards its emphasis on the politics of identity as a retreat from classical sociology's concern with material structures. We cannot, he says, explain violence just with reference to patriarchy because there are multiple situational factors involved in any violent confrontation. MacInnes further criticizes Connell and Messerschmidt for confusing the symptom (gen-dered hierarchies) with the cause – what has made people imagine they possess gender in the first place? – for which we need to look at the sexual division of labour and division of private and public domains.

In the last chapter we saw how post-Fordist restructuring has had profound impacts on urban space and violence. Hall (2002) argues that hegemonic mas-culinity theory plays down political economy and class power in a theoretical 'evacuation of capitalism's global socio-economic process'. For Connell, legal violence and street violence combine with economic discrimination to enact domination which establishes 'destructive masculinity' as the hegemonic form from which most men receive a material reward, whether or not they enact the dominant form of masculinity. However, following Bourdieu, Hall argues that the rule of capital is more dependent on symbolic cultural capital than on overt violence (it competes with words and strategies rather than swords), and anyway vast fortunes are accumulated by very small numbers of men. Connell, he suggests, ignores the 'less exotic young men who populate streets, pubs and clubs of every western town and city' (2002). It is difficult to depict a crude caricature of destructive masculinity as legitimating a 'natural order'.

Capitalism rather creates a hyper-masculine proletarian 'other', whose inse-cure and peripheral social inclusion depends on their serviceability. Further, to regard violence as social domination neglects the dimorphic nature of vio-lence as symbolic and material practice. Capitalism deemed the pacification of internal territory essential to its social reproduction, but this meant that violence was not the route to power or privilege. Chapter 4 shows how seri-ous forms of interpersonal violence (especially homicide) are more common among marginalized fragments of the working class. What Hall calls the 'use-less inter-male violence in these locations' (2002) represents little 'reward' for hegemonic masculinity, while violence, death and imprisonment do not seem to indicate the successful application of an institutionalized dominance strategy.

Connell and Messerschmidt (2005) respond to some of these and other cri-tiques but present a reformulated concept of hegemonic masculinity that is explicitly ambiguous. They concede that they had developed too simple a model of the social relations surrounding hegemonic masculinity, especially in terms of its global dominance. They wish to retain the core idea of a plurality and hier-archy of masculinities, while the 'hegemonic' mode might not be the most com-mon and is open to challenge and variation. They recognize that there is a hybridization of styles of masculinity and that heterosexual men might appro-priate 'bits and pieces' of gay lifestyles but they do not regard these as hegem-onic. At the same time they reformulate their understanding of reciprocal relations and the influence of masculinities on each other. There are, for exam-ple, claims to power by regional hegemonic masculinities among local working-class, ethnically marginalized men which will include 'protest' mascu-linities.[7] These might include the participation of otherwise marginalized men in sports such as rugby that value domination, ruthlessness, competitiveness and commitment. They further suggest that the concept needs to develop a more sophisticated understanding of social embodiment, in which men's bodies are seen as both objects and agents of social practice. Finally, this should acknowl-edge that the dynamic of masculinities does not necessarily translate into satisfy-ing experience.

The empirical support for the theory in relation to violence is mixed. Krienert (2003) undertook a study of 704 offenders in Nebraska and found that masculine traits alone failed to predict violent events. But men with very high 'masculine' traits and few acceptable outlets to assert masculinity (such as education, marital status, children, employment, and income) *were* more likely to have been involved in violent incidents. Similarly, Dutton and Corvo (2006)

---

[7]We might note, though, that protest masculinities can embody the most extreme, essentialist and violent aspects of cultural masculinity – as Ferber (2000) argues in her comparison of white supremist and mythopoetic men's movements.

claim that there is no evidence that men who perpetrate acts of violence have 'traditional' or stereotypical 'sex role beliefs', but that the roots of violence lie much deeper in personality formation. Age is a critical variable in offending, as noted above, and a willingness to fight in response to a perceived slight might be an aspect of performative masculinity for some young men (and women). But as Hall argues, this is not necessarily institutionally hegemonic nor it is the norm for mature adulthood. Day et al. (2003) found in interviews with men about fears in public spaces that despite the way 'masculinism condones confrontation in public space, the young men in this study rejected confrontation as a means to establish masculinity' and did not regard this as part of being 'mature'. Phillips (2003) found a similar pattern among girls who had been violent in their teens, but who subsequently regarded this as wild and immature behaviour. So even in its reformulated version, the theory is indeterminate and cannot show why some men are sometimes violent and (most) others are not. Like many theories of crime, it over-predicts the incidence of offending. Nonetheless, the emphasis on performativity and 'doing gender' is a significant advance on more deterministic theories. The next section examines a different possibility – that violence is better addressed through an understanding of the intersection of social exclusion and marginalized masculinities.

Crisis of masculinity?

Under the heading of a 'crisis in masculinity' there has been attention over the past decade to problems of men's health, boys' educational attainment and the unsettling of traditional masculine expectations. MacInnes (1998) argues that men's material privileges are under scrutiny and attack, but this combines with deindustrialization, long-term unemployment and social exclusion in some places. The movement of manufacturing overseas has forced a re-evaluation of muscular work as a validation of masculinity and the idea of the traditional macho man in control of his life creates false expectations. But this has prompted an articulation of muscular masculinity as 'toughing it out' and taking refuge in the cultivation of hyper-masculine bodies (Bairner 1999). In this context, men and adolescents 'with dead-end lives' might find allure and meaning in guns, violence and the gangsta lifestyle (Bairner 1999).

With the post-Fordist restructuring of work, dominant forms of masculinity are thrown into crisis. Segal (1990) noted that men's desire for dominance at work is connected with the preservation of masculine identity, which is diminished by unemployment, and therefore, one might add, of potential shame. Similarly Hatty (2000: 6) comments, 'Violence is the prerogative of the youthful male, especially when confronted by the contradictions and paradoxes of thwarted desire and personal and social disempowerment'. The implication of this line of argument is that violence or youth subcultures of violence might be part of a response to perceived crisis rather than an expression of a dominant masculinity. Hatty's account suggests that unemployment and the decline of traditional working-class male occupations, combined with increasing women's equality, provokes a 'crisis of masculinity'. Whereas the fathers and grandfathers of today's young men spent their lives in male spaces of manual work and associated leisure activities, young working-class men are often unemployed and spend time at home or on the street. However, home is still a female space, whereas the street offers opportunities for alternative experiences of dominance and risk-taking (joyriding, theft, burglary, competition) and 'business' (drugs and organized crime). At the same time, youth cultures emerge that emphasize and exaggerate features of traditional white working-class masculine appearance and behaviour. Nayak (1999) argues that skinhead culture, for example, represents a violent consolidation of masculinity, sexuality and white ethnicity in working-class culture. Similarly, Hebdige (1987) regarded skinheads as expressing a nostalgic exaggeration of white working-class characteristics and a 'mime of awkward masculinity' that was a macho, working-class, white (often racist) 'geometry of menace'. The uniform – boots, braces and cropped hair – represented a caricature of the traditional dress mode of a working man.

Bourgois's (2003) study of Puerto Rican migrants to the USA exemplifies this argument. This is an ethnographic study of street-level drug dealers in East Harlem (USA) who had found that the work they had migrated to do was disappearing, but they would not take work in service sector, which was regarded as 'women's work'. However, their wives and girlfriends did take this work and gained more financial independence than they had previously had, thereby threatening the basis of male dominance in the household. The men often took refuge in the drug economy, where there were very violent norms of gang rape, sexual conquest, abandonment of families and 'real manhood' based on devotion to group membership. Thus, the crisis of masculinity is more acute at lower socioeconomic locations where violence is a way of confirming status in a street culture. Moreover, this is more consistent with the dynamics of shame and violence described by Scheff and Retzinger (2001) than an outcome of the confidence of enjoying 'hegemonic' power. In this context, Scheff says:

> Hypermasculine men are silent about their feelings to the point of repressing them altogether, even anger. … Repressing love and the vulnerable emotions … leads to either silence or withdrawal, on the one hand, or acting out anger (flagrant hostility), on the other. The composure and poise of hypermasculinity sees to be a recipe for silence and violence. (Scheff 2006)

If resources for the performance of hegemonic masculinities are available in the dominant culture, then film media is one source from which cultures of masculinity might be derived, but which might also reflect changing moods of perception of masculinity and violence. In post-World War II war films and westerns, masculine heroes showed little emotional sensitivity and were prone to impulsivity and anger. War was 'what good men do' and its portrayal was unproblematic, especially since in the war zone sexual differentiation was reaffirmed. During the 1950s, though, there were films that conveyed the internal emotional violence of characters, such as *In A Lonely Place* (1950) and *Vertigo* (1958), that in the 1960s developed into a genre that was subversive of traditional gender categories, exemplified by Hitchcock's *Psycho* (1960) where, as Slocum (2005: 18–19) notes, a tale of adultery and promise of heterosexual desire turns into obsessive and homicidal psychosis. Yet the fact that the killer had assumed his dead mother's persona and dress suggested that the violence did not come from traditional masculinity, and in a succession of films (*Baby Jane* 1962, *Repulsion* 1965 and *Rosemary's Baby* 1968) terror was domesticated but psychotic (Schatz 2004: 4–5). Later, Scorsese's *Taxi Driver* (1976) and *Raging Bull* (1980) possibly 'encouraged viewers to reflect on the exploitation of violence for the purposes of entertainment' (Carter and Weaver 2003: 61).

In the 1980s the action genre reflects a mood of 'back to basics' and the legitimacy of masculine power (Carter and Weaver 2003: 62), although with an edge that perhaps also acknowledges departure from lived experiences. In the 'hard body' films, such as the *Rambo* series and *Die Hard* (1988), violence and single-handed rescue fantasy is unproblematic and unchallenging but also exaggerated, suggesting uncertainty about real-life masculine roles. Hard masculine body cinematic representations of combat – robotic masculinity of *Robocop* (1987) and *Judge Dredd* (1995) – concealed a growing crisis in masculinity, in which an alienated individual experiences potency through experiencing and inflicting pain. This idea becomes thematic in films around this time. For example, in *Falling Down* (1993), a middle-class man, 'D-Fens' (Michael Douglas), divorced and unemployed, unable to visit his children, engages in an escalating spree of violence that ends with his own demise. Playing to the theme of compromised masculinity, D-Fens is successfully pursued by Detective Prendergast of the LAPD (Robert DuVall), who took a 'safe' desk job some years ago to appease his 'bossy' wife. The denouement, in which D-Fens is shot while carrying only a toy gun, compounds the sense of masculine aggression as impotent rage. David Fincher's *Fight Club* (1999) offers a more complex exploration of the crisis of masculinity and violence. Though sometimes regarded as an overtly masculine film, the powerful white masculinity of the 1980s and hard body films of the 1990s is absent. It features Jack (the narrator) and Tyler Durden, his destructive *alter ego*, whom we find first in a support group for men recovering from testicular cancer ('remaining men together') where, following chemotherapy, one character, Bob, has lost his testicles and grown breasts ('bitch tits'), symbolizing both masculinity's demise and the hatred it engendered. Indeed, the threat of castration recurs throughout the film 'like a hysterical leitmotif' (Windrum 2004: 308). Jack's addiction to self-help groups has replaced his addiction to consumerism (again, 'feminized' activity), which is then replaced by a search for authentic masculinity in the self-inflicted violence of the fight club. But the lead woman character, Marla Singer (Helen Bonham-Carter), is dominant in the unfolding plot and enables Jack to renounce violence. However, when the film looks as though it has reverted to a familiar hero-rescue fantasy, Jack is unable to prevent the terrorists of Project Mayhem from blowing up large commercial buildings, their falling symbolizing the failure of the masculine corporate world (Saw 2002). Multiple cultural representations of masculinity and femininity are then available, and these can be deployed in various ways – but one contemporary theme is that violence may be an outcome of a perceived *failure* to perform traditional masculine roles rather than necessarily an emanation of power. These kinds of filmic representations resonate with analysts, who suggest that violence is a manifestation of (perceived) powerlessness rather than of power.

However, despite the *trope* of subverted masculinity, there may not be a 'crisis of masculinity' as such, but rather a modification in the modalities and cultures of social power and gender. Even so, as Hall (2002) argues, it is difficult to regard marginalized men as 'hegemonic' when deploying a destructive masculinity in the forms of delinquency, reciprocal fear of violence and possible imprisonment. Hall (2002) concludes that there is not so much a 'crisis of masculinity' as a crisis on the traditional capitalist order where the boundary between criminality and legality is blurred, where hyper-masculinity is deeply embedded and pointless hostility rages on the margins of neo-capitalism. The injuries of class – shaming and self-doubt – set the scene for contests for dignity. A recurrent theme in this book is that violence is largely a response to situations of exclusion, marginalization and inequality, in which traditional modes of masculine identity might well be deployed to provide a framework of justification for confrontational behaviour.

Debate over 'girl gangs'[8]

There is a dispute over whether women's violent offending might be increasing. Juvenile justice officials generally express doubts about the perceived rise in girls' violence and instead see it as an artifact of the shrinking permissiveness of

---

[8]Gangs in general seem to be more a US than a UK form of street life, if, that is 'gang' requires a name, identifiable colours, a formal authority structure, and endurance over time (Batchelor 2001).

law enforcement agencies. At the same time, it is suggested, girls today face struggles in maintaining a sense of self while confronting more complex and contradictory sets of expectations as to appropriate behaviour. The effects of these contradictions may be intensified by the greater exposure of young women to stressful economic circumstances following recent changes in community social organization and family structure (Steffensmeier et al. 2005). Further, the UK Youth Justice Board suggests that:

> Overall, the ... data indicated that girls appear to be being 'policed' more heavily than previously. Older girls are receiving relatively more Final Warning and Reparation Orders and there has been an increase in the number of younger girls being convicted. Girls are increasingly likely to be remanded into custody and this accounts for the increase in use of custodial placements, rather than there being an actual rise in custodial sentences for girls. (Youth Justice Board 2009: 57)

This issue has been raised, too, in the debate over women's violence (specifically 'girl gangs') in relation to hegemonic masculinities. Miller (2002) argues that there is value in a situated action approach to explaining the gendered nature of crime, which challenges the notion that there are 'natural differences' between male and female behaviour. However, she argues that women's participation in crime then remains unexplained except as an anomaly. For Messerschmidt, Miller says, the street gang is an ideal setting for 'doing gender', and girl gangs actively participate in the construction of gender relations and orchestrate forms of heterosexuality – they 'do difference differently' via a form of 'bad girl femininity'. So when women are involved in violent gangs they still enact 'femininity'. However, Miller sees this approach as flawed and risks tautology since anything women do 'accomplishes femininity', which collapses gender back into biological sex. Rather, she argues, people have the ability to draw from a wide range of schemas (conventions, habits of speech, gestures, etc.) in ways that include 'role experimentation'. Among mixed gender gangs she finds that some girls do 'gender crossing' and construct a masculine identity in which gender markings are minimized – 'just like a dude in a girl's body' (2002a). There are greater rewards for women to 'cross' into culturally defined masculine terrain – creating distance from a denigrated sexual identity and getting status as a 'true' gang member. However, in all-female gangs Miller found more evidence of Messerschmidt's 'bad girl femininity' in that members did not situate themselves as 'one of the guys', but dressed in ways that more distinctively highlighted sexuality and used sexuality for gang purposes. This might include carrying drugs or guns while playing on police officers' lack of suspicion of girls and using gender stereotypes to lure men off guard by feigning sexual interest as a prelude for performing a robbery. Miller concludes, then, that it is not sufficient to examine women's crime as a means of accomplishing femininity since cultural gender is fluid and people strategically use prevailing norms to accomplish particular tasks.

In reply, Messerschmidt (2002) argues that Miller has misread his thesis, which is that 'bad girl femininity' constructs gender in different situations of the gang setting, showing the 'unique fluidity of gender'. However, he disagrees with Miller since this does not involve embracing a masculine identity, but rather girl gangs maintain bodily empowerment (for example, through violence) combined with displays of femininity. Where girls do engage in behaviour that is culturally masculine, this does not always have the same meaning as for men. He cites third-wave feminist literature to the effect that toughness and femininity are not mutually exclusive and there is a 'lived messiness' through which people engage with difference. Girl fighting, for example, might be a strategy for preserving or earning position as a girlfriend of a male member or to deter male members from 'messing' with them. In this largely sympathetic exchange, Miller and Messerschmidt agree that it is necessary to move towards a more disaggregated concept of agency as a means of examining not just normative gendered action but gender as a taken-for-granted background.

A few comments here are in order. First, while the emphasis on fluidity, agency and hybridity might seem to capture a complex reality that evades simple theoretical constructs, it is not clear what remains of a theory when it is stretched to encompass all possibilities. Second, the emphasis on 'agency' in this exchange is problematic – as though the women (and men) in violent street locations are simply making lifestyle choices and playing with gender categories in an ironic postmodern way. Neither Miller nor Messerschmidt directly address the likelihood that many women gang members have escaped abusive families and use drugs as sedation to block out traumatic experiences that may go back to early childhood. Interviewed by Neustatter (2008), Batchelor says that 'powerlessness defines the experiences of most young women who turn violent. ... They believe they have no value except for their sexuality.' Miller and Messerschmidt further avoid the issues of violence and sexual exploitation against women by male gang members, which can be followed by self-harming, and street fights, often with vulnerable people, such as recent migrants (Neusattter 2008). Neustatter further reports comments from women gang members such as 'The boys would treat us as their bitches, phone whoever they felt like fucking' and 'order them to come over' but 'by doing that [violence] I got what felt like respect' (Neusattter 2008).

Batchelor (2009), however, suggests moving away from the dichotomy between girl gangs as either sexually exploited or liberated 'postfeminist criminals'. Most gangs, she says, are not involved in serious criminal activity, though many have had difficult family backgrounds and experiences of bereavement and loss, bullying and neglect. Even so, Phillips (2003) points out that 'while girls appear to be less involved as victims and perpetrators of aggression and violence, their involvement in physically aggressive behaviour seems to be rather more common than previous research would suggest'. But unlike the US literature reflected in the Messerschmidt/Miller exchange, in the UK most young women do not 'join' the group and there is no evidence, for example, of initiation rites. Indeed, Batchelor (2001) did not find evidence of the existence of girl gangs – not one of the 800 teenage girls interviewed in their research claimed to be in a girl gang nor did they know anyone else who was a member. They are more likely to purse thrills, engage in fights and cause more trouble than male members as a form of fun risk-seeking, 'not [as] liberated young women but young women who are severely constrained by both their material circumstances and attendant ideologies of working class femininity' (Batchelor 2009). At the same time, there is evidence of social learning in that young women learn by example that violence is poised to erupt at any moment and that respect and reputation are founded on physical force. In this context, their violence is neither hysterical nor irrational, but rather 'a reasoned response to intimated or actual harms' (Batchelor 2005). Further, the media interest in 'girl gangs' is driven in part by its very impact on gendered stereotypes since it challenges the way 'nice girls' behave in contrast to the presumed naturalness of men's aggression (Batchelor 2001).

Sport, masculinities and the civilizing process

Sports exemplify traditional gendered performance and while sport 'is a domain of contested national, class and racial relations ... gender is its central organizing principle' (Bairner 1999). Such is the significance of sport to mapping gender identity that until just prior to the 2000 Olympics in Sydney women international contestants had to submit to chromosomal 'gender verification' tests. But sport also occupied an important place in Elias's civilizational theory as being indicative of a shift in the balance between external and self constraint (Dunning 1999: 62). Sports exemplify the civilizing process – Ancient Greece was based on an ethos of warrior nobility, with high levels of violence reflecting the importance of war in everyday life. In Medieval Europe, tournaments became mock displays of combat, although folk games in villages tolerated forms of violence that are now prohibited and often resulted in extensive injuries. During the eighteenth century sports become more organized and regulated, with rules governing boxing, fox hunting, horse racing and cricket (McCormack 2008: 182 and *passim*). From the mid-nineteenth century, associations such as the Rugby Football Union and the Football Association defined rules and regulated contact, kicking, handling and throwing, etc., while also generating community and identity among supporters. Thus, sport became less a training for war and more an end in itself – often simulating violence, as in wrestling, rather than doing the real thing.

However, contemporary sport also poses challenges to the civilizing thesis. If sport is a quest for excitement that is regulated to prevent actual violence, how does the theory account for on-pitch violence between players and spectator violence, especially 'football hooliganism'? Further, Hargreaves (1992) argued that Elias's theory failed to acknowledge the dynamics of gender and masculinity in sport and leisure, marginalized women in sport and thereby perpetuated the view that sport is more suited to men than women. These issues will now be examined.

Masculinities have become significant in explanations of violence in sport. It was noted above that in contact sports (such as American football, baseball, soccer, ice hockey, rugby, boxing and martial arts) actions are permissible that in a different context might be considered 'violent'. It is non-legitimate violence that we are concerned with here that 'causes harm, occurs outside of the rules of the sport, and is unrelated to the competitive objectives of the sport' (Terry and Jackson 1985). King (2001) describes the conventional paradigm that violence arises as a result of an interactional dynamic of heightened confrontation and masculine self-understandings. The performance of aggressive masculinity is closely bound up with toughness and an ability to withstand pain. In their study of US collegiate rugby players, Muir and Seitz (2004) argue that the self-image of the male rugby player is dependent on meeting peer expectations. So the cruder his behaviour with regard to women or homosexuals the greater will be peer esteem, while hesitation to adhere to the group's norms will likely be met with ostracism. Further, suffering and the endurance of excessive pain reinforce heterosexual masculinity and bravado – so they found that 'non-injured players would look at a bleeding teammate or opponent and remark, "He's just having his period"'. Machismo, misogyny and homophobia were core to subcultural identities, but also underpinned 'deviance' on and off the field. Bairner (1999) concludes his study of soccer in Northern Ireland by saying that 'far from playing a role as aggression-displacer, sport ... and especially sport spectatorship, feeds hegemonic masculinity, which in turn can encourage violence by men at large'.

Moreover, the idea of sport as an end it itself and a simulation of actual aggressive contest is arguably limited by at least two other factors. First, however regulated the contest is, the emotional appeal of competitive sports is based on an actual play of offence and defence, which stimulates collective emotional effervescence, as Collins (2008: 296) suggests. The struggles for dominance in front of audiences will raise confrontational tension so sport is a stimulus rather than a sublimation of violent impulses. Secondly, sport as an end in itself has been eroded by commercialization, more intense competition, privatization and the need to win-at-all-cost (Mennell 1992: 153).

Attempting to counter the criticism that Elias's theory ignores gender issues (particularly in relation to sport), Dunning (1999: 219–39) argues that the thesis explores sport and gender by providing an explanation of the significance of sport in traditional male identities, the empowerment of women who challenge this and develop a new 'female habitus', along with the reactions of men who thereby feel threatened. It is not immediately clear how this is a specifically 'figurational' analysis. However, he continues that in a 'pacified society', sport is an enclave for the legitimate expression of masculine aggression and a 'male habitus' (1999: 234) and one of the few occasions for men to be 'heroes' (1999: 219) in a male-dominated context (1999: 223). This theme is evident in much of the literature here, although it does not necessarily support the civilizational thesis. Kreager (2007) writes of sport as a hyper-masculine culture in which violence is an acceptable means of developing valued male identities. He further argues that this is not evidence of a lack of self-control but rather stems from learned normative definitions that are favourable towards violence. On-pitch confrontations play to audiences and might encourage violence against opposing supporters. In the USA, football players are at the centre of their school's peer culture, so their behaviour is not explained by weak social bonds but might rather involve over-conformity to competitive norms that results in anti-social behaviour. He argues that in heavy contact sports there are 'endlessly renewed symbols of masculinity' that confirm a sense of superiority relative to women and other masculinities, such as non-sporting and therefore 'effeminate' 'puissies' and 'fags'. These definitions of masculinity, Kreager suggests, derive from childhood relationships with male role models. There is a similar analysis of Australian rugby as positively sanctioning violence within a context of performed masculinity as the 'flag carrier' of masculinity in Australian society (Hutchins and Mikosza 1998). The segregation of men into a homosocial environment and locker-room culture limits social contact with women and fosters an 'oppositional masculinity' that sustains traditional gender stereotypes, although when the same men participate in gender-integrated sports they 'positively reformulate their attitudes toward women' (Anderson 2008).

The other issue here is spectator hooliganism. Dunning (1999: 64) argues that there is a 'civilizational downswing' – a de-civilizing process (of uncertain duration), linked to the growing commercialization and competitiveness of sports, that has given rise to spectator violence, especially around UK soccer matches. These, for Dunning, are expressions of male aggressiveness among the 'rougher' sections of the working class, where the civilizing process is less embedded, although this can also be viewed in Connell and Messerschmidt's (2005)'s terms as seeking masculine validation where other outlets have been blocked. Dunning uses the theory of 'segmental bonding' to depict a processes in which young men have not been incorporated into pacified social spaces but rather experience high deprivation, poor education, are unskilled or unemployed, raised with low adult supervision and involved in street corner gangs (Dunning 1999; Mennell 1992: 153). In this context, the formation of gangs and the pleasure of the fight are associated too with a process of informalization and enjoyment of the carnival of the game – which is also apparent in non-violent cultural manifestations such as face paints and 'soccer casual lifestyle'. However, the football match is also a space for a 'moral holiday', permitting displays of excitement, pleasurable emotional arousal, hard masculinity, territorial identifications, individual and collective reputation management and solidarity (Spaaij 2008). These events are about controlling and occupying public space in which rude and obnoxious behaviour is aimed at shocking bystanders and mostly attacking the weak, while backing away from evenly matched confrontations where there is a serious risk of injury. A further dimension of supporter violence might be to transcend the subordinate role of 'fans' and achieve equality with the players – 'take the manor' to emancipate themselves from the subservient role of supporters (Collins 2008: 331).

Collins (2008) focuses on the situational factors in spectator violence. He argues that sports violence cannot be about 'masculinity' *per se*, since fights are unheard of among weightlifters and male gymnasts, who nonetheless display hard body masculinity. For Collins, struggle for dominance is crucial, and some large-scale disturbances are governed by rhythms of dramatic tension but are also deliberately contrived for the sake of having a good time. These do not depend on the events in the game but rather confrontation is sought out in pursuit of emotional thrills. The participants in this violence are not necessarily the poorest but, in common with other forms of mobilization, they are led by those who have the necessary resources, including the financial means to attend matches. Organized violence involves learning techniques such as the capacity to manoeuvre through the streets and public areas while managing performance so as not to alert the police before the action is due to 'kick off'. Supporters know that the police want to move them on and probably will not intervene in low-level fights and vandalism. King (2001) similarly sees violence as a resource deployed by fans in the maintenance of the gang identity. Most confrontations are quick and indecisive, but the discursive re-creation of the fight is lengthy and enters the memory of the gang – the telling of the account of a fight contains emotional rhythm that is important for engendering group solidarity, but it has to be told well and with the right resonance. While actual violence will often involve weaker victims, such as lone rival supporters, to admit to attacking unequals is to risk unmanning oneself in the eyes of the gang. Thus, the social group provides a framework in which memory and the re-telling of a narrative of violence is given meaning and through which groups must periodically gather together to re-affirm their collective memory.

It has been noted that the process of containment is part of the civilizing process. There is an ongoing struggle for containment of sports both within grounds (for example, separating rival supporters) and in the management of crowds moving to and from the match. Slaughter (2003) points to the Home Office (2001) *Working Group on Football Disorder* that identified the problem in terms of alienated young males demonstrating frustration in anti-social and violent ways. However, Slaughter argues that 'the crowd' is a social fact that changes in its structure, purpose, profile and organization in ways that interact with the systems of law enforcement. The crowds that invaded the pitch at the end of the 1966 England–Germany World Cup were viewed as 'innocent bad time keepers' (as in the genial 'they think it's all over'), but by the 1980s pitch invasions became major public order and control issues that were met by the practice of containment through caging fans behind fences. After the Hillsborough disaster[9] control measures were refined and enacted through stadium design (all seated games), a 15 per cent reduction in ground capacity, high-profile policing, banning orders for offenders (following the 1999 Football [Disorder] Act) and CCTV surveillance. The diminution of violence in sports, however, is not only a reflection of a general civilizational process, but is also crucially bound up with shifting forms of hegemonic masculinity and its intersections with age and class. The spaces of 'decivilization', moral holidays, and public entrainment generally involve the deployment of traditional hard masculinity and the exclusion of women in complex contexts where traditional masculinities are challenged in everyday life.

Conclusions

There is a cultural association between masculinity and violence. The theory of hegemonic masculinities indicates how gender is performative but highly structured by class, social position and age. There is not *a* hegemonic masculinity, but rather multiple articulations of oppositional and embodied masculinities. These have been crucially influenced by global economic restructuring and its interaction with traditional cultures of work and masculinity. These create conditions for pathways into violent offending that will be facilitated by the range of alternative avenues to status and success in local illicit markets and cultures, along with opportunities for thrill-seeking behaviour. In this context, 'girl

---

[9]On 15 April 1989 at Hillsborough Stadium, Sheffield, 96 Liverpool fans were crushed to death on the terraces at the Leppings Lane End during the FA Cup semi-final match between Liverpool and Nottingham Forest. Hundreds were injured. When the police opened exit gates to relieve a crush at the stadium entrance and 5000 people attempted to enter, there was nowhere for the supporters already in the ground to go because of the cages.

gangs' can perform both gender-conformist and transgressive behaviour, although one should not see this just in terms of 'playing with style', but also as expressions of situations of deprivation and exclusion. While the civilizational thesis is non-linear and can therefore account for most outcomes – so sport can be both a medium for legitimate thrills and a focus for violent confrontation – this does not offer an explanation of the *particular* configurations violence, youth culture and masculinity. To understand these one needs to look to the conditions for the destruction of social bonds in spaces of abandonment, combined with cultures of masculine validation, where there are few routes into legitimate society.

6

VIOLENCE AND THE PRIVATE SPHERE

The distinction between public and private is crucial to sociological understanding of violence for at least three reasons. First, for the civilizational thesis, the enclosure of the 'private' was linked to increased sensibilities towards public aggression and therefore to the pacification of society. Second, the focus of the criminal justice system on street crimes and public violence has in the past occluded much private violence and its relationship to masculinities and patriarchal power. Third, the exposure of private violence over the past three or four decades has contributed to an *erosion* of the public/private divide as relationships between the individual, communication media and the state are transformed. These issues are explored here.

Intimate partner violence can take many different forms, including physical assault, rape and sexual violence, psychological or emotional violence, torture, financial abuse, dowry-related violence, and control of movement and of social contacts. The legislative definition of domestic violence in England and Wales is:

> any incident of threatening behaviour, violence or abuse [psychological, physical, sexual, financial or emotional] between adults who are or have been intimate partners or family members, regardless of gender or sexuality. (CPS 2009a: 10)

There is, however, a question of whether 'domestic violence' is too broad a term for the multiple forms of intimate partner violence (IPV) and whether we need to differentiate more specific types. The largest volume of work is on spousal, and especially male, violence but families and intimate relationships are sites of violence in diverse ways. Collins (2008: 137) says 'one spouse can attack another; adults can beat up children, but also vice versa. ... There is also elder abuse of aged parents by grown children, and similar patterns of abuse by elder-care workers.' Collins and Gelles both note that the most common form of domestic violence occurs among siblings

(Collins 2008: 137; Gelles 1997: 96ff). Terms such as 'intimate partner violence' (IPV), 'wife battering' and 'family conflict' have different connotations, especially for the gendering of violence. It is increasingly accepted that violence against men is also an issue (e.g., Loseke et al. 2005), although the extent and seriousness of this is still disputed. There is literature that claims evidence for gender symmetry in family violence, although when men commit most violent crime it would be curious if this were dramatically different in IPV. This chapter will not consider all possible instances of domestic violence, since this would require a longer study, but will focus on the general theoretical issues and controversies. The theoretical field is frequently, though unhelpfully, divided into apparently mutually exclusive terrains – family conflict theory and its critics, social structural explanations, psychopathologies and feminist theories – often with the assumption that each excludes the other. Many writers run through several explanations of domestic violence – 'individual pathologies', 'social structural', 'moralist' (such as family breakdown) and 'feminist' – as though the latter could not also include social structural and individual factors. It is also possible that the various theories are highlighting particular aspects of the issue and are not in themselves sufficient. It has been noted already (pp. 99–100) that the persistence of violence against women is sometimes seen as a limitation of Elias's thesis. The social movement activism that increased legislative intervention into intimate violence could itself be seen as exemplifying the civilizing process, although some have argued that the growth of legislation suggests a failure of the more informal forms of social control that underpin the civilizational process.

Privatization of violence and transformation of intimacy

It is often pointed out that for centuries domestic violence was not considered a serious problem – it was sanctioned in Roman and medieval law and the early modern period – although campaigning for the protection of women from violent husbands goes back at least to the eighteenth century in England.[1] It is claimed that in 1782 the English Judge Francis Buller ruled it permissible to 'beat a wife with a stick no wider than a thumb'. There is some

---

[1] It might be more accurate to say, as Gadd (2002) does, that violence against female partners was 'simultaneously condoned and condemned through a multitude of contradictory social discourses'. For example, while the legal protection for women was weak, until the 1880s effigies of known wife-beaters were paraded through the streets of English towns, in the name of 'patriarchal gallantry'.

doubt as to whether the ruling was ever given; it does not appear in William Blackstone's treatise on English common law, although Buller was parodied in the enlightened press at the time (Gelles 1997: 22). Whatever the truth about this particular ruling, though, domestic violence was not generally considered a serious issue unless the injuries were severe. It is only recently, from the 1980s, in the USA and the UK, in response to feminist campaigning, that the police have more seriously begun to pursue offenders and have established Domestic Violence Units and specially trained officers. There are various government initiatives, such as the National Delivery on Domestic Violence in the UK[2] and the STOP Violence Against Women Grant Program in the USA.[3]

Debates over domestic violence are central to the theoretical trends discussed here – the civilizational process, privatization and the spatalization of violence. Cooney's (2003) thesis of the privatization of violence was noted in Chapters 1 and 2. He concludes that 'Disputes outside the family come to be less fraught with danger. A greater share of violence comes to be committed by intimates. Violence privatizes' (Cooney 2003). However, the privatization of violence was not merely a consequence of the transformation of the normative structures of public conduct, but also, as Warrington (2001) says, the physical embodiment of the 'home' as a territorial space within the house, which during the nineteenth century became an index of worldly success, emotional nurture and an idealized environment of 'security'. On the one hand, life for many became more centred around the family, with increasing owner-occupation and a privatized, consumption-based lifestyle, along with increasing affluence during the twentieth century. This coincided with the idealization of 'the family' as the spatial embodiment of patriarchal and heterosexual norms. But by the later twentieth century the family became a site of conflict over authority and subject to what Habermas (1975) calls the 'crisis of socio-cultural reproduction'. Modernization eroded traditional and taken-for-granted norms, while the welfare state in the second half of the twentieth century assumed or regulated many of the traditional functions of the family, such as socialization, health care and education, which in turn reduced the role of the family even more to one of privatized consumption. The result was a 'consciousness of the contingency, not only of the *contents* of tradition, but also of the techniques of tradition, that is, of socialization' (Habermas 1975: 72, original emphasis). Elias (1997: 210) too observed that as the power imbalance in families decreases, people rely increasingly on working out their own *modus vivendi*, which he regarded as

---

[2]See www.crimereduction.homeoffice.gov.uk/violentcrime/dv017.htm.
[3]See www.wvdcjs.com/justiceprograms/violencewomen.html.

'an example of the civilizing process'. The private sphere, then, becomes one in which traditional norms of sexuality, patriarchal power and authority come to be increasingly challenged and renegotiated as typical family relations become more informal.

For Elias, informalization was an aspect of the civilizational process, although it has also been noted that the relationship between informalization and violence is ambiguous. Durkheim (1969: 77) speculated that increasing equality between men and women might risk increased violence against women, and Giddens (1993) suggests similarly. He says that women no longer accept male dominance, but as traditional norms give way to 'everyday social experiments' (1993: 8) the risk of violence increases. Fearing a 'new castration', men's declining control 'generates a rising tide of male violence towards women' (1993: 3), driven by repressed rage at their emotional dependence on women (1993: 153). At the same time, this ambivalent dependence is not confined to men and can also induce 'shame-fuelled rage' among women (1993: 153). Giddens suggests, then, that the decline of patriarchy and the informalization of previously more structured intimate relations risks increased intimate partner violence. Because of the hidden nature of much IPV, judging whether it has increased is difficult, although actually some evidence does point towards a recent decline.

Legislating against intimate violence

The criminalization of domestic violence and, in particular, mandatory arrest laws represent a significant shift in public policy. But the primary motivation might have had more to do with controlling police behaviour and a more punitive approach to crime rather than reducing violence *per se* (Iyengar 2009). While mandatory arrest has become common practice across the USA, this has not been followed by the UK, although police powers of arrest have increased. In England and Wales, the Domestic Violence, Crime and Victims Act 2004 amended and extended the legislative framework for responding to intimate partner violence. According to the Home Office (2005a: 27), this recognized that the criminal justice system often failed victims whose cases were brought to court, which 'resulted in extraordinarily high attrition rates amongst domestic violence cases'. This Act aimed to address this by improving the effectiveness of the protection offered to victims and police powers to arrest perpetrators. The report continues that the police and the Crown Prosecution Service (CPS) are taking a more proactive approach to prosecution, even where the victim does not want to press charges. See the summary below that identifies its key provisions.

KEY POINTS OF THE UK DOMESTIC VIOLENCE, CRIME AND VICTIMS ACT 2004

- Common assault became an arrestable offence by adding it to the list of offences for which a police officer may arrest without a warrant.
- It became an arrestable, criminal offence to breach a non-molestation order, punishable by up to five years in prison (non-molestation orders were created by the 1996 Family Law Act).
- It extended the provisions of the Family Law Act to cohabiting same-sex couples and to couples who have never lived together or been married.
- It enabled courts to impose restraining orders when sentencing for any offence rather than only on offenders convicted of harassment or causing fear of violence.
- It enabled courts to impose restraining orders *on acquittal* for any offence if they still considered it necessary to protect the victim from harassment.

These changes in perceptions of the seriousness of domestic violence arose from at least four developments (Pahl et al. 2004):

- Feminist activism in the 1970s identified this as an issue that would give practical expression to their more general concern about the position of women.
- The opening of women's refuges made visible what had previously been hidden.
- The growth of Women's Aid, as a coordinating body for the growing number of refuges, brought the activists together to share ideas and experience and to work for increased political visibility for their analysis.
- Feminist scholars and activists were energetic in researching the issue and in pressing for more effective and appropriate action by relevant agencies.

The political context of this campaigning was given additional impetus by the growth of victim movements, through which have emerged new types of rights in which social suffering became politically relevant. Sznaider (2001: 36) notes how nineteenth-century 'campaigns of compassion' eroded supposedly natural rights to use violence in the private domain. Motivated by outrage over criminal victimization, these were highly charged moral protests over the duties of state government, although they also 'counterposed the righteous pain and suffering of victims and the public against "unworthy" criminals' (Barker 2007). They contained an implicit view of a 'good society' in which 'experience of victimization was regarded as significant [and] traumatic'. But these movements had both civilizational and decivilizational aspects, increasing victims' rights and establishing restorative forms of justice but also populist and punitive demands for vengeance. However, the more deliberative and democratic the movement,

Barker suggests, the more likely will people make 'informed decisions about crime control policy ... that are not inherently punitive' (2007).

There is some debate, however, about the unintended consequences of criminal justice interventions, especially in the USA. Fagan (1995) argues that the formation of special prosecution units created an atmosphere and organizational context in prosecutors' offices in which domestic violence cases had high status. On the one hand, these units created incentives for vigorous prosecution without competing with other units and high-visibility cases for scarce trial or investigative resources (Fagan 1995: 15). On the other hand, though, 'There is little conclusive evidence of either deterrent or protective effects of legal sanctions or treatment interventions for domestic violence' (1995: 25). Formal (legal) sanctions are effective when reinforced by informal social controls and weakened when those informal controls are absent (1995: 26). The sources of informal social control of domestic violence may lie either within the individual, in the form of internalized beliefs and social bonds, or may be externally reinforced through normative behaviours within neighbourhoods and other social contexts (1995: 26). Thus, 'like many other legal reforms, criminalizing domestic violence may have unintended consequences, reflecting the social organization of the courts and processual contexts, rather than legal statute' (1995: 27).

Frye et al. (2007) argue that mandatory arrest has had unintended consequences in the USA. These include no arrest, when the perpetrator has left the scene (subsequent arrests being lower in poorer and ethnic minority localities), unwanted arrest (where the victim wants a different resolution), and victim arrest where officers cannot identify the primary aggressor and so arrest both parties. Iyengar (2009) found that an unintended consequence of mandatory arrest could be decreased reporting and therefore an increased risk of domestic homicide since an escalating pattern of assault might go undetected. Fagan also says that those who do report appear to be individuals who have few non-legal resources for protection or deterrence (1995: 29–30). In other words, calling the police to intervene might happen more frequently where people do not feel they have other social capital and recourses for support. On the other hand, Hester et al. (2008: 32) found in their review of the 2004 Act that 'the area where greatest impact could be discerned was in relation to common assault being made an arrestable offence' and that a pro-arrest policy had had a deterrent effect, although a degree of police discretion was retained.

How extensive is IPV?

Despite the widespread association of violence with public street crime, domestic violence represents a significant proportion of crimes known to the

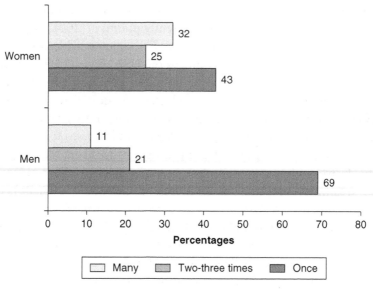

Figure 6.1 Domestic Violence Repeat Victimization Since Age 16
Source: Walby and Allen (2004: 13)

police. The London Metropolitan Police Service (MPS) receives around 100,000 domestic violence calls each year, accounting for one in twenty notified offences.[4] Domestic violence is more likely to involve repeat victimization than any other type of crime and is more likely to result in injury than other offences against the person. Figure 6.1 shows British Crime Survey (BCS) data suggesting that, among women, repeated attacks follow in the majority of cases (57 per cent) although among men this is less frequent (31 per cent). Domestic violence typically escalates and previous violence is a predictor of further violence – 35 per cent of second incidents occur within five weeks of the first (Farrell and Pease 1993). According to the MPS, domestic assaults account for one-third of all Common Assaults, over a quarter of Actual Bodily Harm, and one-eighth of Grievous Bodily Harm (MPS 2003: 16). Domestic homicide (the killing by one family member of another, including current or former partner) accounts for approximately 25 per cent of all homicides in London and 35 per cent in England and Wales (MPS 2003: 5). In the UK in 2001/02, 148 homicide victims were killed by their partner or ex-partner, of whom 116 were women and 32 were men. Further, self-report studies from the USA indicate that IPV happens in between 25 and 48 per cent of female and between 15 and 33 per cent of male same-sex relationships (MPS 2003: 9).

---

[4] In the first quarter of 2001 there were 23,000 calls to the MPS relating to domestic violence, which is around 10 calls an hour, 24 hours a day (MPS 2001).

In data derived from crime surveys, the figures vary considerably with the types of data source used and the questions asked. In the UK, BCS data record respondents' experience of domestic violence both during the past 12 months and during their lifetime. In answer to the question 'Have you experienced domestic violence during the past 12 months?', 4.2 per cent of women *and* men experienced assault, although twice as many women as men had been injured, suffered repeated violence and frightening threats. Although this may create the impression that men and women experience domestic violence roughly equally, victimization takes two distinct patterns. One, which both women and men perpetrate, is marked by occasional anger and aggression; the other, which is more likely to be 'male', is characterized by severe escalating violence and terrorization (Mirrlees-Black 1999). When asked about lifetime prevalence, a ratio of 1:4 women report being assaulted by male partner, 1:8 women have been assaulted repeatedly; while 1:6 men reported occasional assault and 1:20 repeated assaults. Young women are at the most risk, while oldest groups were least likely to report violence. This could mean that IPV has increased over time or that young people have a greater number of relationships and are therefore at more risk. Or again, it may be that older age groups are more reluctant to report experiences, especially if the incidents took place a long time ago.

Globally, reported domestic violence varies considerably and definitions vary too. According to the World Health Organization's report on violence and health (Krug et al. 2002: 89), the percentage of women who reported having been assaulted by a partner in the previous 12 months varied from 3 per cent in Australia, Canada and the USA to 27 per cent in Nicaragua, 38 per cent in South Korea and 52 per cent in the West Bank and Gaza. Further physical aggression in intimate relationships is generally repeated over time and is part of a syndrome of sexual, psychological and physical violence (Krug et al. 2002: 91). Ellsberg et al. (2000) interviewed 488 women between the ages of 15 and 49 in León, Nicaragua. Among ever-married women, 52 per cent reported having experienced physical partner abuse at some point in their lives. A considerable overlap was found between physical, emotional and sexual violence, with 21 per cent of ever-married women reporting all three kinds of abuse. Thirty-one per cent of abused women suffered physical violence during pregnancy. The period between marriage or cohabitation and the onset of violence was short, with over 50 per cent of the battered women reporting that the first act of violence took place within the first two years of marriage. Significant associations were found between partner abuse and physical abuse of children. In the UK, among children staying with their mothers in refuges, 70 per cent had themselves been abused by their father; even those who do not suffer abuse are likely to be aware of what is taking place (Women's Aid 2009: 16). Data indicate that battered women frequently experience feelings of shame, isolation and entrapment, which, together with a lack of family and community support, often contribute to women's difficulty in recognizing and disengaging from a violent relationship. Thus, statistics alone offer only a limited insight into the issue. Questions such as 'Have you ever been abused?' or even behaviourally-specific questions fail to take account of the atmosphere of terror in violent relationships and its effects on children.

However, regarding Giddens' expectation that violence against women would increase with the increasing informalization of domestic relations, the evidence seems to point to the contrary. Finney (2006: v) found that:

> Long-term trends in violent crime, as measured by the BCS, have shown a significant decline since their peak in 1995, in particular there have been large falls in both domestic and acquaintance violence. Between 1995 and 2004/05, domestic violence fell by 59 per cent and acquaintance violence by 54 per cent.

A similar fall was reported in the USA during the 1990s (Chancer 2004) but it is possible that under-reporting to both the police and crime surveys could account for some of this. However, this is a sustained trend that coincides, as Walby and Allen (2004: 91) suggest, with a period in which survey methodology has been considerably refined[5] and during which there 'have been major transformations ... in the way that public services address domestic violence, sexual assault and stalking', which might further increase reporting. So although there will be an unknown level under-reporting, there is a trend towards decline in instances of domestic violence.

Power, masculinity and violence

Data collated by the World Health Organization (WHO) indicates that the triggers for domestic violence are remarkably consistent across all countries and cultures (Krug et al., 2002: 120). These include:

- 'Not obeying the husband'
- 'Arguing back'
- 'Not having food ready on time'
- 'Not caring adequately for children or home'

---

[5]For example, the use of laptops to complete questionnaires, so avoiding the re-telling of traumatic experiences to an interviewer, and more precisely defined descriptions of forms of sexual and non-sexual assault – for example, defining specific acts such as 'pushed you, held or pinned you down, or slapped you', 'kicked you, bit you, or hit you with a fist', and 'choked or tried to strangle you'.

- 'Questionning about money and girlfriends'
- 'Going out without permission'
- 'Refusing sex'
- Pregnancy.[6]

What does this tell us about IPV? A usual conclusion that is drawn from this is that domestic violence is primarily about the exercise of power and a response to perceived challenges to male power. Particularly following Dobash and Dobash's work in the 1970s, feminist researchers suggest that rather than look for specific pathologies among perpetrators, we should recognize that domestic violence is ubiquitous and a routine means of maintaining patriarchal power and authority. Feminist researchers emphasize factors such as:

- The historically subordinate position of women within marriage.
- Women's responsibility for childcare (and consequent exclusion from the labour market and weak economic position in the household).
- Patriarchy reproduces male power/female dependence at all levels – social, cultural and economic.
- Machismo cultures and tacit or explicit approval of male violence.

For feminist theory of the 1970s and 1980s, the linkage of power, violence and sexuality 'has been one of the foundations of feminist analysis' (Kelly 1996: 37). Kelly claims that violence is ubiquitous to masculinity since 'violence is a power turn on for men' (Radford et al. 1996: 3) and Mooney (2000: 91) argues that all male violence against women is a means of social control and maintaining patriarchy. Again, Horvath and Kelly (2006) say that 'perpetrators of violence are more likely to select someone over whom they have a privileged position', although later (in relation to elder abuse) they say that abusers 'may be dependent on the elderly person for housing, money, transport, food and cleaning'. The latter suggests a more nuanced and complex dynamic of power than the former. Kelly and Radford (1998) argue that sexual violence is the outcome of women's inferior status since sex and sexuality is the arena in which men attempt to maintain dominance. Thus, 'heterosexuality as an institution … requires violence' to enforce it (Kelly and Radford 1998: 64). Radford and Stanko (1996: 62) likewise see sexual violence 'used by men as a way of securing and maintaining the relations of male dominance and female subordination' central to the patriarchal order. Some men may enjoy inflicting violence. One of the women interviewed by Hanmer (2000: 12) reported that 'the more

---

[6]Mezey et al. (2002) found that 2.5 per cent of pregnant women suffered assault in the last 12 months, lifetime prevalence was 13.4 per cent, and that violence during pregnancy was ten times more likely if violence had been experienced during the past 12 months, although it is possible that age rather than pregnancy might be the critical factor.

violence he did to me the happier he would be. ... After he had hit me, he would say "Sit there in front of me, if I see any tears in your eyes then see what happens"'. Again for Hatty (2000), violence guarantees individual and social control and the persistence of hierarchy and violence (especially rape) are legitimated both in marriage and in war.

Dobash and Dobash (1992) argue that the structural and ideological character of patriarchy is a set of hierarchical institutions within which violence is a means of control and of diminishing the resistance of women. But they also point to the dangers of reifying patriarchy. Using data largely from the 1970s, Dobash and Dobash (1998: 1) claim that the idea of heroic masculinity is associated with aggressive bodily display, 'allowing men to be violent because of their position' (1998: 145). They say men demand from women household chores and their dinner on the table, so where this is not forthcoming their authority is at stake. There is, however, a tension between this general claim and their suggestion that there are complex and context-specific forms of violence, since violence is chosen in a structural context. Men's violence is variable between different contexts and is specifically focused, and Dobash and Dobash point to the need to analyse the concrete nature of the act and its dynamic development. They further suggest that men who perpetrate violence have specific personality characteristics – they lack empathy, are narcissistic, evaluate their needs above others and their morality is 'out of step with the moral prescriptions of other men and the society at large' (Dobash and Dobash 1998: 163). Even so, they claim that men who are not violent receive affirmation from the violence of others (1998: 166), a claim some research questions.

Talk about violence often combines justification with denial. Reporting interviews with violent men, Hearn (1998: 38) likewise argues that violence is part of enforcing power and control, but those perpetrators often minimize their violence, present it as 'out of character' and suggest that they were a different 'alien' person at the time. Violence to known women was usually regarded by perpetrators as 'incidental' to life histories (1998: 86), although Hearn's transcripts also contain shame cues and accounts of the rage associated with violence, as in 'angers ... come up in my throat, my chest, ... I want to rip it out. I want to completely destroy the object in front of me' (1998: 103–4). There are several techniques of neutralization (see pp. 17–18) in Hearn's accounts (1998: 108–9) – repudiation (deny it happened), quasi-repudiation (minimize its seriousness), justification ('she pushed me to the edge'), but also, rarely, confessions (recognition and accepting responsibility). At the same time (cf. Glasser 1998), men may blame women for provoking violence and adopt the posture of victims, which is a common feature of other violent offenders (Ray et al. 2003). Hearn found that violence was normatively justified by his interviewees, some of whom gained a thrill from the display of power.

The 'right' to use violence to defend hegemonic masculinity is frequently deployed in accounts by male perpetrators of domestic violence. However, the dynamics of power and powerlessness in domestic violence might be more complex than these arguments suggest. While violence is sometimes seen as a ubiquitous expression of patriarchal power, much research suggests that violence mostly occurs within a complex of threatened masculinity, resented dependence and threat of loss likely to be characteristic of shamed but controlling personalities. There is ambiguity here as to whether violence is an enactment of hegemonic masculinity or a response when it is threatened. Mooney (2000: 106), for example, says that violence is a resource for the socially powerless, where male power is threatened. Schrock and Padavic (2007) argue that 'men who harm women often do so when their sense of traditional manhood – such as being a breadwinner or having women meet their often-unspoken needs – is threatened'. Anderson and Umberson (2001) found that perpetrators of domestic violence 'felt emasculated and depicted female partners as dominating' and attempted to reconstruct what had become a contested masculinity by reproducing in their partners a passive femininity. Snider (1998) says sexual violence is more common where gender differences are polarized and general social inequalities are high. Thus, 'many … violent men … are frustrated individuals who see women as easy, weak and available targets. They are often jealous and insecure, they believe in traditional sex roles … [and] frequently they witnessed or experienced physical or sexual abuse as children' (Snider 1998). Violence is therefore both instrumental and expressive – claiming male entitlement but also reinforcing a culture of male dominance.

The issue of vulnerability is complex. Vetlesen (2005: 11) argues that vulnerability is the 'capacity to be affected by the affectedness of the other' and 'much evildoing' arises from vulnerability and dependence on the other, which can lead to narcissistic rage and decivilization. Gelles (1997: 75) argues that perpetrators often experience low self-esteem, vulnerable self-concepts, feel powerless and inadequate. Again, Horvath and Kelly's point about 'elder abuse abusers' suggests that in an abusive relationship the abuser's dependence on the victim is experienced as vulnerability which generates unacknowledged shame. Snider (1998) points to the insecure attachment that can follow from an experience of abuse among people who carry this into their adult social relationships, where an unstable sense of self combines with difficulty in inhibiting action when aroused. Messerschmidt (1997) argues that wife-beating is a resource for constructing 'damaged' patriarchal masculinity and re-affirming a man's right to dominate his wife. However, it is a perceived *powerlessness* rather than power that motivates men to choose sexual violence as a suitable resource for asserting themselves as 'real men' (Messerschmidt 1993: 143–50). Kimmel (2002) similarly says men use violence against their partners or ex-partners 'when they fear their control … is breaking down … not as an expression of their power but as an instance of its collapse'. Therefore, if male violence is placed in the context of the erosion of patriarchy and the transformation of intimacy, then it is more the case that *some* men (and some women) attempt to exercise control through violence while deploying cultural resources of hegemonic masculinity.

To recap, there are two different claims being made in this literature. The first is that violence is a normalized means of exercising and sustaining patriarchal power linked perhaps to a masculine emotional gratification derived from the exercise of violence. The second is that violence is a response to the informalization of traditional family relationships and the loss of power experienced by some men. It is a toxic or hyper-masculinity with particular social and psychological characteristics. This implies a less essential link between violence and masculinity and resonates more with the crisis of masculinity arguments considered in the last chapter and with Arendt's view of violence occurring in the absence of power. It further suggests that violence is more particular to certain people and social locations than a phenomenon in general. This will be developed in the following sections.

Some critiques

Fagan (1995: 38) argues that to assume that patriarchy and power relations alone cause domestic violence leads to missing the full array of explanations. Further, 'power' is generally untheorized in these accounts. Power is normatively embedded in cultural values that sanction its exercise and these vary between cultures. Similarly, as most researchers acknowledge, domestic violence occurs more in some settings than in others, and this patterning requires more specific explanations. Critique of this approach has focused particularly on the application of the theories of Dobash and Dobash and others in the influential Duluth model of offender intervention.[7] Although this programme claims high levels of success, Dutton and Corvo are among the most strident critics of the patriarchal power paradigm. They argue that violence between intimates and

---

[7]The Duluth Domestic Violence Intervention Project, launched in 1980, is a 26-week course aimed at male perpetrators and based on the theory that violence is a strategy for the control of women. The curriculum is designed to be used within a community, using its institutions to diminish the power of perpetrators over their victims and to explore with each abusive man the intent and source of his violence and the possibilities for change through seeking a different kind of relationship with women. Its aim is to change long-held patterns and requires the men to acknowledge and take responsibility for the destructive nature of their behaviour. It is accepted that they are not responsible for creating the many forces, and in particular the hierarchies, that have shaped their thinking and behaviour. See www.eurowrc.org/05.education/education_en/12.edu_en.htm.

family members stems from complex causal processes; that intimate partner violence is committed by both genders with often equal consequences, violence is not committed because of 'sex role beliefs', but rather the formation of an intimate abuser begins early in life, and the stereotype of male perpetrator–woman victim is the least common form (Dutton and Corvo 2006).

Dutton (1999) argues that a triad of childhood events is typically found among violent adults: witnessing violence towards their mother, shaming and insecure attachment and child abuse. These events generate personalities that are hyper-vigilant, have an unstable sense of self and a proneness to shame and rage. He draws on social learning theory (discussed on pp. 86–88), but adds that this does not account for the acquisition of the psychological states that sustain abusiveness – depression, chronic anger, blaming the victim and accumulation of internal tension. These cannot be 'imitated' but are rather generated by early trauma. This argument is similar to Scheff's shame–rage cycle (see pp. 39–42), in which violence protects the self from what is perceived as looming annihilation. Thus, an assertion of independence by the spouse (or possibly other intimates) triggers violence which suggests a high level of dependence. Even so, the enactment of the violence and its subsequent justifications (as Hearn shows) deploys the normative structures embedded in masculine cultures.

There is nonetheless the issue raised in the last chapter as to what forms of masculinity are hegemonic? After all, men accused of domestic violence stand accused of 'the emblematic masculine sin of our age' (Faludi 2000: 7) rather than sanctioned behaviour. Gadd (2002) argues that most men do *not* regard violence against women as an acceptable means of accomplishing masculinity, but suggests that there is a complex relationship between masculinities and violence. He claims that among violent men persecutory feelings too acute to be verbalized and contained are released through destructive behaviour. There is also a psychological process of splitting and projection, in which the self splits off from 'unwanted parts' which are projected on to others where they can be attacked. He presents the case study of 'Mark' who had a history of abusive behaviour towards his partner 'Maria'. Mark's own experience of abuse is initially repudiated by identifying with his abusive father, who is perceived as 'powerful'. But later compelled to recognize the social reality of his father's abusiveness, Mark reworked his memories and identified with his mother yet also split off those aspects of his behaviour that were like his father's. When confronted with this – for example, if Maria says 'You are like your father' – in his 'fantasy Maria became a feared persecutor, heightening both his desire to control her and his fear of dependence on her'. For men like Mark, women are viewed as passive and vulnerable, establishing a dependency that is also experienced as threatening. Thus, the performance of adult 'masculinity' (as protector and provider) depends on a desire to control his partner while remaining dependent on her and upon a rigid but precarious reworking of childhood memories. In this kind of analysis, power and patriarchy are still present – Gadd points out, for example, that Maria had at times wanted to leave Mark but was too socially and economically dependent to do so – but the dynamics of power/powerlessness and the legacies of past traumas are more complexly presented.

Dutton and Nicholls (2005) further claim that the gender disparity in domestic violence is less than originally portrayed by feminist theory. There are disputes over the extent and motives for women's violence, although even if this is rare compared with male IPV, the question still remains of its theoretical explanation. Kelly says that sexual violence is the outcome of men's power and 'it is entirely possible for women to identify with, even want, the kind of "power over" that the sexual frequently provides for men' (1996: 38). But this is tautology. When women perform sexual violence they are 'becoming men' in the way Messerschmidt suggests for 'girl gangs' (see pp. 96–98). It is also frequently claimed that women's violence is self-defence following long-term violence by a male partner. A recent study found that 'few of the women [interviewed] could be considered as the primary aggressor in their relationship' (Henning et al. 2006), and Melton and Belknap (2003) cite similar findings. On the other hand, Ehrensaft (2008), also working with the theory of developmental trauma, questions such claims. Exposure to violence in the home, she argues, influences subsequent stages of development in a cycle of disadvantage and conduct disorder which is explicable in terms of psychopathology rather than patriarchy. Her research followed a cohort of 1000 men and women over 20 years from birth, through early adulthood. Among those in clinically abusive relationships, she found an overlap of 55 per cent between adult spousal violence and child abuse, and that couples in violent relationships were 'often' both from abusive backgrounds. These results, she says, do not confirm long-standing assumptions about the gendering of IPV in that perpetrators were often women. However, in 'clinically abusive' relationships it was more often women who needed medical treatment, a finding that is confirmed by many other researchers.

However, Dutton and Corvo are in turn criticized on a range of methodological and theoretical grounds. Gondolf (2007) argues that while there are multiple factors associated with abuse, only a few of these are significant, and Dutton and Corvo are selective in their use of research and portray a caricature of the projects they criticize. In response to their critique of 'gendered violence' Gondolf points to the disproportionate levels of male violence – there are six times as many female and male victims of domestic violence and Dutton and Corvo's model is static and cannot capture the dynamics of violence over time. He nonetheless agrees that typical perpetrators have narcissistic and anti-social personalities and high displays of egotism and self-righteousness. Melton and

Belknap (2003) aimed to clarify the debate over gender symmetry or asymmetry in IPV and conclude that:

- Evidence from shelters, hospitals and police reports indicate a preponderance of male perpetrators and female victims (perhaps of 90 per cent).
- Gender symmetry arguments do not deal with the context and different meanings of violence, where women experience more intimidation, deploy violence expressively or in self-defence.
- Interviews with both partners rather than only one produced higher rates of male violence.
- The severity of male violence is more serious than women's (although this is based on a review of pre-trial cases, i.e., those serious enough to go to trial).
- Gender differences are more pronounced in qualitative data, which reveal sequences of violent behaviour that can be missed in quantitative surveys.

Patriarchal terrorism vs. family conflict

There is a divergence in the literature over the gender symmetry of IPV and its relationship to power and patriarchy. The remainder of this chapter will explore ways of developing a more integrated theoretical approach. One possibility is that the divergences in the literature arise because they are addressing two different phenomena: one generated through community samples; the other from clinical phenomena. Johnson (1995) makes an often-cited distinction between 'common couple violence' and 'patriarchal terrorism'. Common couple violence is central to the family violence perspective (e.g., Straus and Gelles 1990) that emphasizes factors such as stress, the normative acceptability of violence and inability to express feelings as underlying IPV. These are occasional outbursts of violence in response to everyday stimulus. The concept of 'common couple violence' resonates with Glasser's (1998) theory of 'self-preservative' violence that is triggered by danger, which could include humiliation, attacks on one's self-concept and gender identity. It is also consistent with Scheff's research on the dynamics of shame–rage cycles where repeated conflicts are generated by dysfunctional communication patterns and unacknowledged shame, creating a repetitive cycle of insult and revenge (Scheff 1997: 205). In this type there is greater gender symmetry and generally less severe injury. By contrast, (the more rare) 'patriarchal terrorism' is 'rooted in ... ideas of male ownership of female partners', is overwhelmingly male perpetrated and more often results in serious injury. While common couple violence is intermittent, patriarchal terrorism escalates, especially where a partner resists or even if she submits since no amount of compliance will avoid violence. Escalation follows what Collins (2008) calls 'forward panic' – a manic unleashing of violence where the vulnerability of the victim is itself the ground for overcoming inhibitions. Glasser (1998) also argues that self-preservative violence can become 'sadomasochistic' violence, where inflicting suffering becomes a source of gratification. Like those who see a specific psychopathology in terroristic violence, Glasser also suggests that these perpetrators will have led a 'self-castrating' life, always backing down to their father (rather like Mark, above), thus concealing hidden sadism of identification with the oppressor. There is not a continuum between these – in which the first can escalate into the latter – but they are different forms of violence. This distinction is consistent with studies of clinical violence such as Melton and Belknap (2003).

While these theories emphasize psychodynamic properties of IPV, Mihalic and Elliott (1997) emphasize in addition the importance of learned norms supportive of violence. This connects the analysis with a wider cultural normative masculinity that is an available resource legitimating violence. They argue that there are powerful effects of witnessing violence on subsequent normative development that impair coping mechanisms and engender a sense of powerlessness. However, the effects are greater for men than for women. Male witnesses of violence are prone to lose faith in the 'fairness of the world' and develop a tolerance of violence, although they also emphasize that there is no simple correlation between sex role typing and violence. 'Males with the most traditional attitudes', they say, 'had less serious marital violence' (Mihalic and Elliott 1997). The issue is not one of 'traditional attitudes' but the impact of the experience of violence and the acquisition of normative rationalizations for violence. There seems little doubt that serious and escalating IPV is highly gendered, although there might be forms of domestic conflict, with a largely different socio-psychological basis, in which both women and men participate. Even so, it is possible for family conflict to enter shame–rage cycles and generate more extreme violence. IPV is complexly bound up with issues of power and masculinity.

Spaces of intimate violence

The theories examined above emphasize the micro-dynamics and developmental factors that can underlie IPV. However, it is also important to note that there are socioeconomic and spatial patterns of intimate violence. The Metropolitan Police Service (MPS) notes that perpetrators of domestic violence are often engaged in other criminality – 'by viewing perpetrators of domestic violence as separate from perpetrators of other crimes it is possible that crucial intelligence is lost. ... Recent research shows that police know a large proportion of domestic violence perpetrators [43 per cent – LR] for a variety of other criminal matters ranging from drugs to firearms to murder' (MPS 2001: 12; see also Walby and Allen 2004: 89). The family conflict model would suggest that poverty causes stress, feelings of inadequacy, a 'crisis of masculinity' and makes it more difficult for women to leave abusive relationships. This approach should not be seen as offering a *cause* of IPV. These accounts do not, for example, explain middle-class domestic violence (Mooney 2000: 158 and 219; Pahl et al. 2004), but they do offer some markers of the social distribution of risk. Gelles (1997: 83) says that 'Irrespective of the method, sample, or research design, studies of marital violence support the hypothesis that spousal violence is more likely to occur in low income, low socio-economic-status families'. More deprived localities will often have lower social capital, which is the trust that facilitates coordination, cooperation for mutual benefit and reciprocity within a community. With low social capital there will be less stable social networks and support, more tolerance of violence but more uncertainty about status and identity, including gender performance. These factors in interaction are likely to predispose certain individuals to violence.

Snider (1998) argues that men construct masculinities in the same way as any other identity – by choosing among options that are available and satisfying peer norms of conduct. In localities of deprivation, (poor, marginalized, ethnic minority) men 'may find identities based on possession of turf or defence of honour appealing ... perhaps because a block of contested cityscape, a muscular body and a gun are among the few resources they can claim' (Snider 1998). Domination over women and willingness to use sexual violence might be the locally dominant hegemonic masculinity. This model may explain why some societies and locales are more violent than others, by combining factors of increasing risk. There is an association between domestic violence and low socioeconomic status, as there is for violence in general. Finney's analysis of the 2004/05 BCS report on *Domestic Violence, Sexual Assault and Stalking* claims:

> Indicators of socio-economic status such as household income, vehicle ownership, tenure type and council/non-council areas, suggest fairly consistently that higher prevalence rates of intimate abuse are associated with relatively lower levels of socioeconomic status. ... it is the more vulnerable groups that are more likely to experience intimate violence or abuse. (Finney 2006: 9)

Figure 6.2 shows data on the distribution of reported IPV (based on reports to the BCS) by occupational social class, as indicated in the key below the chart. This chart indicates that there is a relationship between social class and the risk of domestic violence for women and men, although the class gradient is clearer among men than women. For women, reported violence is overall lower in classes I–IV than V–VII but highest in V (self-employed). It will need further research to assess whether this is an artefact of the methodology or reflects an underlying process. Further, Walby and Allen (2004) found that BCS data indicate that the risk of domestic violence varies by social and situational characteristics. Economic factors are the important risk factors for women and vulnerability is associated with a lack of access to financial resources, so in households with income less than £10,000 per annum the risk is 3.5 times greater than in households with over £20,000 (2004: 75).

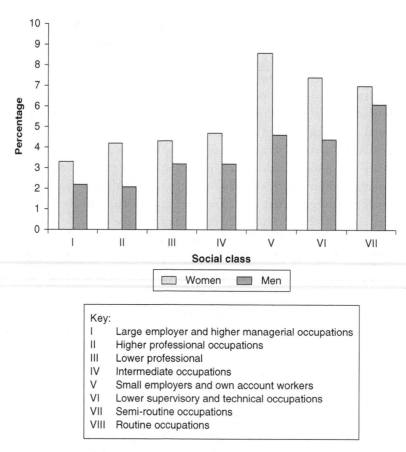

Figure 6.2 Social Class Distribution of Domestic Violence
Source: Chart based on Table 9.A in Finney (2006: 20)

There are significant differences in risk between employed and unemployed men and women (see Figure 6.3). Macmillan and Gartner (1999) analyse the symbolic dimensions of employment in terms of exchange theory. This predicts that the party with less 'reward power' is more likely to resort to coercion, and where masculinity is tied to being a breadwinner, so (we might infer) unemployment will generate shame and threat to self-concepts. They found that the risk of violence was higher (by three times) where only the female partner was employed, while women's entry to the labour market lowered the risk where the male partner was also employed.

We have seen in Chapter 3 how multiple social processes embed into spatial relations. This is also the case with IPV and there is research that suggests that neighbourhoods with the most resource deprivation also have dramatically higher rates of violence between intimates. Some note that this has not featured strongly in the domestic violence literature (e.g., Miles-Doan 1998),

Percentage of all adults reporting intimate violence	Women	Men
Employed	4.9	4.0
Unemployed	12.1	7.7

Figure 6.3 Employment and Unemployment and Reporting Domestic Violence
Source: Chart based on Table 9.A in Finney (2006: 20)

although interest in the spaces of domestic violence is growing. Miles-Doan (1998) tested the theory that concentrated poverty undermined social capital and community regulation, thereby increasing the propensity to interpersonal violence, which in turn will permeate intimate relationships. She cautiously (because reporting could also be skewed by social location) concludes that part of the neighbourhood effect is a result of the concentration of poverty. Her conclusions are further tested by Wooldredge and Thistlethwaite (2003), who included race variables and found comparable effects of neighbourhood disadvantage among African-American males. Further, in densely populated urban areas rates of IPV follow rates of property crime and other violence, and living in a neighbourhood with high social disorder, economic disadvantage and substance use increases women's exposure to IPV (Fox and Benson 2006; Raghavan et al. 2006). The intersectionality of multiple neighbourhood effects – hegemonic masculinity, economic disadvantage, individual economic distress, residential instability, unemployment and subjective strain – together increase the risk of IPV.

A broader approach that incorporates feminist analysis would be a more multifactorial one that estimates the risk of domestic violence across a number of dimensions. Krug et al. (2002: 98) develop a model that attempts to combine individual, relationship, community and societal levels of analysis while identifying markers of risk, rather than causes of violence. In this model, poverty causes stress, inadequacy, a 'crisis of masculinity' while making it more difficult for women to leave abusive relationships. This model may explain why some societies and individuals are more violent than others, but we do not know the specific and relative weights to give the factors nor how they operate on different levels. Heise (1998) has further developed an ecological model that aims to explain IPV on multiple levels and incorporates specific situational and spatial factors as well as patriarchy. The layered ecological model in Figure 6.4 identifies personal history, the microsystem (family and immediate context, including the ways decisions are made and behaviour is controlled), the exosystem (socioeconomic position, whether peers are sexually aggressive and desire to be held in high esteem) and the macrosystem (cultural values around masculinity and violence). The risk of perpetrating

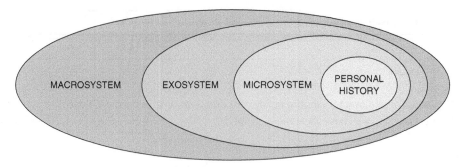

Figure 6.4 Ecological Model of Violence

Source: Heise (1998)

domestic violence would be increased if there is an intersection of several levels. For example:

- At a personal level, someone has witnessed violence from a rejecting father, developed traumatic reactions, depression and unacknowledged shame.
- The microsystem valorizes male dominance, male control of wealth, heavy alcohol consumption and conflict resolution through violence.
- The exosystem was one of low socioeconomic status, the isolation of women, urban disadvantage, unemployment and high levels of local crime.
- The macrosystem was one of male entitlement, masculinity linked to aggression and dominance.

These examples suggest the way in which multiple factors might intersect to increase the tendency to intimate violence, especially in conditions of social stress. This model acknowledges the role of gendered inequality on several dimensions – the relative economic powerlessness of women in many locations, the way hegemonic masculinities provide legitimation for the exercise of power and control in intimate relations and the 'right' to exercise violence. However, rather than view IPV only as an outcome of these structural factors, this model also builds in an understanding of the intra-psychic dynamics of trauma and shame in forming violence-prone personalities. It further positions these within a wider context of structural inequalities and urban enclosure within spaces of disadvantage. While the majority of perpetrators of severe IPV are men (though not all are), there is a greater gender symmetry in family conflict models – there is a need for further analysis to work through the dynamics of these within a nested ecological context.

Conclusion

I have argued here that modernization entailed a privatization of violence, since while interpersonal violence in public diminished, there was a relative rise in intimate violence as the family became both the site of enforced gender identities and of their contestation. This has been especially the case in recent decades with increasing informalization and transformation intimacy. Domestic violence is gendered, although violence in families is multifarious. A distinction was drawn between family conflict in which violence is deployed and terroristic patriarchy. The former might present greater gender symmetry than the latter, which is predominantly perpetrated by men and systematically bound to the cultures and structures of patriarchy. However, such violence is not necessarily simply a manifestation of power but might be a hyper-masculine response to the erosion of patriarchal power through the informalization and de-traditionalization of intimacy. However, it is not informalization alone that generates violence since many manage to negotiate this flux into non-traditional gender performances. The manifestation of violence might best be approached though a spatial model that mediates among factors of personality, social context, socioeconomic location, and wider cultures.

7

EXPLAINING HOMICIDE

The most extreme form of violence is homicide.[1] In the discussion of Elias in Chapter 3 it was noted that there was a steep reduction in homicide rates in Europe between the fourteenth and twentieth centuries and this can be cited in support of Elias's thesis. The civilizational process entailed an increased level of restraint of violent emotions through the consolidation of the state's monopoly of the means of force, and legal and informal social regulation. However, it was noted in Chapter 4 that Elias gave too little attention to economic processes and, in particular, to the spatial localization of inequalities and economic transformation. This criticism is relevant to the analysis of homicide too since it will be argued that economic transformation in the later twentieth century has had consequences for trends in homicide rates in developed societies. After several centuries of declining homicide rates, these rose fairly consistently in the UK during the twentieth century, with the exception of the post-Second World War years, during which they fell. Can this rising trend be explained with reference to the decivilisational effects of socio-economic changes and, in particular, growing social inequality in the later twentieth century, which dislocated social solidarity by weakening social cohesion? This chapter examines the long-term trends in homicide in the western world while also identifying the importance of shorter-term trends and their relationship to possible decivilizational downswing. It will also be noted that there is a marked spatial distribution of homicide, which might correlate with inequality and social disadvantage. However, despite considerable evidence for the inequality effects on homicide, other factors might also be relevant, such as concentrations of poverty and particular national intersections of economy and culture.

---

[1]Homicide is any form of unlawful killing and includes murder, manslaughter and infanticide. Rates cited in this chapter are subject to the usual health warnings about official crime data. It should be kept in mind too that there is evidence that the homicide rate today would be higher were it not for the increased survival rate from serious violent assault facilitated by increased medical sophistication (Zimring and Hawkins 1999: 95).

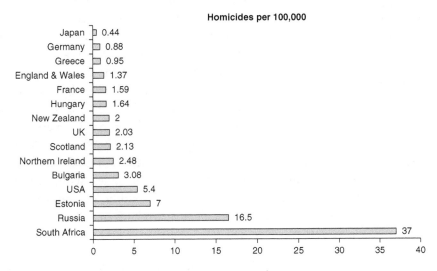

Homicides per 100,000

Figure 7.1 International Homicide Figures 2008–09[i]

Homicide is rare in the UK and in most other developed countries – generally ranging from 1–2 per 100,000 of the population per annum (see Figure 7.1). According to the Home Office (2005b), homicide generally accounts for 0.1 per cent of violent crime in England and Wales and 0.01 per cent of overall crime. The rates for Scotland and Northern Ireland are significantly higher than for England and Wales. Around two-thirds of victims are male and men are more likely (by about two-thirds) to be killed by strangers. The highest risk of

---

[i]There are multiple sources for this graph:

http://www.saps.gov.za/statistics/reports/crimestats/2009/categories/murder.pdf (South Africa);
http://www.gks.ru/bgd/free/b09_00/IssWWW.exe/Stg/d01/7-0.htm (Russia);
http://pub.stat.ee/px-web.2001/Dialog/varval.asp?ma=JU001&ti=RECORDED+OFFENCES+BY+DEGREE%2FTYPE&path=../I_Databas/Social_life/07Justice_and_security/03Crime/&lang=1 (Estonia);
http://www.fbi.gov/ucr/05cius/data/table_16.html (USA);
http://www.unodc.org/pdf/crime/seventh_survey/7sv.pdf (Bulgaria);
http://www.unodc.org/pdf/crime/eighthsurvey/8sv.pdf (Scotland);
http://www.statcan.gc.ca/pub/85-002-x/85-002-x2006006-eng.pdf (New Zealand);
http://www.statcan.gc.ca/pub/85-002-x/85-002-x2006006-eng.pdf (Hungary);
http://www.statcan.gc.ca/pub/85-002-x/85-002-x2006006-eng.pdf (France);
http://www.homeoffice.gov.uk/rds/pdfs08/hosb0308.pdf (England and Wales);
http://66.102.9.132/search?q=cache%3Ahttp%3A//www.unodc.org/pdf/crime/eighthsurvey/8sv.pdf (Northern Ireland);
http://66.102.9.132/search?q=cache%3Ahttp%3A//www.unodc.org/pdf/crime/seventh_survey/7sv.pdf (Greece);
http://66.102.9.132/search?q=cache%3Ahttp%3A//www.unodc.org/pdf/crime/eighthsurvey/8sv.pdf (Germany)
http://www-rohan.sdsu.edu/faculty/rwinslow/ (Japan).

victimization in the UK is among Afro-Caribbean men aged between 21 and 25. Women are most at risk from spouses or former spouses, with 20 per cent of all murders occurring among spouses and over half of women victims knowing the suspect. The overall risk of being a victim of homicide in the UK is around 14 per million but this varies greatly by age and social location, with the risk generally decreasing with age. Children under 1 year old have the highest risk of homicide at 38 per million of the population and, in contrast to every other type of violent crime, the perpetrator is most likely to be female. Despite recent concern about gun crime and related homicides, and unlike the USA, shooting accounts for around 9 per cent of UK homicides, while a sharp instrument is the single most common method of killing (30 per cent). In terms of the circumstances of the homicide, a quarrel, revenge or loss of temper reportedly accounts for over half the homicides where the suspect was known to the victim, whereas when the suspect was unknown to the victim this was the circumstance for less than a quarter of the homicides (Home Office 2005b: 5). Within the category of 'homicide', then, there are acts with differing motives and relationships to wider patterns of social relations.

Homicide and the civilizing process

Chapter 3 noted the long-term decline in European homicide between the fifteenth and twentieth centuries, which is a possible source of support for the civilizational thesis. Elias's core thesis is summarized in the box on p. 51. Eisner (2001) identified a long-term decline in homicide in Europe that was linked to modernization and appeared first in the 'pioneers of modernization' England and Holland, with a decline appearing later and more unevenly in Scandinavia and Italy. In England, he calculates the homicide rate falling from about 20 per 100,000 of the population in the high Middle Ages to one per 100,000 in the mid-twentieth century and an 'all time low of 0.6 in the early 1960s'.[2] He suggests that Elias's processes are relevant – a growing moral concern about cruelty and violence and a decline in violence among the gentry from the late sixteenth century combined with a stabilization of state structures from the late sixteenth

---

[2]However, there are considerable methodological issues with this kind of research. In relation to Eisner and Spierenburg (see below), Schwerhoff (2002) says that this analysis is 'fraught with so many problems that a comparison between these figures or even the determination of a trend ... seems to be methodologically inadmissible'. Eisner acknowledges that there are problems of measurement and incomplete data, but uses a variety of data sources – such as county assize courts, post-mortem records, local and national records and takes an average of different results. On balance, the case for a long-term trend seems persuasive.

century. Eisner explains the declining trend in terms of a variety of emerging disciplinary arrangements, the growth of moral individualism and more centralized administrative and juridical organizations. These included cultural and social resources for a more ordered life and increased moral control through expanded schooling and work discipline that reinforced power structures. His analysis of increased social disciplining, while broadly consistent with Elias's thesis also highlights the contribution of Durkheim, who himself said that 'with the progress of civilization homicide decreases' (Durkheim 2003: 113). Eisner uses Durkheim to suggest that in opposition to Elias's notion of pre-modern unregulated affects, violence is always a product of specific moral and cultural conditions. For example, where the legal system is undeveloped, cultures of honour are a means of mediating individual competitive and aggressive inclinations, mostly among men (Spierenburg 2006). The decline in homicide, by contrast, is linked to the rise of moral individualism and reduction of honour cultures, since violence declines to the extent that individuals are liberated from sacred obligation to the group. Thome (2001) notes that this change was signalled by the declining birth rate at the end of the nineteenth century. In smaller families, in which children were no longer economic assets, there were stronger emotional attachments and a greater sense of personal value, all of which encouraged moral individualism. This at least might explain a decline in lethal impulsive violence and male–male confrontation violence.

Cooney (1997), like Gould (2003), further emphasizes that the decline of homicide follows the establishment of the rule of law as a means of mediating disputes and the consequent decline of honour codes. Lethal conflict such as feuding, brawling and duelling, he says, is a function of the unavailability of law, and a situation where law is effectively unavailable to disputants. This can occur when the agents of the law are either too high or too low in social status. In this case the availability of law is itself linked to increased democratization and the reduction of extreme social hierarchies. Drawing on Black's theory of law (e.g. Black 1993), Cooney argues that 'the poor, marginal, unconventional, and unrespectable' are largely outside the state's legal system and hence are more likely to use aggressive tactics such as fighting, burning, seizing and killing to resolve conflicts. Homicide is concentrated, then, in spaces of 'virtual statelessness' where law is effectively unavailable. This happens in two circumstances. The first is when legal officials are too high in status relative to the principal parties or disputants. The second is when legal officials are not high enough in status relative to the disputants. The former places low-status disputants beyond the law; the latter puts high-status disputants above the law. For example, he notes that 'when the British Prime Minister, the Duke of Wellington, duelled at the age of 60 in 1829, he was the sixth holder of that office in the previous 100 years to do so' (Cooney 1997). This reflected an elite honour culture that was beyond the law. At the other end of the social hierarchy, 'if low-status people do invoke the law, their experience is often frustrating'. Cooney says this was expressed by a young black man from an impoverished, inner-city, all black neighbourhood, one of 75 homicide perpetrators he interviewed in 1989–90: 'Don't be pushed around; if somebody insults you, assaults you, or steals your property, handle the problem yourself; do not run to the police because if you do, you might get into more serious trouble on the street' (1997).

In sum, then, historically the availability of the law increased as the state acquired more wealth and organizational capacity and its officers came to represent a body of high stature, while elites came to accept that recourse to a court was compatible with their personal dignity. Increasing functional democratization also increased the availability of law to non-elites and weakened cultures of honour and vengeance. State formation is gradual as it extends its reach to the most remote corners of its territory, and secures enough wealth to fund an elaborate, permanent bureaucracy. The converse of this is that a decline in the availability of the law will increase honour cultures and extra-legal social order, as we saw in Chapter 4.

Cooney (1997) further points out that criminal homicide encompasses very different behaviour, including feuding between gangs, infanticides, contract killings, domestic slayings, murders committed to facilitate a robbery, as well as certain kinds of road traffic fatalities. It cannot be assumed that the social conditions underlying these different types of homicide will be the same. A distinction is often drawn between primary homicide rates, generally involving family members or friends, and non-primary homicides, often involving strangers, such as those occurring in the course of a robbery. It is sometimes suggested that while social structural explanations are relevant for the former, this is less the case for the latter (e.g., Pridemore 2008). However, since many social theories of homicide are also more general theories of violence, then different types of homicide might still be amenable to social structural explanations. Spierenburg (1994) similarly identifies a long-term decline in European homicide from the Middle Ages to the mid-twentieth century and, following Elias, he attributes this to the growth of psychical 'equipment of emotional control'. One consequence of this, he says, is that there has been a decline in impulsive lethal violence but a proportionate increase in family homicides. In Amsterdam, between 1650 and 1750, 60 per cent of recorded homicides were the result of tavern conflicts between strangers, but between the seventeenth and nineteenth centuries the ratio of stranger to intimate homicides declined from 4:1 to 1:3. Spierenburg (1994) argues that pre-modern homicide tended to be impulsive and 'ritual expressive' violence, embedded in cultural codes, while modern violence tends to be planned and instrumental.

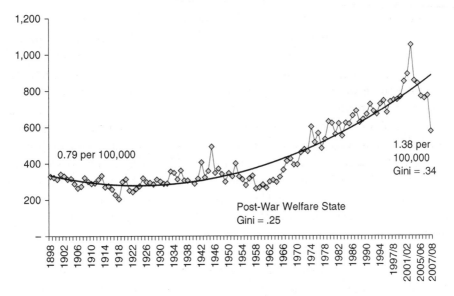

Figure 7.2 Homicide in England and Wales 1898–2008

Source: Home Office http://rds.homeoffice.gov.uk/rds/pdfs07/recorded-crime-1898-2002.xls

However, this pattern changes in the twentieth century. If we look at Figure 7.2, an upswing in homicides in England and Wales is evident, especially in the latter half of the twentieth century.

The number of homicides in England and Wales has more than doubled since the mid-1960s, while, as we have seen, general recorded crime fell significantly in the 1990s.[3] In the USA, national data from the early twentieth century are not readily available but estimates suggest that homicide increased moderately between 1900 and 1933 and then sharply rose between 1933 and 1974. Overall, the US homicide rate doubled from the mid-1950s to 1980 and afterwards fluctuated, going up to 9.8 per 100,000 in 1991 and then decreasing through the late 1990s (Zahn and McCall 1999). Hall (2007) argues that the long-term decline was a 'pseudo-pacification' process driven by capitalism's aversion to arbitrary violence that inhibited the protection of property. In order to stabilize conditions for capital growth, capitalism cultivated behavioural codes and emotional sensibilities with gradual democratization and diversion of threatening energies into 'fake revolts' of style. This was not merely a 'façade', Hall says, but neither was it a 'complete civilization of the soul', and in the wake of globalized consumerism, economic crises, extreme anomic hedonism eroded solidarities and decontrolled lethal interpersonal

---

[3]This is a paradox that needs further research, since intuitively we might expect there to be a connection between homicides and general levels of violence. This might reflect problems in recording violent crime noted above.

violence. The notion of 'pseudo' pacification implies there is some other presumably more permanent type, which Hall does not elaborate. Nonetheless, versions of this argument are widespread. Thome (2001) accounts for the homicidal upswing by arguing that there was a reversal in the civilizational process – there was a weakening of the state's monopoly of violence with the privatization of prisons and security so that the 'purchasing power of clients in security markets' normalizes the use of violence in social relations. The state needs adequate regulatory power to secure sufficient measures of justice, equity and equality, along with social welfare. However, neoliberal globalization erodes the territorial integrity and authority of the nation state and in particular its tax basis. Echoing Habermas's critique of the intrusion of systems of money and technology into the lifeworld, Thome suggests that rising inequality and social marginalization, combined with an instrumentalization of the body through biotechnologies, all contribute to a decivilizing process. At a psychological level there is a growing gap between the demands for self-control and people's diminishing ability to supply it, since the 'intrusion into the private sphere of mass media and business communications' generates an ethos of instant gratification. Following Durkheim, Thome argues that while declining homicide was a result of the pacifying effects of increased 'moral individualism', an egoistic individualism created conditions for increased violence in the later twentieth century. He identifies a process of *Entgrenzung*, that is, the dissolution of boundaries between public and private and sacred and profane, reducing sensitivity to vulnerability and capacities for self-control.

The specific connection between these processes, though, is left unclear in Thome and others. There is the problem of tautology here that has been noted already, when a 'decivilizing process' is inferred from things like rising violent crime, but this is also invoked as its explanation. Further, the claim that the increase in lethal violence during the 1960s was a consequence of the hedonistic culture of gratification needs (Thome 2007; see also Ouimet 2004) at least needs to show in detail how this informalization and transgression of cultural boundaries made people more likely to kill. This is especially so since the counter-cultural movement associated with the late 1960s also involved anti-war, pacifist, anti-racist and civil rights campaigns, and can thus plausibly be seen as part of the civilizational process. Within the context of general socio-cultural processes we also need more specific explanations. If one looks at Figure 7.2 again, it is apparent that the pattern is of a gradual rise in homicides during the first half of twentieth century but then a decline in the post-war decade. This was also the period of the Keynesian Welfare State and post-war political consensus on the desirability of a mixed economy (nationalized and capitalist industries), during which income inequality was very low.

In order to understand fluctuations in the homicide rate, greater attention needs to be paid to economic processes and the interplay between state and economy. This might be more significant than the generalized processes referred to above. Mares (2009) points out, like Schwerhoff (2002), that there is not a linear fall in homicide rates between the thirteenth and twentieth centuries, but rather rates are uneven and fluctuate on shorter time scales. He suggests that they decline most in periods when state institutions of social incorporation were more dominant. The development of the civilizing process, Mares continues, is periodically undermined by limits to economic growth, when the state loses the capacity to control the erosion of interdependencies. Mares identifies three phases of state formation. In the first phase, of early industrialization, capital concentrates in areas of political power but growth is uncontrolled, the state is coercive and social mobility is limited for those outside the dominant groups. In this phase interpersonal violence will increase. So in England there was an upsurge in homicide and gang violence between 1750 and 1860. In the second phase of mature and stable industrialism, the state is effective in developing institutions of social integration such as education, public utilities and provision for the poor. With democratization and increased powers and rights for workers there is also greater social cohesion, pacification and a decline in violence. So homicides in the UK declined from 4 per 100,000 in 1860 to 0.7 in 1900. In the third phase of deindustrialization and global restructuring, the legitimacy and cohesion of state institutions is undermined, social cohesion is fragmented and the Keynesian Welfare State is dismantled or eroded, social mobility becomes limited and there is a disruption of the 'social contract'. Violence again increases and in the developed world generally homicide trends rose in the 1970s through the 1990s and peaked, after which there was a slight decline, which is visible in Figure 7.2.[4]

The debate over homicide and the civilizing process has been further addressed in relation to 'American exceptionalism'. That is, the US rate is over three times that of other 'established market economies', a situation that Monkkonen (2007: 17) describes as 'a medieval phenomenon occurring in a modern world nation'. He argues that prior to 1850 the US pattern was similar to that in Europe, but with industrialization, mass manufacturing and migration the continents moved in opposite directions. The European pattern was that, with modernization, cultures of honour and feuding yielded to larger organizations as force was concentrated in the state and institutionalized in the legal system. In the USA, Monkkonen suggests, a monopoly of force was seen as undesirable since democracy, which for white male Americans quickly

---

[4]The peak in the England and Wales figures in the early 2000s was caused by exceptional events. In 2000, 58 Chinese nationals suffocated *en route* to the UK, the Harold Shipman serial killings (at least 215) were recorded and in July 2005, 52 people were killed by the London terrorist bombs.

followed independence, was widely equated with the right of self-defence.[5] Further, in the slave plantations of the *anti-bellum* South, social relations were more akin to the unpacified Middle Ages where honour violence was widespread and justifications of self-defence were accorded plausibility (Monkkonen 2007). The system of racial exclusion and slavery was based on rationalized violence which continued into the twentieth century and Spierenburg (2006) suggests that among both white and African Americans an honour code became widespread. While the US homicide rate is often attributed to wide gun ownership (Zimring and Hawkins 1999), Monkkonen argues that Canada has similar levels of gun ownership to the USA but a much lower homicide rate. The types of gun owned (pistols as opposed to hunting rifles) might be more significant. But other factors, especially gender roles and the culture of masculinity, are more significant for explaining high homicide rates. Further, in the South there were historically low conviction rates for homicide, partly because juries were reluctant to convict, often tolerating honour-motivated violence with a 'there but for the grace of God' attitude. In addition, with high levels of geographical mobility both informal and formal social controls were weak.[6] To summarize, then, the claim is that the US homicide rate did not match the fall in European rates in the later nineteenth century because the civilizational process was less embedded there and the particular process of US state formation limited the establishment of a monopoly of force while promoting 'private self-help' in resolving conflicts (Mares 2009).

Spaces of homicide

The civilizational process depicts macrosocial transformation over several centuries. Yet although there is a long-range homicide trend, this is subject to shorter-term fluctuations that need more specific explanations. There is evidence that homicide rates generally respond to short-term social and cultural changes rather than to specific policy and policing initiatives, although there is debate about the influence of the latter. The rapid decline of the New York homicide rate between 1991 and 1997 has been the focus of much discussion of the underlying determinants of lethal violence. Although this fall in homicide was often claimed as a success for 'zero tolerance policing' (the aggressive enforcement of minor offences), Bowling (1999) aims to show that this claim is largely circumstantial. He argues that homicide rates were at an all-time high in 1990–91, had begun to decline before any radical changes in policing policy

---

[5]And still is by the US National Rifle Association. See, for example, www.nraila.org/legislation/read.aspx?id=5416.

[6]See also Mennell (2009) on Elias and American exceptionalism

were instituted, and the decline was more closely related to contraction of crack cocaine markets in the 1990s. This is supported by Karmen (2000), who argues that the fall in New York murder rates was not the result of a single factor but a 'fortuitous confluence' of underlying factors. As the local economy recovered, inner-city poverty was reduced. Occupational mobility increased and a rapidly growing migrant population committed fewer crimes and helped preserve the city's tax base by replacing the middle class who fled during the 'bad old days'. A further factor was demographic change (fewer men aged 20–24) and a changing youth culture less involved in violence and criminality. This latter change was encouraged by enabling high school graduates, many of whom were unlikely to graduate, to enrol in colleges since higher education 'is a sound collective investment ... counteracting the values of street culture' (Karmen 2000: 265). The decline in the crack trade combined with removal of some 43,000 dealers through imprisonment, homicide, drug overdoses and AIDS. Again Ouimet (2004) points out that while homicide is three to four times higher in the USA than in Canada, both countries saw rates falling during the 1990s following demographic changes, especially the diminishing numbers of young men in the population, but *before* the adoption of new styles of policing. He also attributes such fluctuations to shifts in collective cultural ethos and long-term changes in social organization.

Homicide is highly spatially distributed in a way that could be described as 'localized decivilization' and there is a strong statistical association between homicide rates and rates of both poverty and inequality, although these may reflect different processes. Discussion of overall trends is not sufficiently nuanced to develop differential explanations of local trends. For example, although homicide in the UK rose during the late 2000s, this was highly spatially concentrated and created little increase in risk for the majority of people. Economic globalization has left many people vulnerable to anomie, especially in communities on the margins of modern economic life. Thus, in the USA rates vary considerably between extremes of 11.9 per 100,000 in Louisiana and 1.9 in Wyoming and there are further marked spatial distributions within cities. In large US cities rates can be as high as 80 per 100,000 in areas of high deprivation. In New York, for example, the rate varied during 2003–09 between 11 per 100,000 in the Bronx, 6 in Manhattan and 3.6 on Staten Island (*New York Times* 2010). Although there was a long-term decline in serious violence during the sixteenth to twentieth centuries, Hall (2007) sees a return of interpersonal violence as a routine aspect of everyday life and murder rates in economically run-down locales have increased. In England the rate rose from 0.8 per 100,000 in 1950 to 1.4 in 1998 but in economically run-down locales the 1998 rate was 8 per 100,000. Similarly, Shaw et al. (2005) argue that high levels of spatial polarization (residential segregation into rich and poor) were accompanied by dramatic increases in poverty and income inequality during the 1980s and

1990s. The UK's national murder rate increased without any increased risk for the majority of the population when age and geographic location are taken into account. They found that during 1981–85 in the poorest 10 per cent of localities the risk of being a victim of homicide was 4.5 times the risk in the richest 10 per cent. By 1996–2000 this had risen to 5.7 per cent. In the least poor 20 per cent of localities, a low risk of victimization fell even further, so that 'the rise in murder in Britain has been concentrated almost exclusively in the poorest parts of the country and among men of working age'. 'The lives of young men', they say, 'have been polarised and this inequality has curtailed opportunities; hopelessness appears to have bred fear, violence and murder' (Shaw et al. 2005).

A large body of research dating back to the 1960s generally concludes that there is a strong association between inequality and homicide rates. The process suggested by studies like these is that relative poverty causes feelings of stress, inadequacy, 'crisis of masculinity' and undermines social capital.[7] This in turn creates a context conducive to risk taking, criminality and increasingly violent competition for resources such as street business and dominance. Wilkinson and Pickett (2009) argue that more unequal societies have higher levels of crime and lethal violence because greater inequality is accompanied by increased status competition and status anxiety, leading in turn to reduced trust. This increases mental illness and vulnerability to emotional distress and shame when one fails to maintain one's social position (2009: 34ff). Young men in particular strive to preserve their social self and are vigilant to potential threats to self-esteem. Further, in neighbourhoods where life is shorter and people die prematurely from many other causes, more risky strategies are necessary to gain status. Inequality, they argue, is structural violence (2009: 132) that creates conditions for interpersonal violence, including increased family breakdown and stress, children experience more conflicts while people have fewer protections and buffers against shame and humiliation as status becomes more important. It was noted in the discussion of masculinities and violence that Bourgois's (2003) ethnography of the violence culture of East Harlem crack cocaine dealers exemplifies this process.

However, there is debate over whether it is inequality *per se* that produces a high homicide rate or other related factors. A great deal of research measures homicide rates against measures of the distribution of household income such as the Gini coefficient.[8] The relationship between income inequality and the

---

[7] Social capital here refers to the extent of voluntary groups, involvement in the community, social networks and levels of social trust.

[8] This is frequently used in cross-national analyses. The Gini coefficient measures the percentage difference between a hypothetical model of perfect equality with actually income inequalities. If income were equally distributed across a population, the Gini index would be 0. But actual income distribution will always be skewed and approaches 1 when

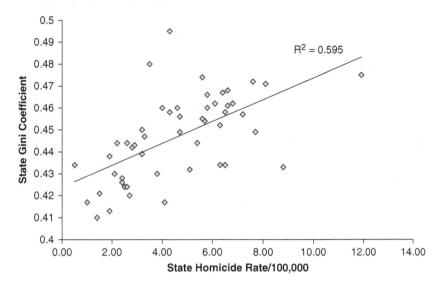

Figure 7.3 US Homicide and State Gini Coefficient

Sources: Homicide FBI Uniform Crime Reports 2008; US Census Bureau 2006.

homicide rate is remarkably consistent cross-nationally (Daly et al. 2001). However, it is less clear that the Gini can explain all variations in the rate and changes over time, which suggests that other factors will also be relevant. Daly et al. (2001) suggest that despite the evidence for an association between inequality and homicide, this claim remains controversial partly because of the difficulty in identifying the independent effects of variables. For example, poorer areas with low average income and high disadvantage and poverty will often also have high levels of inequality so that distinguishing inequality effects from those of concentrated poverty can be difficult. This raises a further question of whether the determining factor is actually inequality, which is a relative measure, or rather concentrated poverty – an issue that has been raised already in the discussion in Chapter 4. Moreover, a society could (though this is unlikely) have high inequality but little absolute poverty – in this case, which is the more significant factor: relative income inequality or deprivation?

Let us look at this more closely. US state-level data on homicides and many other social indicators is readily available. It is true that these data are for whole states and there will be many local variations, as Lee and Shihadeh (2009) indicate. Nonetheless these data might point to the importance of looking further at the processes that generate poverty and exclusion. Figure 7.3 correlates

---

all income accrues to the single wealthiest unit, which is again hypothetical. The figure will always be between 0 and 1 and higher Gini coefficients indicate greater income inequality.

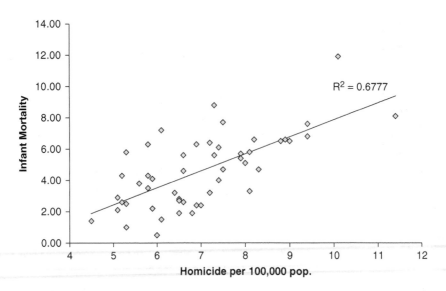

Figure 7.4 US Homicide and State Infant Mortality

US state homicide rates with state Gini coefficients and generates a visible pattern of clustering which is statistically significant (r=0.5954). There is clearly some clustering around the trend line, and states with higher Gini coefficients also often have higher homicide rates, but there are also some outliers where states have high Gini scores but low homicide rates and vice versa. So there are other factors influencing the outcomes. Daly et al. (2001) add data from Canada into their correlations of inequality and homicide and find income inequality 'a strong and significant predictor' of homicide rates. They further looked at variation over time (16 years) in Canada and found that at a national level there was no significant co-variance between changes in the Gini and homicide rates since homicides fell without any significant change in the Gini. But at province level, the relationship was more significant and fluctuations in the Gini did predict changes in the homicide rate. They concluded that inequality is a strong predictor but this might still reflect something other than an effect of income *distribution*.

Perhaps we really need to assess the effect of a measure of poverty rather than simply inequality? One such measure is infant mortality (as Pridemore (2008) suggests) since poverty is a prime cause of high infant mortality. Figure 7.4 plots state homicide rates against infant mortality rates and there is apparently a closer fit (r=0.6777) than with the Gini coefficient. This might suggest that poverty is more relevant to the homicide rate than inequality alone (r=0.595). But if we also take a direct measure of the poverty – the percentage of people in each state whose income is less than the poverty

	Unstandardized Coefficients		
Model	B	Std. error	Sig
1 (Constant)	–3.010	1.216	.017
infmort	1.087	.170	.000
2 (Constant)	–3.591	1.201	.004
infmort	.847	.197	.000
poverty	.185	.085	.034
3 (Constant)	–19.759	5.547	.001
infmort	.757	.185	.000
poverty	.083	.085	.337
gini	40.392	13.577	.005

Figure 7.5 Coefficients for Infant Mortality, Poverty and the Gini[ii]

threshold[9] – and build each variable into a model (Figure 7.5), the results look different. When the variables (the Gini, infant mortality and poverty) are entered individually to see if each is adding something more to the model, it seems that infant mortality and the Gini are significant predictors of homicide but poverty is not, once the other two effects are included (Model 2). Interestingly, these results suggest that it is indeed *relative* inequality rather than poverty that has greater predictive significance for the homicide rate. Furthermore, the effect of infant mortality declines when income measures are included, but remains significant, which suggests that something associated with infant mortality, other than economic differences, correlates with homicide.

There will be complex structural processes that generate these outcomes. The data discussed above suggested that the percentage levels of poverty across each state might not predict the homicide rate but that does not mean that poverty is not relevant. Few studies specifically examine the spatial clustering of high poverty and its relationship to violent crime rates. Stretesky et al. (2004) argue that the effects of social disadvantage are amplified through inter-action with poverty to generate social isolation and cultures of violent retaliation in response to disrespect. Lee (2000) presents a version of anomie theory, argu-ing that there is 'considerable evidence that the spatial distribution of poverty positively interacts with city-level disadvantage to produce higher rates of homicide'. The severe economic and social dislocations experienced by many city neighbourhoods (see also pp. 74–80) remove traditional routes to status. Then the readiness to use violence and a 'predatory demeanour' may become secondary routes to status, while violence becomes a means to both status and

[ii]I am grateful to Lynn Prince-Cooke for assistance with preparing this data.
[9]Poverty data was taken from the US Census Bureau 2008: www.census.gov/hhes/www/cpstables/032009/pov/new46_100125_01.htm.

material resources. When urban areas are segregated (especially on racialized lines) isolation becomes self-reinforcing and communities' ability to govern and regulate members' activities may be compromised. This 'opens the door' to criminal activities, including a greater prevalence of homicide. He argues further that families tend to have little in the way of childrearing or problem-solving skills and have a proclivity to act in a violent and abusive manner towards both their own children and others with whom they may have disputes. In this manner, violent, aggressive behaviour as a problem-solving device is transmitted to children as a legitimate mode of interaction.

Spatial patterning that is structured by hierarchies of wealth and status will generate harmful characteristics and might also support cultural conditions for homicide. While developments of anomie theory (detachment from dominant norms) often feature in these accounts, there is also a rather different emphasis on local norms and values that are tolerant of violence. The Southern USA[10] has often been the focus of debates about spatial concentration because homicide rates are generally higher in Southern states[11] and there is a long-standing claim that there is a 'culture of violence related to the history of slavery and Confederacy violence' (e.g., Cohen and Nisbett 1997). Cohen and Nisbett argue that attitude surveys reveal among Southerners a 'culture of honour' that is supportive of violence – compared to the rest of the USA, they oppose gun control more, favour the death penalty more, are sympathetic to those 'provoked' into (especially domestic) violence and approve more of physical punishment. In this vein, Lee and Shihadeh (2009) examine how the spatial concentration of *native* Southern whites is associated with white argument-based lethal violence. They examine native white Southerners to focus on communities that have resisted outside influences and access 'traditional' culture, especially in rural areas. They claim that argument-based homicide rates are higher where white Southerners are more spatially concentrated. They account for this in terms of the cultural transmission of pro-violent attitudes that occurs within spaces of concentrated poverty, where identities are reinforced and where there is limited recourse to the law to resolve disputes. Greater concentration, they argue, increases both exposure to and support for norms tolerant of retaliatory homicide.

Where social divisions coincide with racial division the effects of inequality are more severe. The mechanisms through which this occurs are matters for debate, though. Massey and Fischer (2000) argue that underlying shifts in

---

[10]The South generally refers to the 11 states that seceded during the Civil War to form the Confederate States of America and which share commonalities of history and culture (South Carolina, Mississippi, Florida, Alabama, Georgia, Louisiana, Texas, Virginia, Arkansas, Tennessee and North Carolina).

[11]Homicide rates are twice as high in cities with populations under 200,000 and 1.2 times higher for larger cities (Cohen and Nisbett 1997).

socioeconomic structure can have very different effects on the concentration of poverty experienced by different groups, depending on the degree of racial/ ethnic segregation they experience. The economic and geographic trends of globalization and deindustrialization affected all racial and ethnic groups, but the consequences were especially severe for African Americans because they were already highly residentially segregated. Indeed, they identify 20 metropolitan areas in which racial segregation was so complete and occurred on so many dimensions simultaneously that they call it 'hypersegregation'. By contrast, Lee (2000) says, in relation to the disproportionate representation of African Americans in homicide statistics, that spatial inequality is 'a strong, consistent, and primary determinant of homicide levels'. But he argues that this is an effect of concentrated poverty rather than race in itself. He continues that this implies that the crucial factor for urban homicide rates is urban disadvantage, which is manifest in the spatial clustering of poor populations. Simple measures of the percentage poor in the city do not fully capture the spatial dimension of this form of disadvantage, where the crucial factor is poverty concentration. He says that there is therefore no need for race-specific theorizing, which may actually impede our understanding of homicide. But Krivo et al. (2006) suggest a strong influence of racial residential segregation on levels of lethal violence. Segregation will affect localities whatever their ethnic composition, but since whites use their more privileged position to reside in the most advantaged neighbourhoods, African-American and Latino disadvantaged communities will bear the brunt of lethal violence. That is, economic exclusion and segregation interacts with racialized divisions. One could add that the visibility of racial inequalities and spatial segregation has profound implications on the lived perceptions of inequality, especially for those in the ghetto.

This brings us to a further critical issue – for explaining homicide, it might not just be a matter of the existence of inequalities but *of how inequality is generated*. In a classical statement of institutional anomie theory, Messner (1989) argues that, in addition to inequality, an aggravating factor is the *mechanism* by which inequality was reproduced – so that, for example, inequality based on racist exclusion would result in high levels of diffuse hostility and low empathy. Structural discrimination then might have more bearing on homicide rates than income inequality alone. Institutional anomie theory (IAT) focuses on the intersection of culture and social structure, and Messner et al. (2008) argue that the type of institutional configuration conducive to high levels of crime is one in which the economy (more particularly the market) is dominant. This 'marketness', he says, generates the processes noted above – social marginalization and violence, loss of social bonds, egoistic individualism, loss of empathy and high risk taking, all of which are conducive to higher levels of homicide. Violence might be appealing as a response to human problems and is more likely to enter the interaction process where normative constraints are weak. This is consistent with the view that violence requires an overcoming of social inhibitions. Where inequalities are further generated by mechanisms of exclusion based on ascribed characteristics, notably race, their effect is intensified through an experience of injustice and in-group solidarity, exclusive values, pent-up aggression and diffuse hostility. Messner et al. (2008), however, argue that these tendencies are constrained by social welfare protection, which encourages social solidarity, and the moral economy (law abidingness in everyday life), and thereby reduces crime and especially lethal violence. It was noted above that the period in which homicide in England and Wales was lowest in the twentieth century coincided with the post-war welfare state (Figure 7.2) and this was also the period of lowest income inequality.

Savolainen (2000) similarly argues that the effect of economic inequality on the level of lethal violence is limited to nations characterized by relatively weak collective institutions of social protection such as welfare states. He tests this hypothesis with two cross-national data sets drawn from Finland and Mexico. Both settings suggest that the effects of income inequality on homicide can be mitigated by the strength of the welfare state. Nations that protect their citizens from the vicissitudes of market forces appear to be 'immune to the homicidal effects of economic inequality'. This again suggests that it is the social disorganization caused by sharp inequality rather than the inequality itself that is the determining factor. Similarly, Kawachi et al. (1999) argue that the degree of cohesiveness in social relations among citizens, measured, for instance, by indicators of social capital, affect the level of violent crimes, including homicides, that were 'consistently associated with relative deprivation (income inequality) and indicators of low social capital'. Hall and McLean (2009) argue similarly. It is worth noting in this context that South Africa, which has one of highest homicide rates in the world at 37 per 100,000 per annum (see Figure 7.3), has experienced the persistence of racialized inequalities after the long and bitter history of apartheid *and* has an exceptionally high Gini of 0.65 (World Factbook 2009).

Further factors could be the decivilizational effects of social deregulation, state failure, and the rapid increase in inequality such as occurred in the post-communist societies after 1989–91. Following the end of Communism in Russia, inequality increased (with marked regional variations) from a Gini coefficient of 0.26 to 0.38 during 1991–95 (Outhwaite and Ray 2005: 51–9) and then to 0.42 by 2008 (World Factbook 2009). The 1990s level was not exceptionally high by international standards, but its effect on social cohesion was dramatic when combined with the rise of mafia capitalism and the collapse of the economy and governmental institutions against a background of a remaining popular commitment to equality. By the mid-1990s the Russian homicide rate was six times that of the USA, albeit with considerable local variations and higher rural than urban rates (Pridemore 2005). Pridemore also found that the proportion of the population in poverty increased on average during 1991–95 from 12 per cent to over 25 per cent, but in some regions, such as the centres of the former Soviet defence industry (for example, the Tula 'rust belt'), to 75 per cent. In these areas of high concentrations of poverty in particular, there were high increases in homicide, though they were higher still in the 'frontier' regions of the east Urals, where there was most freedom from the state and violence was a means of informal social control and everyday negotiations.

The social processes here are complex and much of the debate focuses on detail. Generally, it is reasonable to conclude that homicide rates are higher where inequality is greater and possibly compounded by spatial concentrations of poverty. This may be a more relevant factor than poverty averages across large communities. This effect is likely to be further pronounced when inequality and spatial concentrations of poverty are racialized and where the highest deprivation is experienced by minorities. There is, though, some uncertainty as to how to theorize this. Many writers use anomie theory and emphasize the effects of inequality – the loss of social bonds, rampant egoistic individualism, increased risk taking, criminal economies (especially drug markets), and lack of empathy, all of which increases the risk of lethal violence. However, other writers emphasize not the absence of social bonds but the importance of social bonding to values tolerant or, indeed, encouraging of homicide in some circumstances, especially defence of 'honour'. This is often seen to pertain in areas that have resisted the establishment of legal conflict regulation and have remained or become frontier zones with the collapse of state structures and welfare-based social integration. One poignant example is the rise of homicide in 1990s post-communist societies, where there was 'more shock than therapy' (Hall and McLean 2009), combined with violent organized crime (Outhwaite and Ray 2005: 80–5). There is a wider global process here that we saw in Chapter 4 – the spatializing consequences of capitalist development that presupposes pacified spaces but through creative destruction creates rustbelts and other spaces of abandonment. The converse of this is the considerable evidence that homicide is lower in social democratic welfare systems where there are longer chains of interconnection, less experience of inequality and more restraints on 'marketness'.

Performative homicides

Macro sociology develops theories of homicide risk based on historical and socioeconomic conditions, but these explanations need to be compatible with the micro-level conditions in which action takes place. Collins (2008: 2–3) argues that if we 'zero in on a situation of interaction – the angry boyfriend with the crying baby, the armed robber squeezing the trigger on the holdup victim, the cop beating the suspect – we see patterns of confrontation, tension and emotional flow' that define the situation of violent confrontation. Collins argues that this illustrates how background conditions such as poverty, race and childhood experiences of trauma are remote to the dynamics of violent incidents. He further makes the familiar point that most people who experience conditions of deprivation and trauma do not become murderers, while some affluent people do. Moreover, Collins says, the correlations between social conditions of the kind discussed in the last section do not hold up well beyond criminal violence. They do not explain 'legitimate' state-sanctioned violence by police, soldiers and perpetrators of genocide. Finally, whatever makes individuals violent cannot happen without a prior career of learning the interactional techniques that overcome inhibitions based on confrontational tension (Collins 2008: 187). Regarding the latter point, Collins is right in regard to certain premeditated killing, such as those of professional hit-men (whom he discusses in Collins 2008: 430–40), although the argument set out above was that social conditions do not directly cause homicides but might create circumstances of increased risk taking and reduced inhibition.

Katz (1988) similarly argues that 'social background' (class, ethnicity, inequality) are unable to get at the motivational dynamics of actual individuals, for whom the *meaning* they attribute to action is crucial for explaining it. This is, of course, a very old debate in the social sciences between those who seek to explain action, with reference to objective factors, versus those who understand actors' subjective meaning. Much of Weber's sociology, and in particular his Protestant Ethic essays, attempted to show how explanation and subjective understanding (*Verstehen*) could be combined. Katz also, in principle, aims to reintegrate social explanation into his analysis, but relies heavily on ethnographies and description of the moral dynamics of killing. His concept of 'righteous slaughter', which was referred to above (pp. 10–11), suggests that people murder to 'defend the "good"' and in this way justify their actions, at least at the moment they act. These murders emerge quickly, are fiercely impassioned and are conducted with indifference to the consequences, so, for example, these perpetrators typically make no attempt to escape (Katz 1988: 7). By defence of the 'good', Katz means that the killer interprets the victim as having attacked some eternal value and that the situation requires a last-stand defence of his basic worth.

Echoing in some ways Scheff and Retzinger's theory of unacknowledged shame, Katz argues that the killer transforms what is initially experienced as humiliation into rage and 'forges a momentary sense of eternal unity with the "good"' (1988: 23). Righteousness is a 'stepping stone' from humiliation to rage. But whereas Scheff and Retzinger (2001) regard violence as a loss of the social bond, for Katz lethal violence can invoke a strong social bond of the defence of honour. Indeed, resonant of Girard's theory of sacrificial killing, Katz suggests that violence has a ritual purpose (for the killer) of ending the chaos of a threat to eternal values and re-establishing social order. The victim is transformed into a 'morally lower, polluted, corrupted, profanized form of life' (1988: 36), particularly in domestic murder where the 'typical killer is familiar with the victim, feels at home in the setting and has often practiced variations on the themes of sacrificial violence' (1988: 39). Crimes from the most banal to the most brutal have a transcendent meaning for offenders. While Katz might appear to be describing the typical *crime passionnel*, he suggests that apparently 'instrumental' killings also have moral dimensions. Cold-blooded, senseless killings aim to create fear but also create a 'transcendental identity', showing that the perpetrator cannot be controlled. These are important concepts to which we will return in the analysis of genocide in Chapter 9.

Katz is not insensitive to the social class and gender dynamics of offending (see 1988: 43ff), but as Turk (1991) says, 'the class–crime relationship is left essentially unexamined' and leaves actors 'floating about in some undefined social space'. The social and spatial patterning of homicide discussed above still requires explanation, which, as Turk further argues, is going to be difficult if 'discrimination and deprivation are rejected as explanatory elements' (1991). How it is that differentials in structures, motives and behaviour originate, persist and change and, in particular, how they are organized within geographic space, needs to be central to a comprehensive theory of homicide or of violence more generally. The models developed in the last section suggest that social conditions interact with the dynamics of social and psychological stress and with prevalent performances of masculinity and violence. These do *not* generate specific murders in particular places, but rather an increased risk of a higher homicide rate in some social spaces as opposed to others. This point, it seems to me, is also a response to some of the arguments made by Collins against the influence of 'background' structures.

This does not mean that we should neglect the performative dimension of homicide in which killings intend to convey a moral or political message. Rampage shooting such as high school killings is an example of performative premeditated homicide that often exemplifies 'righteous slaughter', where through extreme violence perpetrators escape a situation that is experienced as inexorably humiliating. It is common for perpetrators to commit suicide after the mass killings and to leave a video justifying their actions – a practice often shared with suicide bombers. These are spectacles of murder that send a message to various audiences, often ones of revenge for rejection, bullying and failed masculine achievement. Indeed, the media spectacles surrounding school shootings themselves play into the fantasies of celebrity, revenge and masculine dominance, as Frymer (2009) suggests, and might thereby provide a script for further shootings. However, school shootings are also socially and spatially structured. They occur more in some types of places than others. Between 1966 and 2010 there were 96 school shootings in the USA, the most infamous (though not the most deadly) being that at Columbine High School, Colorado, where senior students Eric Harris and Dylan Klebold murdered 13 people and injured 24 on 20 April 1999 before committing suicide. Since 50 of these shootings occurred since 2000, their frequency appears to be increasing. These killings are much less frequent in other countries. Since 1913 there were nine in Canada and 15 Europe, of which seven were in Germany. Further, the perpetrators have almost all been male and most of them white. Indeed, school shootings have 'come to stand for an entire constellation of threats and troubles' arising from 'formerly harmless white suburban youth' (Frymer 2009). Dramatic crimes like these invite a focus on the individual perpetrators but this overlooks the considerable influence of socio-cultural forces (Tonso 2009).

School shootings occur mostly in small towns rather than large cities. The small town organization seems to combine with a culture of competitive hypermasculinity and exclusion. Kimmel and Mahler (2003) argue the violence was retaliatory against threats to masculinity in a context where this was crucial to both peer and official school culture. While there is no evidence that the shooters were gay, nearly all had stories of homophobic bating because they were different – shy, bookish, artistic, theatrical and, importantly, non-athletic and 'geekish'. This, Kimmel and Mahler (2003) suggest, prompted the desire both for revenge but also to demonstrate overt masculine performance. While this is the case with many boys, it assumes a pivotal role in school shootings where, in the face of humiliation, they lacked any alternative sources of validation. Further, Newman et al. (2004) says that most rampages have occurred in small communities which are often those idealized by many as close, family-oriented and with low crime. In Columbine, potential warnings from Klebold and Harris, such as threats and an obsession with killing, were missed, which she suggests is also a feature of small-town organization, where there is little communication between agencies about marginal youth and deviance is driven underground. She argues that these densely interconnected networks can be oppressive when combined with school status hierarchies and an absence of alternative sources of validation for troubled young men. Since schools are among the few public stages for identity performance in small towns, they are also obvious symbolic targets for rage. Kimmel and Mahler (2003) suggest that the absence of alternative identities explains why it is white boys who are shooters. African-American boys face formidable challenges – racial stereotypes, low expectations and under-achievement – but they do not plan and execute random and arbitrary mass shootings. Cultural marginalization plays differently where people can tap into collective, narrative repertoires of resistance.

Thus, one of the conditions for rampages, Newman suggests, is that the perpetrator is marginal to his social worlds with low status in peer hierarchies and having experienced bullying and ridicule. This marginality is then magnified by psychological vulnerabilities, paranoia and obsession with social rejection. But within a prevailing social context that associates masculinity with violence and in particular firepower, the shooters had access to 'cultural scripts' (Newman et al. 2004: 230) that validated armed attack and the terrorizing of innocents as a means of achieving masculine status. They all had access to guns, which were a mark of status. As Michael Carneal, the 14 year-old perpetrator of the 1999 Heath High School shooting, said: 'More guns is better. You have a lot of power. You look better if you have a lot of guns' (Newman et al. 2004: 6). Tonso (2009) further argues that the schools are complicit in reproducing hyper-masculine cultures of aggressiveness, such that the shooters believed they could get no help from the school itself and that reinforced a culture of exclusion. They were, in a sense, 'hyper-conformists' who aspired to the hegemonic masculine ideals from which they were excluded. In her analysis of five shootings where boys targeted girls who had rejected them, Klein (2005) argues that this lethal attempt to reverse subordination also traded on a tacit cultural acceptance of gender violence.

Conclusion

The above example indicates that homicide rates are not simply explicable in terms of inequality but rather the outcome of complex historical, cultural and gendered intrapsychic processes. Conditions of social strain create an increased homicide risk, although homicide is at the same time a deliberative act that often invokes 'the good'. At the macro-historical level, there is evidence for the Eliasian long trend of falling lethal violence, but there are also shorter-term fluctuations that respond to changing configurations of state, welfare and social inequality. The conclusion of this discussion is not complex or new. It is that at a macrosocial level the homicide rate will be higher the greater is social inequality, combined with concentrated poverty and weak social welfare, since these create spaces of local decivilization. The effects of these are likely to be magnified when inequalities are created through ascribed (usually racialized) social exclusion that creates segregated urban spaces. There is scope for further research to work out and theorize the effect of different possible relationships and the intersection of economic and cultural factors. Although nineteenth- and twentieth-century socialists and liberal reformers were well aware of the connection between violent crime and inequality, this needs restating in the face of prevailing neoliberal policy commitments and a likely assault on social welfare throughout the mature market economies in the 2010s.

8

THE POLITICS OF 'HATE CRIME'

This chapter examines the concept of 'hate crime' and hate-based violence. The phenonomon is not new in human history but has been thrown into relief by the civilizing process. Until the second half of the twentieth century the use of extreme and everyday violence in enforcing hierarchies of social class, religious observance, race and ethnicity, sexuality and gender was widespread. In post-Civil War USA 'several thousand African Americans, mostly young black males who challenged the racial status quo', were lynched in the Southern states in public spectacles that had the active or tacit support of local state authorities (Clarke 1998). By the later twentieth century, in most developed countries and following the USA, 'hate crime' statutes and policing strategies were widely established. 'Hate crime' (also called 'bias crime') refers to crimes in which the victims are chosen because of particular characteristics, such as race, ethnicity, disability, gender, sexuality and religion, although the scope of this legislation varies between jurisdictions. 'Hate crime' refers to a 'family of legislation' (Jacobs 2003: 412) that includes reporting statutes, enhanced penalties where an offence is motivated by bias, civil rights laws and new substantive offences.[1] Hate crime statutes are sometimes linked to the rise of identity politics in the 1980s (e.g., Jacobs 1993). But Levin (2002) argues that they are more deeply rooted in the history of the USA – in particular in the 1865 13th Amendment abolishing slavery and the 1866 Civil Rights Act, which conferred equal legal citizenship to all Americans and prohibited employment discrimination based on race and colour. The emancipation of slaves was violently challenged by the formation of the Ku Klux Klan in 1867, and there followed a century of struggles against racist violence and criminality, which culminated, Levin suggests, in legislation against hate crime. This might be an overly linear view of steady progress since it is also suggested that the civil rights movement faltered during

---

[1] Hate crime often adds penalties to existing crimes (called the 'basis offence') but an example of a new offence is the 1999 Football Offences and Disorder Act (S.9) in the UK, which made chanting of an indecent or racist nature at a football match an offence.

the Reagan administrations (1981–89), during which time several civil rights statutes, notably the Equal Rights Amendment, were defeated (Craig 2003). Even so, the 1980s was also a period of intense social movement activism – of feminism, gay and lesbian rights, identity and anti-racist movements. The post-Reagan development of hate crime statutes perhaps reflected how 'our sensitivity to, and distaste for, group prejudice and hatred have sharply increased' (Jacobs 2003: 412). This chapter will first consider the origins of this legislation and then discuss ways of explaining hate-based violence, especially where this becomes a means of social bonding among perpetrators.

Context for the hate crime agenda

Habermas and Rehg (2001) ask 'what basic rights free and equal citizens must mutually accord one another in post-traditional societies if they want to regulate their common life legitimately?' Part of the answer to this question could be the development of a legal framework of rights and constitutional protections since 'morality alone cannot meet the demands for regulation and organization in societies that can no longer rely on a common ethos for purposes of social integration' (2001). Virtually all societies now are 'multicultural' in that they include complex and hybrid patterns of ethnic, religious and cultural diversity which is premised upon cosmopolitan and pluralistic ethics and law. However, the extension of rights and entitlements based on universalistic principles (such as the struggles for suffrage and for civil rights) has been among the hardest fought political battles of the twentieth century. Social movements were central agents around which new conceptions of rights and entitlements were formed and institutionalized.

The movements to establish hate crime laws can be placed in the broader context of modernization and informalization, which, as Elias noted, places an increased onus on the self-regulation of bodies and emotions. However, this is a complex process. We have seen that the civilizational process 'incrementally develops stable forms of self-constraint on individual drives and the social relations through which they operate' (Slocum 2005). Cooney (1997) noted that whereas violence was in earlier periods an elite way of resolving conflicts, by the twentieth century 'aggressive tactics – fighting, burning, seizing, killing, and so forth' are viewed as the preserve of non-elites in places where the state's rule is ineffective. A similar process might have occurred with expressions of racism and other forms of hate-based behaviour. In developed societies, overt expressions of hate have largely diminished among elites and in public spheres. O'Brien (2000: 29) says 'Today, it is pejorative to be called a racist. No-one with sense wants to be associated with racism. Nor do they want the organisation which they work for to be regarded as racist.' In our interviews with racially motivated offenders in Greater Manchester (e.g., Ray et al. 2004), we found that respondents were often more willing to justify their perpetration of violence than the racist aggravation for which many had been convicted. This reflects a strong cultural prohibition on public expressions of racism, which has developed along with juridical controls on hate speech and behaviour, beginning in the UK with the 1976 Race Relations Act, which criminalized incitement to racial hatred.

The nature of 'hate' requires some reflection. Citing Gordon Allport's concept of hate, Iganski (2008: 2) describes hate as a sentiment rather than an emotion – 'an enduring organization of aggressive impulses' and 'habitual bitter feeling and accusatory thought'. That is, cold hatred rather than the heat of anger. Hate is bonding. Alford (1998: 68) similarly says that 'hatred is enduring. ... It can define a self, communicating it to others, anchoring it in the world, while at the same time acting as a fortress.' Hatred, he continues, 'consolidates the unconscious identification' between victim and victimizer. It energizes the self while keeping at bay feelings of helplessness (1998: 74). Hate, he suggests, is a medium of social bonding and is the 'simulacrum [i.e., a likeness or resemblance] of love' which gives meaning and purpose to life and chains individuals to those they hate, such that even when the victim dies the fetters remain. Hatred traps the victim and perpetrator in a 'world of bodies' in that the body comes to symbolize the world reduced to bare essentials of 'pain and power' (Alford 1998: 71–4).

Iganski (2008: 2), however, says that such definitions would confine the concept to 'extreme bigots' rather than the more common forms of confrontation violence that constitute 'hate crimes'. But this is not necessarily the case if we view hate in terms of what social movement theorists call a 'sentiment pool' of shared grievances that can be mobilized in certain situations. For example, in the UK there were 2,000 attacks on asylum-seekers between 2000 and 2002 (Kushner 2003) and such periodic manifestations of hatred can be mobilized by the mass media or political parties because they tap into widely shared grievances about housing, employment, schooling, welfare benefits and, 'less tangentially, about a threatening future and a rapidly changing and increasingly complex global community' (Kushner 2003). Asylum-seekers, then, became tangible scapegoats for multiple anxieties that were mobilized though not necessarily created by sections of the mass media. In this way, hatred that is directed towards people who are marginalized and have little power is socially produced while reinforcing established status and power hierarchies (cf. Perry 2002). This enables us to view hate actions as invoking structures of power and exclusion even in situations of confrontation violence that might not have been premeditated by 'extreme bigots'.

Hate takes as its object the surface of the body since physical appearance is here the essential marker of difference. As Shilling (2005: 52) says, 'the very construction of race has been dependent ... on classifying humans on the basis of corporeal characteristics such as skin colour'. Social hierarchies are inscribed on to bodies and ways of feeling as signifiers of gender and sexual difference, religion, ethnicity, race and disability. Michael John (1999) says 'As a "raced body" I do not have the luxury of entering spaces as a "race neutral" body. My body carries certain signifiers such as the drug dealer, car jacker, rapist, and sexual promiscuity'. The body of the Other has been constructed variously as inferior, diseased, licentious, menacing, primitive, cunning and world-controlling, and therefore fit only for displacement, segregation, cleansing and genocide. The ghetto is a space for the disciplining and quarantine of stigmatized bodies within physically, symbolically and socioeconomically constructed walls. Describing the violent exclusion of two black students (James Meredith and Autherine Lucy) from the universities of Mississippi and Alabama in 1955 and 1956 respectively, Jackson (2006: 22) says that 'by denying Meredith and Lucy admittance … the university was saying to them that their black bodies were despicable and disturbing, that the mere fact of their racial existence was reason enough to justify horrid treatment'. This extreme othering can also be a prelude to genocide, discussed in the next chapter.

However, we saw in Chapter 4 that gender identities are performative rather than fixed, and a performative approach to stigma, exclusion and identity is also productive. The body is dressed and presented in ways that mark, subvert or challenge dominant culture or again to 'pass' as not visibly different. 'Passing' is also about managing personal appearance in the light of anticipated stigmatizing responses of others. Passing evokes 'normality', as Goffman said, by controlling 'the information conveyed through … bodies'. However, while some signs are congenital (such as skin colour), some vary in their permanence and some are 'less stable' and subject to 'slips' (Goffman 1961: 61). The crucial thing is that these boundaries are maintained by the implicit threat of retaliation for stepping out of line – for example, entering the 'wrong' neighbourhood or holding hands in the wrong place. Thus, Perry (2001: 55) says:

> When we do difference, when we engage in processes of identity formation, we do so within confines of structural and institutional norms. In so doing … we reinforce the structural order. However, not everyone always performs 'appropriately'. … We step out of line, cross sacred boundaries, or forget our place. … Hate crime often emerges as a means of responding … to perceived violations.

Both passing and hate violence confirm the 'natural' orders of race, sexuality, body form, dress, etc., and mark their boundaries. Racist discourse is part of a 'reservoir of procedural norms' that not only tacitly inform routine activity but also legitimate racist practices (Perry 2002).

The violence referred to here can be extreme and has a high rate of repeat victimization. In prosecuted cases in the England and Wales, offences against the person are the most frequent (67 per cent) with criminal damage and public order offences at 11 and 12 per cent respectively (CPS 2009b: 13). Further, according to the Institute of Race Relations (IRR), around 160 people were victims of racially motivated murders in the UK in 1999–2006 (IRR 2010).

Legislating against hate

However, the meaning of hate crime is often unclear, contested and differs between national jurisdictions, where they are informed by particular national histories and collective memories. Moreover, the development of laws against hate crime can be viewed in two contrasting ways. On the one hand, they can be seen, as Levin (2002) argues, as extensions of the long struggle for rights-based equal citizenship. On the other hand, the extension of legislation in this area can be seen as evidence of the 'new' regulatory state attempting to 'impose civility through coercion', on a par in the UK with ASBOs and community safety initiatives (Crawford 2006). In either case, though, hate crime laws define the quality of an action differently depending on the putative motive underlying it. While judgements of motives do have a well-established place in the criminal justice system (CJS), as Lawrence (1999: 106–9) points out, the judgement here is not simply about culpability – to what extent was the harmful outcome intended by the perpetrator? – but also about its meaning. In many jurisdictions the penalties for bias or hate-motivated crimes will be enhanced where the offence was motivated or accompanied by expressions of religious, racial and sexual hate.[2] These are 'signal crimes' in a way that say muggings are not, in that their significance is enhanced because of the message sent by both the crime and the sentence.

Is hate crime 'stranger violence'? Two conditions are sometimes suggested for identifying hate crime. First, that the victims are interchangeable so long as they share the relevant characteristic of the stigmatized group; second, that there is little pre-existing relationship between victim and perpetrator that might give rise to some other motive for the offence (Lawrence 1999: 14–17). But both of these conditions are problematic. For example, domestic violence is frequently included within the category of hate crime (e.g., in the US 1994 Violence Against Women Act) and women who are subject to intimate partner violence are by definition known to the perpetrator. Further, much research (including Ray et al. 2004) suggests that true stranger violence is atypical, and

---

[2] A significant ruling in England and Wales in 2008 extended the category of hate crime to violence motivated by the victim's appearance. In 2007 Sophie Lancaster was murdered in Stubbylee Park, Lancashire, where she and her boyfriend, Robert Maltby, both dressed as Goths, were victims of a vicious attack. Judge Anthony Russell, sentencing the teenage perpetrators to life imprisonment, classified the offences as 'hate crimes'.

that victims of racist and homophobic crimes are often known to their attackers, though not as intimates (Mason 2005). Kielinger and Paterson (2007) similarly found that in the majority of hate incidents reported to the police in London, perpetrators were people with whom victims came into contact in their daily lives. Victims are not generally 'known' but for the perpetrator are symbolic of some perceived external threat. The crucial question really is whether the victim would have been selected had it not been for their particular identity? For example, in Greater Manchester there are frequent attacks on taxi drivers, many of whom are South Asian. These incidents might arise (as perpetrators often claim) from a disputed fare, but the important question for the legislation is whether the dispute would have arisen or become violent were it not for the ethnicity of the victim?

Legislative regimes vary between countries. Hate crime legislation in the USA is founded on five key Federal Acts: the 1990 Hate Crime Statistics Act, the 1994 Violence Against Women Act, the 1994 Hate Crimes Sentencing Enhancement Act, the 1999 Hate Crimes Prevention Act and the 2009 Matthew Shepard Act,[3] plus over 150 state statutes. By contrast with the UK's victim-centred Macpherson (1999: Chapter. 47, para. 12) definition ('A racist incident is any incident which is perceived to be racist by the victim or any other person'), the 1990 US Hate Crime Statistics Act requires, for the recording of an event as a 'hate crime': 'manifest *evidence* of prejudice based on race, religion, sexual orientation or ethnicity', which entails a 14-point checklist to be completed by the recording officer (Jacobs 2003). In UK legislation 'hate crime' does not feature explicitly, although the term is widely used in the annual reporting regimes for the Crown Prosecution Service and divisional police forces and in posters encouraging reporting.[4] While US legislation is informed by the history of slavery and subsequent struggles for civil rights,[5] the

---

[3]The 'Matthew Shepard and James Byrd, Jr. Hate Crimes Prevention Act' extended the legislation to crimes motivated by hostility to the victim's gender, sexual orientation or disability. It was named after Matthew Shepard, a gay college student who was brutally murdered in 1998 in a bias-motivated attack in Wyoming.

[4]The key UK legislation that creates a framework for hate crime laws are the Public Order Act 1986, which makes it an offence to commit an act which is intended or likely to stir up racial hatred; the Crime and Disorder Act 1998 (as amended by the Anti-terrorism, Crime and Security Act 2001), which created specific offences of racially or religiously aggravated crime; the Criminal Justice Act 2003, which requires courts to treat more seriously any offence shown to be racially or religiously aggravated and includes hostility towards the victim's disability or sexual orientation; the Football Offences Act 1991 (see p. 148, note 1); and the Racial and Religious Hatred Act 2006, which makes it an offence to use threatening words or behaviour with the intention of stirring up religious hatred.

[5]The 1999 Hate Crimes Prevention Act, Section 2 (8) says 'violence motivated by bias that is a relic of slavery can constitute badges and incidents of slavery' (Perry 2003: 484).

UK's approach to diversity is framed by policies of multiculturalism and a post-colonial history of labour migration.

The UK's approach is broad and 'victim-centred' in that hate crime includes 'any criminal offence that is motivated by hostility or prejudice based upon the victim's [perceived]: disability, race, religion or belief, sexual orientation or transgender' (Home Office 2010: 56). Racist violence in the UK came under sharp public scrutiny following the murder of a black teenager, Stephen Lawrence, by a gang of racist white youths in 1993 and the subsequent public inquiry that reported in 1999 (Macpherson 1999).[6] Criticism of the police investigation and a broader suggestion that the police were 'institutionally racist' resulted in widespread scrutiny of institutional practices in the police and other public organizations of ways in which racism might be inscribed in routine practices and beliefs.[7] This also resulted in the creation of many new practices, training, and requirements to report, record and act on allegations of racist harassment and assault, and established the Macpherson definition of a 'racist incident' that removed police discretion from the recording process and encouraged third-party reporting of incidents through organizations such as community associations and schools. Partly as a result of this, the numbers of recorded racist incidents in England and Wales rose from 15,000 in 1988 to 25,000 in 1999 and 57,902 in 2006, although these fell to 38,327 in 2007–08 (see Figure 8.1). One reason for thinking that this was due to an increase in reporting rather than an increase in incidents is that the BCS reported *falling* racially motivated incidents (from 390,000 to 179,000) between 1995 and 2005, which was the period of the largest increase in incidents recoded by the police. Although this rapid increase in reporting of racist incidents was not initially matched by increased convictions, this had changed by 2008–09, with around one-third of reported incidents resulting in conviction in 2008–09 (CPS 2009b).

---

[6]Stephen Lawrence was a Black teenager, murdered on 22 April 1993 in Eltham, southeast London. During the attack, one of the assailants reportedly yelled 'What! What! N*****!' as they charged at Lawrence, who was then stabbed in the chest and shoulder (*The Guardian* 30/1/99). There were five suspects – Gary Dobson, Neil Acourt, Jamie Acourt, Luke Knight and David Norris. The Crown Prosecution Service initiated but then withdrew prosecutions against Dobson, Knight and Neil Acourt. After years of campaigning for an inquiry into the murder and failure of prosecution – an Inquiry, chaired by Lord Macpherson, convened in 1998 and reported in 1999.

[7]Institutional racism was defined as 'The collective failure of an organisation to provide an appropriate and professional service to people because of their colour, culture or ethnic origin. It can be seen or detected in processes, attitudes and behaviour which amount to discrimination through unwitting prejudice, ignorance, thoughtlessness, and racist stereotyping which disadvantage minority ethnic people' (Macpherson 1999: Chapter 6, para. 34).

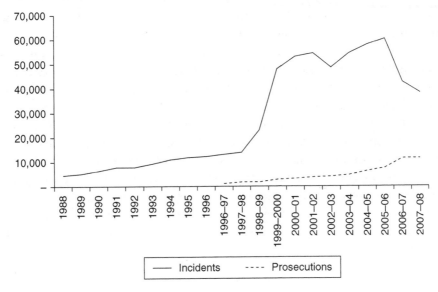

Figure 8.1   Racist Incidents Reported to the Police in England and Wales
Source: Home Office Racist Incident Reports and CPS Reports 1997–2008.

The UK's Crime and Disorder Act 1998 states:

> A crime will count as 'racially aggravated' if it can be shown that it was motivated either wholly or partly by racism or, if it can be shown that even though the motivation for the attack was not racist, racist hostility was demonstrated during the course of the offence or immediately before or after it. (Section 28)

The definition is broad and does not require proof of motive, which is difficult to establish, but only of hostility, which will typically refer to the use of racist speech by the offender. Most of the behaviours included under the 'hate crime' category are already criminal – harassment, damage, assault, threatening behaviour and homicide. The new content of hate crime legislation is the emotion attached to the act, which can attract an enhanced sentence if the prosecution can prove either that the victim was selected because of their race, ethnicity, religion, gender, sexual orientation or disability or that such hostility was evident at the time of committing the act.[8]

Hate crime strategies differ between jurisdictions. The Anglo-American legislative strategy contrasts with that in Germany, where hate crime laws were traditionally framed by the Holocaust and directed against xenophobic crime

---

[8]At a presentation to the Pathfinder working group at the Home Office (2000), the author was assured by someone who had drafted Section 28 that the intention had been to criminalize expressions of racism.

and political extremism. In 2001 these provisions were extended to prohibit 'Incitement ... directed against a person on account of their political opinion, nationality, ethnic origin, race, color, religion, ideology, origin, sexual orientation, disability, appearance or social status' (Bundesamt für Verfassungsschutz 2003: 22). But German initiatives place more emphasis than Anglo-American ones on engagement with civil society organizations and youth services aimed at improving and promoting democratic behaviour. These include XENOS,[9] which undertakes education against xenophobia, racism and discrimination in schools and workplaces, and CIVITAS, an initiative against right-wing extremism in eastern Germany aimed at strengthening civil society, which supports mobile advice teams, victim counselling centres, and networking centres. These are important initiatives, especially in view of the associations between deprivation and racist offending. The importance of anti-racist activism in addition to legislation is further exemplified in the success of movements against racism in sport – such as 'Kick It Out'.[10]

Victim politics

Legislation against hate-motivated crimes resonates with Elias's thesis of growing repugnance of violence and management of unruly passions. However, the increasingly global agenda of hate crime laws reflects ambivalence in the relationship between states and victims. Is hate crime legislation an extension of rights (protection from bias-motivated harm) or does it reflect the weakness of the juridical process? Rock (2002) suggests that although victims were once marginal to the criminal justice process, they have acquired more centrality in the wake of the political impact of victims' movements. He further suggests that the contrast drawn between the 'moral' states and 'immoral' offenders is made more sharply by publicizing 'victims' palpable distress'. Hate crime initiatives have been encouraged by victim movements, anti-racism movements, and lesbian-gay activism. In the USA, civil rights groups, women's groups and lesbian and gay campaigners (often in alliance with more traditionally 'right-wing' victim movements) have argued that bias victimization is 'terrorism' directed against sexual and ethnic minorities (Jenness and Broad 1997). Victim politics can also enable the construction of broad coalitions, such as the campaign for the Stephen Lawrence inquiry, which brought together disparate actors including left-wing anti-racist movements, senior police officers and The *Daily Mail*, a conservative national newspaper.

---

[9]See www.xenos-de.de/Xenos/Navigation/english.html.

[10]See www.kickitout.org/.

Similarly, Wieviorka (2009: 47ff) argues that in the past, crime represented a threat to the social bond and the purpose of justice was to dissuade the majority from wrongdoing. However, victims did not then feature in this exchange of infraction and punishment, whereas 'The contemporary victim began to acquire a certain public visibility in the nineteenth century, in at least two domains ... international ... and internal social life' (Wieviorka 2009: 48). Internationally, sensitivity to war victims, and especially civilians, grew following the formation of humanitarian organizations such as the Red Cross in 1908, psychiatry's interest in trauma and war neurosis, and the welfare state encouraged broader ideas of social protection. In the later twentieth century 'victims enter public space *en masse*' through victimization studies, 1960s collective protest movements and campaigns for recognition of victims of rape, abuse, violence and discrimination (2009: 44ff). That these protest movements coincided with the anti-Vietnam War movement suggests they were part of a broad process of internal and international pacification.

However, Wieviorka (2009: 60) further argues that foregrounding victims of war and crime leads to the state losing legitimacy since the emergence of victims 'reveal failings and dereliction of the political, and the decay of states and political and juridical systems' that can no longer fulfil their classic functions of guaranteeing order. Evidence for this could be seen in the widespread critique of the UK police (especially the Metropolitan Police Service (MPS)) and CJS following the Stephen Lawrence inquiry. Wieviorka continues that victimhood feeds into fear of crime while the infantilized culture of complaint accords power to the complainant, evidenced by the use of victim impact statements. Victim politics, then, can be seen as a challenge to state authority.

However, such a challenge may be followed by a strengthening of the state as power is consolidated through new laws that extend 'security'. While extreme racial violence such as lynching in the Southern USA 'dramatically depicts the state's failure to protect a racial minority group from violent, extra-legal social control' (King et al. 2009), the enforcement of hate crime legislation can be evidence of the state's increasing control over the means of violence. Grattet and Jenness (2003) describe the development of training and intervention policies for specialized enforcement units that also evoke new knowledge of offenders' motivations. Likewise the initial challenge to the UK CJS posed by the highly critical Macpherson Report was met by radical review and revision of the way racism and racist crime is policed. This extension of state power has been contested – in the USA the constitutionality of hate crime statutes were challenged in appellate courts 38 times between 1984 and 1998 (Grattet and Jenness 2003: 399). However, these challenges prompted a refinement of the concept to specify the criteria for a judgment of bias crime. The embedding of hate crime legislation into the routine practices of institutional life, then, which allows the creation of new subjects of intervention, represents an *extension* rather than weakening of state authority.

The hate debate

Hate crime laws are often advocated on the grounds that hate crime is more damaging and the violence often more extreme than other crimes (e.g., Iganski 2001; Messner et al. 2004). Further, they are 'message crimes'. That is, hate crimes are directed at whole communities with a message of hostility and exclusion. The trauma of being selected for crime because of one's identity, it is argued, is greater than for other crime. A respondent in Iganski's (2001) Boston pilot research on harms of hate crime says:

> It is much more difficult I think as a victim to say I was put in the hospital because I'm gay or because I'm Hispanic, or because I'm a woman, than it is to say, you know I was walking down the street and I had my bag around my arm and some guy snatched from me, some guy knocked me over the head and took what I had, because they want property. You're not being singled out. You are beaten or hurt because of who you are. It is a direct and deliberate and focused crime and ... it's much more difficult to deal with ... because what a hate crime says to a victim ... is 'you're not fit to live in this society with me. I don't believe that you have the same rights as I do. I believe that you are second to me. I am superior to you.'

Many sources report that victims feel isolated, depersonalized and deprived of a sense of self-worth, often blaming themselves and experiencing shame and flashbacks (e.g., Patton 1999).

Advocates of hate crime statutes further argue that alongside the additional hurt done by these crimes the law has an expressive function of promoting collective values. As Lawrence (1999: 169) puts it, 'If bias crimes are not punished more harshly than parallel crimes, the implicit message expressed by the criminal justice system is that racial harmony and equality are not among the highest values in our society.' Perry (2001: 237) regards the law as having a transformative role but argues further that there is a need for social practices that disrupt institutionalized structures of inequality, including the reclaiming and empowering of difference. Quoting Iris Young, she says:

> I am just what they say I am – a Jewboy, a colored girl, a fag, a dyke, or a hag – and proud of it. No longer does one have the impossible project of trying to become something one is not, under circumstances where the very trying reminds one of who one is. (Perry 2001: 237)

Critics of hate statutes dispute these claims. They argue that all crimes (not only 'bias crimes') have repercussions beyond individuals. In addition, these laws, they argue, 'fix' identities into *'government*-designated group[s] which benefit from government-mandated preferences' (Sowell 1990: 14). Indeed, hate crime statutes can confirm the status of designated 'vulnerable groups' as victims and promote a 'nanny culture of the victim' (Gates et al. 1999). For Green et al. (2001), this can further heighten intergroup resentment. Hate crime laws punish 'speech' or what the offender was thinking at the time of the offence. For example, Ignatieff (2000: 24) says:

> We do not need to police each other's thoughts and attitudes towards our differences. We simply need to master violence, to punish the kind of attack that occurred at that bus stop in south London, with all the determination that we can muster. And insist – before another courageous mother has to remind us – that justice is indivisible.

In other words, there is no need to for specific anti-hate laws so long as there is sufficient will to prosecute. Moreover, as noted above, most offenders are not committed 'haters'. In their review of the Crime and Disorder Act, Burney et al. (2002: 111–12) say that 'Serious race hate is fortunately rare – which is why the label "hate crime" is so misleading'. Most people, they claim, have prejudices, but those who 'get prosecuted for racially aggravated offences are often too ignorant or unsophisticated to exercise self-control'.

It is also claimed that there are logical problems of determining which groups to include in the legislation, which will, in practice, be set by those social movements with most influence while being denied to those 'whose suffering is less dramatic' (Moran and Skeggs 2004: 42). Use of the coercive state, critics say, further aligns with the 'very emotions that it seeks to challenge', of vengeance (2004: 42). Hate crime laws reduce issues of racism and structural discrimination to individual motives and 'incidents'. They are a liberal way of being 'tough on crime' in that they build on the power of state agencies but avoid addressing issues of structural violence such as healthcare disparities, economic inequalities and police brutality. Hate crimes occur within dynamics of power and exclusion to which the law has paid little attention and which punishment enhancement fails to address (Franklin 2002). There are also free speech objections to the effect that with enhanced sentencing it is *speech* rather than action that is being punished (e.g., Jacobs 1993) since what distinguishes a hate crime from the basis offence is the hate language and sentiment.

Some of these critiques are valid. But the long-term consequences of hate violence can be profound, heightening social divisions, conveying long-enduring messages of vulnerability or empowerment, even to those far removed from the initial violence, provoking potential victims to limit their activities, and shaping a dynamic of contention that can fuel further violence (Blee 2007). The 'free speech' argument – that only actions and not words should be punishable – makes an untenable distinction between actions and speech, suggesting that what is spoken is inactive as opposed to deeds with real effects. Speech act theory argues that speech acts are performative and have intentions and effects. When we speak we do so to achieve effects – to embarrass, persuade, frighten, warn, etc. So if speech does things and is an act, the distinction between words protected by constitutional freedoms and acts regulated by law also becomes problematic. There is clearly a danger of extending this argument into a regulation of speech in general. But certain kinds of speech – oaths, curses, threats, epithets, etc. – do not invite the hearer to enter dialogue, but reinforce and instantiate systems of exclusion and marginalization. Further, hate crime invokes the power of the dominant culture and instantiates a hierarchical order of exclusion (Perry 2001). While hate crime laws define various vulnerabilities, thereby risking encouraging a 'culture of the victim', it is hate-based crime that 'fixes' identities – one becomes acutely aware who one is when this identity can mean a life of security and peace or a life of fear and anxiety.

Where critics might be right is in relation to the individualization of societal issues. This will be developed here because it is relevant to a wider understanding of the politics of hate crime. The ultimate reference point for hate crime is the threat of systematic ethno-national violence and terrorism. Hate crime is thus a harbinger of terrorism. But whereas ethno-national violence and terrorism are viewed in a largely politicized frame of reference, in which individual motivation is largely taken for granted, hate crime is often viewed as expressive of mental or social pathology. One does not generally ask questions about the 'motivations' of ethno-nationalist organizations (Green et al. 2001). In Northern Ireland, as ethno-national conflict declined following the peace process, the frame of interpretation shifted from that of sectarian conflict to one of 'sectarian hate crime'. This view was promoted following criticism of the Police Service of Northern Ireland for failing to intervene in a number of sectarian incidents.[11] Mac Ginty (2001) argues that the key differences between ethno-national violence and hate crime are politicization and the scale of conflict. Other differences, he argues, are that ethnic violence is concentrated in outbursts while hate crime is more stable and ongoing. In ethno-national violence, spatial segregation of communities is critical, with violence often appearing on 'peace lines' such as West Belfast, while hate crime is more territorially diffuse. In ethno-national conflicts paramilitaries monopolize and regulate violence, which has strategic purpose, such as murders of Catholics by Unionist militias to undermine support for the IRA. Hate crime, by contrast, is more informal

---

[11] In 2003 there was a violently anti-Catholic dispute around Holy Cross School, North Belfast, and fierce anti-Muslim sentiment expressed in Craigavon in the context of building a mosque. However, anti-hate provisions were not deployed in either situation (Committee on the Administration of Justice 2003).

and unregulated, and most perpetrators are not willing to subordinate to party ideologies and discipline (Krell et al. 1996).

Even so, the differences between hate crimes and sectarian violence might be matters of degree and of 'range of movement along the conflict cycle' (Mac Ginty 2001). Green et al. (2001) propose an analysis that views 'genocide and civil war' as 'extreme instances of hate crime'. These are actually often spatially structured on borders between residentially segregated communities and in supposedly 'safe' spaces such as gay villages (Mason 2005). They can also occur in outbursts such as the riots against asylum-seekers and migrants in East German cites like Hoyerswerda and Roskock in 1991 and the anti-refugee violence in the UK in the early 2000s. The Northern Ireland peace process was followed by a steep rise in reported sectarian and other hate crimes, which points to a process of informalization of violence (PSNI 2009). Mac Ginty (2001) says 'all hate crime is political in the sense that it involves a statement that goes far beyond' the act itself and 'involves the ... depersonalization of the victim'. Ethno-national violence can manifest with macabre theatricality – as with the 'Shankill Road Butchers' who murdered 30 Catholics in the 1970s, often in familiar and apparently secure places such as shopping malls and transit centres (Jurgensmeyer 2003: 122). These killings had no direct strategic purpose but were public rituals of extreme expressive violence and illustrate how close, at times, the conflict came to being genocidal. Both ethno-national violence and hate crime, then, invoke structures of power and exclusion and might be amenable to broad structural and civilizational analysis. While racist violence can take a cyclical pattern in which its objective is the maintenance of racial hierarchies, it can, especially in a context of weakening state authority, slide into ethnic cleansing and potentially genocidal violence. Offenders dehumanize the victims, who serve as 'scapegoats' for their own feelings of inadequacy and failure (Wieviorka 1995: 74–6).

Hate and discivilization

There are differences between hate crimes and ethno-national violence, especially of degree, politicization and organization, but if, as suggested above, there are also some similarities, then explanations of hate crimes could be placed in a broad socio-political context. A large volume of literature on perpetrators of hate crime focuses on motives and the psychosocial and environmental factors that contribute to intergroup violence. Offenders are generally young, male, under-educated, hostile to diversity, and regard violence as supported by their peer groups (Heitmeyer 1994; Krell et al. 1996; Ray et al. 2003, 2004). Figure 8.2 presents a model of preconditions and offenders.

PREDISPOSING STRUCTUEAL CONDITIONS	FACTORS DISINHIBITING VIOLENCE	OFFENDERS	PERFORMANCE OF 'HATE'	
Socio-economic deprivation; family dysfunction; economic downturn; residential and cultural segregation	Community stereotypes and tolerance of 'hate'; social disorganization; acceptance of violence; resource competition; sense of threat; peer dynamics, media images; alcohol or drugs; local myths and rumours.	Young, mostly male; probably engaged in other criminality; unstable employment and educational history; low or unstable self esteem; cognitive disturbance and hypersensitivity; unacknowledged shame; need for masculine validation; sense of grievance and resentment	Unacknowledged shame turns to fury in situations of conflict that provoke assertion of difference.	
			Typical 'Specialist' Greater severity of violence; victim a stranger; high risk of repeat offending; hate ideology	**Typical 'Generalist'** Less serious offences arising from disputes; victims known, though not well

Figure 8.2   Model of Hate Offending

There are typologies of motivation of which McDevitt et al.'s (2002) has been particularly influential in identifying perpetrators in terms of:

- Thrill seeking – to display power, experience rush of excitement.
- Defensive – to protect the 'neighbourhood' from outsiders.
- Retaliatory – following a rumoured incident or response to attacks.
- Mission – committed 'hater' who seeks to rid the world of 'evil'.

Messner et al. (2004) suggest that the specialist 'mission' offender is three times more likely than others to commit an unprovoked attack that results in serious injury. This type could be described as true 'hate crime', although it only accounts for a small proportion of reported incidents. Martin (1995) points out that 'bias' might be only a secondary motivation – people hurl racist and other epithets in the course of a confrontation that is rooted in more tangible concerns. Even so, in the act of articulating these epithets, whole structures of exclusion and stigmatization, along with stereotypes of minorities are invoked, whether or not perpetrators adhere to a racist worldview.

However, 'motivation' should be placed in a wider structural context. Many theories of hate motivation tend to be theories of prejudice rather than specific theories of violence, and their frequent focus on anomie and social disorganization might overlook the ways in which violent hate can act as a medium of social bonding. Beck (2000) developed an influential cognitive psychological model that draws on classical models of authoritarianism and racism, such as Adorno et al. (1950). Beck (2000) claims that hypersensitivity and 'continual mobilization to fight' combine with pro-violent attitudes towards minorities and women, which arise from archaic beliefs about their inferiority. Like Scheff (1997), Beck argues that the offender is often provoked by a sense of being disrespected. Further, perpetrators feel deprived as a result of the others' presence, their 'success' in life and perceived lack of concern for the perpetrators induces a sense of shame. Target groups become the scapegoat for intra-psychic conflicts and demonizing them gives the in-group a sense of power and identity. Heitmeyer (1994) argues that hostility towards foreigners is based on a process whereby feelings of perceived threat develop into racist violence. First, feelings of 'estrangement' are expressed as 'an attitude of distance' and 'contempt'. Second, this fear of foreigners becomes overshadowed by a 'competitive stance fuelled by economic and/ or cultural considerations'. Third, tolerance disappears and 'complete hatred of foreigners' arises resulting in hostile 'offensive struggle' (Heitmeyer 1994: 17). Bjørgo (1994) focuses on patterns and motives of violence towards immigrants and refugees in Scandinavia where youth gangs, often with criminal records, perpetrate the majority of racist incidents. Though not necessarily members of extreme right groups, they have been exposed to their propaganda and methods. Alcohol is significant in the planning and enactment of attacks, but as a disinhibiting rather than causal factor. These models regard the racist offender as having a distinctive personality that predisposes them to both racism and violence. Violent racism arises from poor and problematic moral reasoning, cognitive defects, including an inability to accept the impact of violence on the victim, a predisposition to resort to violence and a 'distorted worldview'.

However, the 'problem of violent racism', as (Bowling and Philips 2002: 125) argue, is not simply a matter of racist individuals, but of a wider racist culture, which defines people as problematic, 'threatening' and (simultaneously) vulnerable. There is considerable evidence that perpetrators' racist views are shared by the communities to which they belong and provide a source of reinforcement and justification of their behaviour, at least by not condemning it (e.g., Ray et al. 2003; Sibbitt 1997). The association between football and racist violence is not accidental since both summon up identities based on territory, in the context of which prejudice is more a disinhibiting rather than motivating factor (Messner 2004). As Englander (2007a) notes, these 'conformist rebels' are less likely to encounter social disapproval from peers if the victim is 'different'. Blee (2007) points out that the initial motive for violence might not be racism or other hatred, but rather members of violent groups might become racist or homophobic by engaging in assaults which suggests that 'hatred can be an outcome as well as the motive for violence'. It can build groups as well as be an outcome of these groups so 'violence *makes* a group' (Blee 2007).

This illustrates that human behaviour is not simply 'caused' but is embedded in systems of belief, legitimation and justification within which it appears to be acceptable. Sibbitt (1997) argues that prejudice permeates whole communities that have entrenched problems of socioeconomic deprivation and crime and 'spawn' violent perpetrators through mutually supportive relationships between the perpetrator and the wider community (1997: 101). Hence, she speaks of 'perpetrator communities' that scapegoat their problems on to visible minorities who serve to provide an external focus for their dissatisfaction, frustration and alienation. In the racist riots in Hoyerswerda and Rostock in 1991, 'hooligans really did believe they were simply carrying out the wishes of a large number of spectators', and 'that they were so doing was obvious from the applause and approval of the latter' (Krell et al. 1996). Collins argues that 'violence is generated by an entire attention space' (2008: 413) and there is a mutually supportive relationship between the violence of leaders and the crowds from which they derive emotional energy (2008: 430).

However, these interaction rituals take place in a wider social context. In Chapter 5 it was argued that neoliberalism had the localized decivilizing consequences of generating a harsh environment for those who lose out from social and economic restructuring, with the decline in social supports, brutalization and consequent narcissistic violence. But it is not necessarily the economic impact of social changes alone that has this effect since violence is related to dynamics of shame among those 'disadvantaged and marginalized economically and culturally and thus deprived of the material basis for enacting a traditional conception of working class masculinity' (Ray et al. 2003: 112). Iganski (2008) found that 'traditionally white strongholds that have experienced greater demographic change' in terms of increased minority residents 'experience greater rates of "race hate" victimization' compared with communities with a less dominant white population (2008: 70).[12] Likewise many of the offenders in Ray et al. (2004) came from predominately white disadvantaged estates in Greater Manchester.

The intersection of economic exclusion and masculinity is developed by Ferber (1998), who argues that a central goal of the white racists is to re-affirm the masculinity of white men threatened by structural transformations. 'The visible boundaries and borders separating races have been threatened with disruption' she says, and 'as in the past, when secure boundaries separating races begin to break down, fears of racial intermixture … emerge' (1998: 59).

---

[12]This is not to say, as Bowling and Phillips (2002: 115) note, that racism is confined to areas of deprivation – it also affects rural, suburban and prosperous areas as well as blighted inner-city locales..

Anahita's (2006) analysis of the 'global skinhead movement' found that it is largely comprised of white, downwardly mobile, young men who perform a heteronormative, hyper-masculine gender identity'. There are similar arguments in Blee (2007) and Kimmel (2002), who note that the multiple processes of globalization and other structural shifts have reshaped masculine identities in profound ways. By 'hyper-masculinity' Anahita means an identification with an iconographic style: shaved heads, heavy work boots, and other markers of white working-class masculinity. Again, Tomsen (2001) argues that homophobic crimes serve a dual purpose of constructing a masculine and heterosexual identity through involvement with violence and by establishing homosexuals as social outsiders. Thus, fatal gang attacks that are seen as 'hate crimes' can also be read as masculine crimes characterized by the group production of masculine identities. They also reflect the limited material and cultural resources available for the achievement of a masculine status among the groups of young men who carry out these attacks.

Intersections of perceived class disadvantage are interlaced with racialization. So, for example, the targets of hostility are often those perceived as 'middlemen' mediating the worlds of cosmopolitan capital and local communities. It was classically Jews who were scapegoated in this role but more recently this has been extended in different contexts to South Asians in the UK, Koreans in the USA, and East African Asians in East Africa (Perry 2001: 134). Ray et al. (2003) further found that racist offenders tended to scapegoat South Asians for community problems of unemployment, the decline of local manufacturing, and (somewhat paradoxically) for the rise in local crime. We also found respondents drawing a contrast between the global city image of central Manchester and the isolated and deprived life on outer-city housing estates from which many racially motivated offenders came. Offenders frequently expressed hostility at their exclusion that was projected on to South Asians as symbols of an apparently cosmopolitan culture.

These observations suggest that there are links between deprivation, social and personal disorganization and racist violence. Similar themes arise in the inquiry reports into the disturbances in English towns in 2001, which identify a territorial mentality, residential segregation and the deep fracturing of communities on racial, generational and religious lines. The Home Office reports into the disturbances put considerable weight on residential segregation, which is in turn symptomatic of several underlying structural conditions (Home Office 2002: 12). These include:

- Systematic disadvantage in that many members of ethnic minorities can only afford cheaper housing.
- Higher unemployment than in the majority community, especially in Bangladeshi and Pakistani communities.

- Cultural cohesion and choice among minority communities, which is possibly linked to fear of racist attacks and hostility from the surrounding areas.
- Discrimination in council housing allocation that has been a major cause of residential segregation.

Hate and social bonding

Within a context of localized, decivilizational processes hate crime perpetrators are not necessarily best described as 'anomic'. Alford (1998: 68) argues that 'hatred creates history, a history that defines the self and provides it with structure and meaning'. Moreover, 'loving recitation of harms suffered and revenge inflicted constitutes the single most important, most comprehensible and most stable sense of identity'. In his study of US skinheads, Hamm (1994) deploys the antinomy of anomie, that is, 'synomie' to argue that membership of hate groups creates social bonding that was otherwise absent in their lives. Movements such as the Aryan Nation in the USA draw members from among the most marginalized American youth seeking a sense of belonging (1994: 71). They bond through mutual interests in style and music to cultivate what Katz (1988: 89ff) calls a 'bad asses' dramatic style of presentation. Hamm found a profound sense of hopelessness mixed with rage that no one could prevent terrible things from happening (1994: 80). He emphasizes that these youths are conformists, who are not alienated but are well bonded to conventional systems and display a 'hyperactive commitment to American culture' (1994: 130). They are no more alienated than similar youth and in some ways less so since they had 'faith in the future' and 'alienation is not a necessary antecedent' for extreme beliefs (1994: 166). Violence becomes a means of social bonding and is viewed as 'defensive' rather than predatory. Hamm further emphasizes the closeness of skinhead friendships since they 'appear to love and value one another' in a family-like mentality (1994: 184). But their 'souls are full of chaos' and they do 'believe in vengeance' and are 'devoted to vitriolic hatred' (1994: 205). Similarly, Lyons (2007) argues that social disorganization theory predicts more hate crime than we find in disadvantaged areas and that rates are higher in 'defended neighbourhoods' that are socially organized to oppose outsiders.

More organized 'hate groups' develop social practices of bonding and socialization. Balch's (2006) study of Aryan Nation (AN) found that for members:

> Besides Sunday services, church activities included regular Bible studies and holiday celebrations, and church facilities were used for all AN events. The regular attenders were bound together by a dense network of friendships and family ties that were reflected in frequent family get-togethers, casual socializing, and collective projects.

The church was the social hub where talk about Scripture and Bible history lubricated relationships. Similarly, the White Power Movement (WPM) provides children with racist activities such as racist crossword puzzles, colouring pages, and children's white power literature (Blee 2007). Parents utilize web-based home schooling material such as colouring books, children's literature and workbooks. Home schooling is often chosen to escape the contrary influence of public schools. All of these materials are easily accessible in cyberspace, enabling WPM families to integrate them into their daily practices.[13]

Other media of social bonding include the initiation into conspiracies, rumours – which might be formal or informal – into a world of secret and forbidden messages – symbols that transform ordinary realities into 'extraordinary ones' (Hamm 1994: 211). Conspiracy theories have been crucial to hate movements, the most notable being the *Protocols of the Elders of Zion*, a forgery produced in 1903 by the Tsarist secret police, which is still in global circulation (Ben-Itto 2005). This purported to have uncovered the secret records of shadowy Jewish leaders plotting to bring crisis and chaos to the world prior to taking control of national governments. This conspiracy worldview is invoked by neo-Nazis in the epithet 'ZOG' (Zionist Occupation Government) and less overtly in the belief that a 'Jewish lobby' has a stranglehold over American foreign policy. Rumour is also a catalytic element in racist violence, pogroms and lynching. Rumour constitutes community since it binds participants around narratives that condense and displace social problems while offering an experience of empowerment. Racial violence is frequently linked to accusations of ritual crime – child murder or kidnap in anti-Jewish pogroms or sexual crime, as in lynching in the USA. But rumour can operate in more mundane ways too in the form of myths and folklore that legitimate hostilities against minorities. A 29 year-old woman from an outlying estate, poorly served by public transport and visibly suffering from deprivation, damage and violence who was interviewed for Ray et al. (2004) said, 'They get a good deal. What they get causes resentment. Moss Side is all done up now. They should do it round here. People feel left out and let down.'

Conclusion

Hate crime statutes have a complex genealogy in post-Civil War USA and the following century of struggles for civil rights. In the later twentieth century this combined with broad social movement activism and rights-based advocacy,

---

[13]Similarly, hate on the Internet is expanding as racist and extreme right organizations make use of its potential – including 'Aryan dating sites' (Back 2002; Ray 2007b:128–30).

identity politics and victims' movements. The emergence of hate crime legislation across the developed world has been controversial and condemned as inappropriate and counter-productive. However, the legislation is justified by the additional harm, the signal nature of these offences and the way they instantiate structures of inequality and exclusion. Now it would be naïve to expect hate crime legislation to solve structurally and culturally embedded hatreds and divisions. It does, further, carry risks of polarizing divisions and reducing structural violence to individual motivations. Racist and other difference-based violence summons up deeply embedded notions of the 'normal body' and is linked to socioeconomic structures of masculinity and locality. Offenders (as the summary in Figure 8.2 outlines) act within complex determinants, and the risk of offending is high in conditions of deprivation and residential segregation combined with street cultures of unfulfilled masculine expectations. Prejudices held by peer groups will underpin violence, in combination with disinhibiting factors such as a perception of community 'under threat'. The law will not be effective here unless linked to transformative practices such as anti-racism, civic education and engagement with communities designed to shift identities towards non-defensive openness to cultural difference. In this process, the law and policing are not monolithic but provide resources that can be mobilized towards this kind of transformative politics and regulate our common life effectively.

9
MODERNITY AND THE HOLOCAUST

Hier ist kein Warum ('There is no why here', an Auschwitz guard replying to Primo Levi). (Levi 1987: 35)

Previous discussion has engaged with Elias's theory of the civilizational process and developed a framework for understanding violence within the context of the nature and trajectory of modern societies. This final chapter discusses Bauman's challenge to the civilizational thesis set out particularly in *Modernity and the Holocaust* (1999), in which he argues that the Holocaust was made possible by the institutions of rationalized modernity. This will be referred to as the 'modernity thesis'. This thesis has been very influential and is often accepted uncritically, as for example Malešević (2010: 138) does when he says, 'As Bauman argues, the Holocaust was achieved through the imposition of dull bureaucratic routine, where discipline was substituted for moral responsibility'. This discussion will examine Bauman's thesis within the context of his wider theoretical trajectory and his critique of modernity (or in later work, *heavy modernity*). Bauman's thesis is often read as a critique of Elias although, in so far as is this is his intention, the critique is rather oblique – he rarely refers to Elias directly and at no point does he set out the civilizational thesis in any detail. Bauman's arguments further involve particular readings of modernity, the Holocaust and modern genocide, all of which are open to question. I will suggest that Bauman's concept of modernity is too one-dimensional and that bureaucratic obedience might not be as central to understanding the Holocaust as he imagines. Bauman was right, nonetheless, to draw attention to its neglect (at least at the time) within mainstream sociology.

The discussion here will focus on the Holocaust as the epitome of modern genocide.[1] As Fine and Turner (2000: 7) say, 'the world is haunted by the ghost

---

[1]This concept was coined in 1944 by the Polish lawyer Raphael Lemkin from Latin *genus* (people) and *cidium* (slayer) and refers to 'war against whole nations and people' (Freeman 1995). It was adopted by the United Nations in indicting 24 Nazi war criminals in 1945 (Praeg 2007: 1), which signalled a shift towards an international civilizational process.

of the Holocaust' and of Nazi Germany, which was the most genocidal regime ever seen (Mann 2000). There is a debate, which Bauman (1999: 83ff) addresses, over whether the Holocaust was 'unique' or, on the contrary, one instance of many acts of genocide in recent history (see p. 44, note 1)? Fackenheim (1994: 10ff) argues that the Holocaust was unique on the following grounds. A third of all Jewry was murdered (including virtually all East European Jews) and the intention was to exterminate all Jews, who were selected on mere evidence of 'Jewish blood'. With the exception of Gypsies, no other people were killed for the 'crime' of existing. The extermination was not a means to an end (such as Stalin's liquidation of the 'kulaks' as a means to collectivization), but was an end in itself that was of sufficient importance to the Nazis to use resources that could have been used in the war. Further (and this is similar to Bauman), those who carried out the 'Final Solution' were primarily average citizens; not in the main 'perverts or sadists'. Other atrocities, Fackenheim says, do not have all these characteristics. However, his reference to the Roma Holocaust, in which around 25 per cent of European Roma was killed, suggests otherwise, and documenting this has featured increasingly in the memory politics of European genocide (e.g., Kapralski 1997). It might be better to say, as does Bauman (1999: 2), that to view the Holocaust either as unique or as a 'normal' event in a history of genocides is mistaken since both suggest there is nothing in particular to be learned from it. Again, Bartov (2000) says it is more important to explore the significance of the Holocaust for modern identity than to debate whether it was 'unique'. Nonetheless, the Holocaust was exceptional in its use of bureaucratic and scientific planning, the deployment of massive resources to move millions of people across Europe, and creation of a coordinated system of slave labour and factory-style extermination. The camps were linked to 'industrial zones' that would be the foundation for expansion of the Third Reich and of which the Auschwitz-Birkenau complex was to be the prime example.[2] Bauman is right to regard the genocide as integral to the construction of a New Order.

Before proceeding with this discussion, two points should be noted. First, the Holocaust was one of the most complex historical realities with which one can deal, involving millions of victims, perpetrators and bystanders, and raises multiple moral, political, philosophical and empirical questions. It is unlikely that any neatly systematized narrative is going to illuminate more than a fragment of this complexity. Second, as Healy (1997) says, all interpretations of the

---

[2]Auschwitz-Birkenau was a complex of 40 camps linked to industries in the region. Prisoners who were not selected on arrival for extermination performed slave labour, mostly in German coal mines, mills, armaments plants, and building sites for new industrial facilities. When the prisoners had been worked to exhaustion, they were killed.

Holocaust 'must be made with the utmost humility', not only because of its complexity, but also because, as the opening quote suggests, it might not ultimately be understandable. This chapter makes no such attempt but considers some fragments of recent debates.

Bauman's critique of the civilizing process

The core of Bauman's thesis is that the Holocaust was not, as many imagine (or at least used to), the antithesis of modern civilization, but rather was executed in modern rational society 'at the peak of human cultural achievement' (1999: x). Therefore, it 'is not the Holocaust that is difficult to understand. Rather, it is our western civilization which the Holocaust makes it difficult to understand' (Freeman 1995). Bauman does not argue that modern civilization alone caused the Holocaust – it was not its sufficient condition – but it was 'most certainly its *necessary* condition' since without modernity and the rational world of modern civilization 'the Holocaust would be unthinkable' (Bauman 1999: 13). Sometimes though he makes the weaker claim that rationality and civilized habits had been 'incapable of preventing' genocide (1999: 17). Although he does not discuss Elias at any length here or elsewhere (apart from a slightly deprecating review, Bauman 1979), the civilizing process is one of his targets. But he does not always get Elias right. For example, he refers to Elias's 'portrayal of recent history as eliminating violence from everyday life' (1999: 13 and 107), which Elias did not claim. The core of Bauman's critique is that it was precisely the aspects of modernity that appear to entail a reduction in violence that have actually intensified it, albeit displaced from the realm of everyday life on to interstate wars and state-sponsored genocide. The monopolization of the means of violence by the state was crucial to the process of social pacification but the concentration of power actually enabled mass extermination to occur. State violence shows the 'destructive potential of the civilizing process' separates the use and deployment of violence from moral calculus and removes moral inhibitions to violence (1999: 27). Pacification of daily life creates a defenceless and disarmed society, allowing the supremacy of political over social power (1999: 107). The complex division of labour and increasing social distance (figurations) which for Elias increase empathy, for Bauman quash the moral significance of action while moral dilemmas 'recede from sight' (1999: 25). Indeed, the very sentiments of revulsion and disgust that are central to modern sensibilities for Elias, were mobilized by the Nazis to render the very presence of Jews nauseating and repellent since they were represented as physically repugnant and carriers of contagious disease and danger (1999: 124).

However, Bauman's account does not give great weight to antisemitism[3] or other Nazi ideologies. He claims that the Holocaust cannot be explained simply as the outcome of centuries of European Christian antisemitism, which, though violent, had not until the twentieth century manifested as an exterminatory project. Further, he argues that many countries in the preceding decades displayed higher levels of antisemitism than Germany. He is concerned to demonstrate the *modernity* of Nazi antisemitism, arguing that in the late nineteenth and twentieth century a new antisemitism appeared in which the Jews became a target for diffuse anti-modernism and symbolized the chaos and devastation that this brought (1999: 31ff). The mythical association between Jews and the money economy was intensified with increasing Jewish assimilation. Assimilated Jews, who were 'no longer recognizable', posed an even greater threat of surreptitiously driving forwards the destructive force of advancing capitalism. They were strangers *par excellence* – in society but not of it, with no national home (1999: 53). This Jewish 'homelessness' was linked to paranoid beliefs about their controlling national governments and international finance, articulated in the *Protocols of the Elders of Zion*. Exterminatory antisemitism, then, was part of a *modern* racism that promised to create a perfect society by 'cutting out elements of reality' (1999: 65).

Bauman adopts a functionalist rather than intentionalist view of the Holocaust – that is, the Final Solution emerged over time in the Third Reich rather than having been intended by the Nazis from the outset. Every 'ingredient' of the Holocaust, he says, was 'normal' in keeping with the guiding spirit of civilization (1999: 8). The SS division organizing the Holocaust – the Economic Administration Sector of the SS Central Security Office – did not differ in a formal sense from other bureaucratic sections and (Bauman claims) preferred to recruit obedient functionaries loyal to the Führer rather than ideologists and sadists (1999: 20). Once given the objective of making Europe *Judenfrei*, the bureaucracy engaged in an ethically blind problem-solving process. This considered at one point the deportation of Jews to Madagascar, then to the East, which was unrealistic when Germany failed to defeat the USSR in 1941. Following this, the concentration of Jews in ghettos in Eastern Europe was accelerated, from which removal for mass extermination began following the Wansee Conference in January 1942. Bauman argues that violence is the product of a process that is *authorized* by a legally entitled chain of command through which it becomes routinized and requires victims to be dehumanized. This is possible because the moral significance action is quashed by the distance between actions and consequences in bureaucracies (1999: 25).

---

[3]A note on spelling – 'antisemitism' is preferable to 'anti-Semitism' since Semitic and anti-Semitic are not directly opposed to each other. Antisemitism refers specifically to hatred of Jews.

However, Bauman says that while the possibility of the Holocaust is rooted in 'universal features of modernity', its implementation was connected to specific relationships between state and society. His discussion of these is not very specific. He advances two theses on the relationship between state and society. First, the modern state (as opposed to postmodern or later 'liquid' modernity) was a 'gardening' state that aims to bring order, pattern and regularity to society. Nazi Germany and Stalin's Russia perpetrated 'genocide with purpose' with the aim of creating an ordered and rationally designed society (1999: 92ff). Second, the concentration of the means of violence in the state illustrates the destructive potential of the civilizing process where the deployment of violence is removed from moral calculus and inhibitions (1999: 27). The one organized pogrom during the Nazi period, Kristallnacht,[4] was regarded by the high command as too public and disordered and was not repeated (1999: 89). From this, Bauman concludes that 'the non-violent character of modern civilization is an illusion' since what happened in the course of the civilizing process was a redeployment of violence from public to invisible and segregated spaces. It was removed from everyday life to be organized through bureaucratic divisions of labour where, with the substitution of technical for moral authority, knowledge of the final outcome is not necessary, and each person is accountable only to their superior. The victims of this system are dehumanized and reduced to objects (1999: 96ff) which was epitomized by the striped uniform and number tattooed on prisoners' arms.

Bauman was not the first to develop a modernity thesis of the Holocaust. One of the main tenants of Bauman's thesis is the Weberian principle that bureaucratic rationalization generates a type of social action in which the ethical value of goals is separated from the practical achievement of tasks along with submission to authority, which assumes moral responsibility for the ends pursued. The human objects of bureaucratic task-performance are then viewed with ethical indifference (Bauman 1999: 103). Although hardly mentioned by Bauman, a modernity thesis had already been proposed by Adorno and Horkheimer (1973). In the post-war years, Adorno was one of the main voices in Germany challenging the silence on the Third Reich and prompting a 'coming to terms' with or 'working over' [*verarbeiten*] the past. A central motif was Adorno's attempt to create a post-Holocaust sensibility invoking the idea of 'nach Auschwitz' (after Auschwitz) as a caesura in which culture, philosophy and social theory could not be the same as before. Like Bauman, Adorno and

---

[4]On 9 November 1938 the Nazis unleashed a wave of anti-Jewish violence and within a few hours thousands of synagogues and Jewish premises were destroyed, at least 91 Jews killed and 30,000 deported to concentration camps. This became known as Kristallnacht, the night of broken glass. Following this, responsibility for 'solving' the 'Jewish question' moved from the Sturmabteilung (Storm Troopers) to the SS.

Horkheimer invoked Weber's concept of rationalization, and in particular the dominance of means–end rationality in which the capacity for autonomous moral judgement is lost in the face of bureaucratic technological reasoning. In the modern world, the only rational motive bourgeois society could recognize for decent public conduct were the ethics of utilitarian self-interest. This meant that reason vacated the ethical realm and was confined to matters of technical decision – finding the most efficient means to a given end. For Bauman, this created an uncritical and methodical search for 'solutions' to the problem of how to make Europe *Judenfrei* that ended in the Final Solution. But for Adorno and Horkheimer instrumental rationality reopened the way for the return of irrationality and myth. By admitting no public rationality other than self-interest, questions of fundamental value were removed into the 'irrational' realm of personal ethics and private decision. However, if irrational power politics (i.e., fascism) should replace enlightened self-interest in peoples' minds, Horkheimer commented, 'no moralist could object because no moral choice could be condemned as irrational. Reason had committed suicide' (Horkheimer 1974: 25). Paradoxically, for Adorno and Horkheimer, enlightenment that was supposed to liberate humanity from myth and ignorance had allowed myth to return by foreclosing public rational debate about morality and the good society, which were mere values consigned to the 'irrational'.

However, to argue like Bauman, that the institutions and (a)morality of modernity failed to *prevent* the Holocaust is not to offer any explanation of why it happened or what motivated those who participated. Although he shares in some ways Adorno and Horkheimer's 'modernity thesis', Bauman objects to Adorno et al.'s (1950) concept of the 'authoritarian personality' that attempted to identify the personality type (in relation to the familial and class systems) that was most prone to fascist propaganda. Bauman regards this approach, which seeks the social-psychological and familial bases of prejudice, as too subjective and concerned with questions of motivation, which are not relevant once evil has become banal and bureaucratized. Even so, Bauman cannot really avoid addressing the question of the behaviour of individuals who participated; therefore Milgram's (1974) experiments on obedience are central to his thesis. He wants to argue that its perpetrators were not insane, but well-educated, civilized men doing evil in a system of authority that de-legitimated ethical judgements. Arendt had come to a similar conclusion in her study of Eichmann's trial in Jerusalem in 1961, after which she famously concluded that 'the lesson that this long course in human wickedness had taught us ... [was] the fearsome, word-and-thought-defying *banality of evil*' (Arendt 1963: 252).[5]

---

[5]Details of the Eichmann trial, including full transcripts, can be found at www.nizkor. org/hweb/people/e/eichmann-adolf/.

During the 1960s and again in response to the Eichmann trial, the social psychologist Stanley Milgram conducted a famous series of experiments on obedience which demonstrated that a wide cross-section of Americans were willing to torment people whom they did not know or hate as part of an 'experiment' in learning. In the experiment, a 'learner' (actually an actor) is asked to learn a number of word associations and when he makes errors the 'teachers', who are the real subjects of the experiment, are asked to administer electric shocks. The voltage appears to rise from 15 volts to a lethal 450 volts (in reality there were no shocks) and, as the voltage appears to increase, the 'learner' screams and bangs on the wall and would then be silent (was he dead?). When 'teachers' expressed doubts or refused to continue, the 'scientists' in charge insisted that the experiment required them to continue and reassured them that they would not be held responsible for any outcome. Milgram found that (despite often showing acute distress) around 70 per cent of subjects were willing to continue administering severe shocks, although this diminished considerably if the 'learner' was visible to 'teachers'.

Milgram drew three conclusions in particular (Milgram 1974). First was the theory of conformism, that a subject with neither the ability nor expertise to make decisions will surrender responsibility to those in authority. Second was the 'agentic state' theory that people obeying authority see themselves as the instrument of another person's wishes and again surrender responsibility. Third was the claim that the greater the physical and psychical distance between victim and perpetrator, the easier it is to be cruel. The latter is particularly important for Bauman, who argues that inhumanity is a matter of social relationships and proximity to the victim. People will be crueller the more rationally organized and legitimately authorized is the action, the more collective it is and the greater is the physical distance from the victim. Perpetrators are also drawn into a gradual sequence of escalating cruelty which makes it difficult to draw a line and stop (Bauman 1999: 154ff).

Bauman, modernity and Elias

Bauman's thesis is a powerful indictment of modernity and he is right to claim that genocide on the scale of the Holocaust would not have been possible without modern bureaucratic organization and technical knowledge. However, this section identifies some problems with Bauman's argument, which will lead on to a more multifaceted understanding of genocide.

First, there is his concept of modernity. Bauman's thesis is part of a wider critique of modernity, which he sees epitomized in twentieth-century totalitarianism. He says: 'Modernity was a long march to the prison. It never arrived there (though in some places, like Stalin's Russia, Hitler's Germany or Mao's China, it came quite close) albeit not for the lack of trying' (1992: xvii). He depicts modernity in heroic terms, by contrast with the fluid, differentiated and aesthetized cultural forms of postmodernity, which is not 'a stage beyond modernity' but 'modernity coming to terms with its own impossibility' (Bauman 1991: 272). That is, the impossibility of state dreams of total social reconstruction. In later work (e.g., Bauman 2000) he has replaced the modernity/postmodernity couplet with that of solid/liquid modernity, but the contrast between two phases of society is otherwise very similar (Ray 2007a). However, this view of modernity is questionable. Arnason (1993) suggests that modernity is a complex field of tensions and within the civilizational paradigm alternative forms appear via the selective appropriation and re-activation of traditions (1993: 22ff). There is a contrast between the hierarchical statist-warrior modernization associated with ideals of heroism, self-sacrifice and certainty and modernity depicted in, for example, Weber's notions of disenchantment, rationalization, organizational impersonality and formal legality. From the standpoint of the latter, the claim that Nazi Germany was 'modern' would be hard to defend. Rather than develop an ethic of formal bureaucratic impersonality accountable to an open public sphere, the Nazi bureaucracy created a power structure dominated by a pre-modern warrior cult of 'honour'. Weber did identify the risk of an 'iron cage' of bureaucracy, although he thought this outcome was most likely under socialism (Weber 1978, vol. 2: 1402). Within democratic societies, two constraints limited bureaucratic power: first, political pluralism in which politics was a vocation pursued independently from the bureaucracy, and secondly the market with private property and a wage system. Indeed, 'For Weber, the problems with state bureaucracy in Germany arose not from its overarching embodiment of some cultural spirit of "instrumental reason" but from an illegitimate extension of its administrative ethos into the sphere of political leadership' (DuGay 1999).

Second, there is the importance of war for genocide. Bauman's 'modernity' is actually modelled on a war command economy with a single overriding goal, planned state requisition, compulsion and directed labour and finding technical solutions to problems (O'Kane 1997). Indeed, war was an important context for the Holocaust in several ways. Bartov (2000) argues that there is a strong relationship between war, genocide and modern identity. Europe was refashioned by the ultra-violence of the First World War trenches and the precedent this created for industrial killing, which, he suggests, hardened warrior values in Germany in particular (Bartov 2000: 13). Through literature and artistic representations of the War, Bartov argues that glory at the front meant enduring the most degrading, inhuman conditions under constant threat of death and regularly killing others without losing one's good humour, composure and humanity. The ability to switch roles between helpless prey and professional killer, loving son, father and husband while separating the atrocity at the front from normality at the rear – to survive the fighting but also the homecoming – all became glorified as a 'higher existence' (Bartov 2000: 18). Bergen (2009) likewise argues that the First World War affected attitudes to life and death and the defeat was followed by the creation of paramilitary groups like the Freikorps in Germany in 1920s, from which many leading Nazis came.[6] Similarly, Shaw (2002) argues that genocide is 'a type of war' and generally takes place during interstate war in which social enemies are identified with international state enemies. So in Nazi ideology the Jews were controlling both Soviet Bolshevism and international finance. Genocide's aim is annihilation of the stigmatized group, although unlike interstate war, the action is illegitimate and generally denied by perpetrators.

Third, there is the role of the state. Bauman mistakes totalitarianism for modernity. Mass extermination was always implicit in the Nazi project (O'Kane 1997), but Bauman does not distinguish between pluralistic and totalitarian states. For Elias, it was not simply state power that was civilizational, but functional democratization, that is, greater social complexity equalized power ratios between people, reduced hierarchies and enhanced informalization. By contrast, Nazi Germany was a state of extreme hierarchy combined with the arbitrary exercise of power. Primo Levi (1988: 94) said that 'throughout Hitlerian Germany the barracks code and etiquette replaced those which were traditional and "bourgeois"'. Arbitrary terror and the constant threat of arrest by the secret police (Gestapo) created fear and mutual distrust among people, which meant that communication was very limited. This was officially encouraged by the slogan 'Think of it always, speak of it never', as Adorno noted (1974: 40). O'Kane argues that this was an exceptional form of the state in which real power rested with the Gestapo and the SS and not with the formal state institutions that were merely a façade.

Fourth, there is Bauman's concept of reason. Bauman regards instrumentality and rationalization as the epitome of modernity and claims that 'the idea of *Endlösung* [Final Solution] was the outcome of the bureaucratic culture' (1999: 15). It was noted above that Bauman's critique in part echoes Adorno and Horkheimer's. Therefore, Bauman might be open to Habermas's critique of Adorno – namely that Adorno's denunciation of rationalization is one-sided because it fails to distinguish instrumentality from critical reason. The latter, for Habermas, is always implicit in communication that attempts to reach agreement or make judgements about 'good reasons' for action. Questions such as 'what do you mean?' or 'is it right to do this?' imply that we can engage in

---

[6]The Freikorps were extreme-right paramilitaries in post-First World War Germany who were involved in assassinating social democrats and communists (notably Rosa Luxemburg and Karl Liebknecht in 1919) and fought the Red Army in the Baltic States.

open-ended, non-instrumental communication that attempts to reach agreement about the meaning of statements and norms that guide action. Further, critical reason is not just a feature of conversations but is crucial to public life in modern societies and is (partially) realized in institutions of democratic government, civil society, the public sphere, critical debate and rights-based constitutions. The practice of reducing modern rationality to its 'jagged profile' (Habermas 1984: 241) of instrumentality, he criticized as 'being careless of the achievements' of western modernity and giving up on the emancipatory potential of modernity. Healy (1997) draws on Gillian Rose's social theory to make a similar point that Bauman *reifies* reason to the point where the political and historical realities and contingencies that underlay Nazism are overlooked. Bauman did not examine reason *per se*, but rather the deployment of power and domination to destroy it. Many of those who fought against Nazism and Stalinism believed passionately in the values of critical rationalism and justice, but formulations such as Bauman's disclaim the very possibility of critical self-reflection and normative judgement. He can explain why 70 per cent of those in Milgram's experiment continued to obey orders but has no explanation for the 30 per cent who refused.

These arguments suggest that we should not be looking to 'modernity', 'rationality' or civilization for an understanding of the Holocaust, but rather to specific conditions in pre-Nazi Germany. This is the stance Elias takes in *The Germans* (1996). This is often read as a repost to Bauman, although it is a collection of essays mostly written during the 1960s and 1970s and is not a direct response, Bauman being mentioned only in the editors' Preface. But as an historical account of the social texture and customs of German development, this is a very different approach from Bauman's. It can be read as a version of the *Sonderweg* (special path) thesis that German history was aberrant, at least by comparison with western Europe. Some manifestations of the *Sonderweg* were the absence of a completed 'bourgeois revolution', no transition from aristocratic to liberal bourgeois democratic government and strong intellectual and political movements to preserve the 'nobility' of German *Kultur* rather than follow the vulgar, materialistic path of western *Zivilization* and capitalism. In particular, Elias aimed to explore the conditions that made possible the 'decivilizing spurt' of the Hitler epoch (1996: 1). He locates this within an 'exceptionally disturbed' (1996: 401) long-term development that can be traced back to a weak process of state formation as a 'middle bloc' of Germanic states between the Slavic and French kingdoms. The medieval Holy Roman Empire, which was fatally weakened in the Thirty Years' War (1618–48), became an object of nostalgia among subsequent generations, but its legacy was that the German state formation did not 'keep pace' with developments elsewhere in Europe (1996: 4). Within the decentralized system of German states the military role of the aristocracy remained dominant while the middle class was subordinate. The eventual unification of Germany under Prussian hegemony, followed by military conquest in the Franco-Prussian War (1870–71), created a nation with a weak bourgeoisie, no court society and a political culture that idolized Germany's 'past greatness' (Dunning and Mennell 1998). Elias takes the duel, a 'socially regulated fostering of violence', which spread among the middle class after 1871, as a symbol of the dominance of warrior values and a specific habitus-shaping syndrome (Elias 1996: 19). It was also a symbol of a highly ritualized, hierarchical but unpacified society in which, since duels are private wars, the state had failed to gain a monopoly of the means of violence (1996: 67–8). This was a 'pitiless human habitus' in which anyone who revealed himself as weak counted for nothing (1996: 107). Indeed, 'if one asks how Hitler was possible, one cannot help concluding that the spread of socially sanctioned models of violence and of social inequality are among the prerequisites' (1996: 19).

Elias argues that a peculiar conjuncture of circumstances following the First World War established a decivilizing process. Germany's defeat was unexpected and the terms of the Treaty of Versailles were widely regarded as humiliating. Scheff (2000b: 107ff) argues that the pain of post-war humiliation was lessened by blind rage projected on to Jews. Elias also places emphasis on middle-class resistance to the post-war Weimar Republic, and the escalating double-bind of violence and counter-violence on the streets that ended in Hitler's rise. Unable to establish legitimacy beyond Social Democratic circles, the Weimar Republic was paralysed by economic collapse and terroristic violence. Elias stresses how undermining the German state from within through acts of terror and the systematic use of violence (by Nazis and Communists) has 'not been accorded the significance it deserves' (1996: 220). Into this vacuum, he says, there marched Hitler, a 'gifted shaman' 'with his magical symbol the swastika' who 'invoked the *fata morgana* [mirage] of a superior German Reich' and promised to regain the greatness of Charlemagne's empire (1996: 402). In sum, Elias argues that Nazism happened because Germany had not completed a civilizing process (1996: 299ff), although he also stresses that while these developments are specific to Germany's past, such nationalistic yearnings are far from unique.

This account is important because it focuses on the cultural conditions and habitus from which genocide could emerge. It has been noted (e.g., Moses 1999) that Elias defines civilization as a functional matter of self-control (eating with knives and forks), but it has a normative component, which he develops less. This tension, Moses suggests, is evident in the fact that the Nazis ate with knives and forks and that Himmler, in his infamous Poznań Speech, took pride in the 'decency' of his men, because they had not robbed the Jews they had just shot.[7] In other words, perpetrators could maintain an outwardly 'civilized'

---

[7]This was a speech to 100 SS Group Leaders in Poznań, occupied Poland, on 4 October 1943: 'Most of you know what it means to see a hundred corpses lying together, five

persona in some contexts while organizing mass murder in others, which points back perhaps to the 'ordinariness' of the perpetrators. In an attempt to reconcile this, De Swaan (2001) argues that state-organized violence involves a twofold movement of rationalization-bureaucratization *and* regression, breakdown and barbarism. Following Elias, he argues that this happens as a result of 'disidentification' between ethnic groups along with a campaign to strengthen identifications among the rest of the population, thus creating increased polarization. He describes the result as a 'dyscivilizing' process in which society is compartmentalized into areas – one where 'peaceful' everyday life continues and another, in the camps, where extreme violence is perpetrated against the targeted group. But Elias's own account raises another possibility, where he examines the accounts of soldiers who were active in the Freikorps, especially in the 1919 Baltic campaign where they were fighting the Red Army. Elias reported how recruitment to these units created strong social solidarity in opposition to the rest of society, which seemed 'rotten to the core' and from which they were 'detached outsiders' (1996: 220). Further, he identifies a typical career path from serving in the German army in the First World War, through the Freikorps in 1919, on to conspiratorial terrorist sects and into the Nazi Party (1996: 19). This is not simply a matter of moral neutralization, then, but, on the contrary, of an alternative normative and cultural bonding to a 'higher' warrior caste that was observed in the last chapter among hate groups.

Righteous slaughter and social bonds

We have seen in earlier chapters how Collins argues that in order to commit acts of violence perpetrators must overcome confrontational tension-fear arising from reciprocal social solidarity, which Bauman (1999: 20) describes as 'animal pity'. The extreme power chasm between victims and perpetrators of genocide would be such a mechanism. However, there are also complex issues here of intent, choice, sadism and social bonding. Bauman claims that genocide is explicable because organizations have a functional separation of tasks, distance from consequences, and an authority structure neutralizing moral choice. But in some respects this is wrong. This discussion will argue that genocide is *not* impersonal, proximity does *not* necessarily engender pity, and extreme violence can be a means of social bonding for perpetrators. The idea of bonding through violence was raised in the last chapter in relation to hate groups and in some ways transcends the issue of whether the perpetrators were ideological

---

hundred, or a thousand. To have gone through this and yet … to have remained decent fellows, this is what has made us hard. This is a glorious page in our history that has never been written and shall never be written.'

killers or 'ordinary people'. Those drafted into the ranks of the *Einsazgrouppen* (SS 'special-operation units' that perpetrated mass killings) and the Order Police[8] might not have been committed Nazis, but their commanding officers were, and even the ranks often shared career paths: all the guards at Auschwitz, for example, had previously worked at other camps and been involved in the 'euthanasia project' to systematically kill the mentally ill and those with disabilities (Matthäus 1996). Even so, there were situational dynamics to the mass slaughter that acquired ritual aspects which need to be explained with reference to antisemitic ideology. While Bauman talks about genocide 'effacing the face' (1999: 216), it can also be a form of intimate violence.

Moral neutralization is disputable

Bauman regards the perpetrators as having been morally neutralized by the bureaucracy, but the evidence is, on the contrary, that many were morally committed to genocide. In relation to the 'desk murderers', Healy (1997) says that 'given the nature of what the bureaucracies of Nazi Germany were involved in … the desk murderers knew enough, had enough moral education and awareness, to question their involvement in these "bureaucratic procedures" had they chosen to'.[9] The bureaucracy had, moreover, become highly politicized (Vetlesen 2005: 44). Therefore the role of antisemitism in providing a legitimation for killing is more important than Bauman allows for at least two reasons, both of which were noted in the last chapter. Bauman treats antisemitism as largely incidental to the Nazi system, a symptom of its 'modernity', rather than its prime mover. He regards the genocide as the outcome of a bureaucratic ethically-blind problem-solving process. Shaw, on the other hand, argues that genocide does not always involve the slaughter of the majority of 'the enemy', but can involve limited killings combined with terrorizing and forcible deportation of the population (Shaw 2002: 48). In these terms, the Nazi regime was *already genocidal* by the time of Kristallnacht.

Further, it is questionable whether, as Bauman claims, the Final Solution was the outcome of an ethically-blind search for 'solutions'. It was the Nazi doctor Hans Hefelmann who in 1941 proposed sending Jews to Madagascar. Prior to this he had organized the 'euthanasia' programme that had murdered some 70,000 people, in what Proctor (1988: 117) calls a 'rehearsal for subsequent

---

[8]The Order Police were regular police supposedly separate from the Security Police but from their ranks Police Battalions were established for law enforcement in occupied territories. Some of these were directly involved in mass killings.

[9]A 'desk-murderer' (*Schreibtischtäte*) killed thousands by issuing orders from an office in a Reich Ministry, such as the Interior Ministry or Reich Ministry for the Occupied Eastern Territories.

genocide'. As a defendant in the 1964 Frankfurt Euthanasia Trial, Hefelmann said 'I have never been in doubt that legally and in matters of humanity I acted correctly' (*De Zeit* 1964). Another doctor, Viktor Brack, who had advocated sterilizing rather than killing 2–3 million Jewish men who were capable of work, claimed at his trial in Nuremburg that by 1941 it had been an 'open secret' in higher party circles that leaders planned the extermination of all Jews and he and Hefelmann proposed different 'solutions' (Proctor 1988: 200). In other words, genocide was already occurring and being planned *before* the airing of these 'alternatives'. We might also note that these were doctors, not bureaucrats, who, like Mengele and many other professionals 'of high standing', performed 'experiments' on camp prisoners (Proctor 1988: 220). They were committed to the Nazi project, aware of its consequences, and were not simply in an agentic state.

In explaining this, many writers point to the centrality of ideology, and especially antisemitism. There are two questions here: Was antisemitism 'new'? And was it central to the perpetrators' motives? In relation to both of these questions, Furet (1999: 188) claims that:

> Hatred of Jews ... was nothing new in European history. In its many forms it was inseparable from the Christian Middle Ages, from the age of absolute monarchy, and even from the so-called 'emancipation' period. It resurfaced widely at the end of the nineteenth century, notably in the Vienna of Hitler's youth. The author of *Mein Kampf* had no need to search deeply in his memory in order to come up with portraits of plutocratic Jews, defined exclusively by their wealth, strangers to the state, parasites of collective labour, scapegoats of the Right and the Left. He had only to add a new role, that of Bolshevik agents. Whereas the pre-1914 Jews were bourgeois or socialist, postwar Jews were also Communist. In that role, they offered the unique advantage of incarnating both capitalism and Communism, liberalism and its negation. Through money, the Jews decomposed societies and nations; in Bolshevik guise, they threatened their very existence. Jews personified the two enemies of National Socialism – the bourgeois and the Bolshevik. ... Hitler's anti-Semitism ... constituted the core of the Nazi political prophecy, without which it would have lost all direction.

The centrality of antisemitism as the motive for genocide is the theme of Goldhagen's (1997) controversial study.[10] For Goldhagen, it was eliminationist antisemitism (which, like Bauman and Elias, he dates from the late nineteenth century) that moved many thousands of 'ordinary Germans' to willingly slaughter Jews. He discounts explanations in terms of compulsion, following orders, social psychological pressure, petty bureaucratic careerism, and fragmentation of tasks (1997: 12). His explanation is, on the contrary, simple – the

---

[10]The full controversy will not be addressed here but see Kamber (2000) for a good discussion.

killers held the death of their victims desirable.[11] Even if one accepts the functionalist account of 'failed solutions' to the 'Jewish problem' by subordinates, eliminationist antisemitism could still explain how ordinary Germans became 'willing executioners' (Kamber 2000) since it was this that defined the goal of making Europe *Judenfrei* and legitimated the means. He attempts to show that perpetrators were often routinely offered the choice as to whether to participate, which also is claimed by Browning's (1998) study of the reserve Police Battalion 101 in Poland. 'The perpetrators were not coerced to kill', Goldhagen claims, 'Never in the history of the Holocaust was a German ever killed, sent to concentration camp, jailed, or punished in any serious way for refusing to kill Jews. It never happened. Sometimes, such as on the death marches, the SS continued to kill when ordered not to' (Goldhagen et al. 2001:7). Kamber (2000) describes zeal, cruelty and celebratory attitudes in excess of orders, motivated by the belief that Jews and other enemies of the Reich were dangerous and demonic. Many sources confirm that only a few who were ordered to kill in the East refused (e.g., Matthäus 1996).

Genocide is not instrumental in the way Bauman suggests, but rather is expressive violence. Primo Levi (1988: 83ff) describes the Holocaust as 'useless violence' – the deliberate creation of pain and humiliation as ends in themselves. For example, the violence of the registration number tattooed on the forearm of Auschwitz prisoners was gratuitous, an end in itself that 'wrote the sentence in the inmates' flesh' and was all the more humiliating for Orthodox Jews for whom tattooing is prohibited (Leviticus 19: 28). Further, Levi asks why, during the furious round ups in all cities and villages, they 'violate houses of the dying' and force those already dying from infirmity on to the transports? Because, he says, the 'best choice' was the one that entailed the 'greatest amount of affliction' and suffering – the 'enemy must not only die but die in torment' (1988: 96). Further, there was dramaturgical display in the killing, suggestive of Katz's concept of righteous slaughter. Vetlesen says that the SS were 'always on show and dressed to kill', with immaculate presentation, which contrasted with the squalor of arrivals on the transports (and the nakedness of the victims of mass shooting). Thus, technical skill and theatrical showing off were blended to produce gratification for the performer which Katz described as the 'sensual magic' of 'genuinely experiential creativity' (Vetlesen 2005: 38). Similarly, in relation to the 1994 genocide of Tutsis in Rwanda, Dudai (2006) describes how knowledge of their victims' suffering was important to the perpetrators. So babies were 'killed more quickly, because their suffering was of no

---

[11]Goldhagen et al. (2001:1) argues that in relation to other genocide, such as that in former Yugoslavia, Rwanda, Armenia or Cambodia, no one doubts that the killers held the death of the victims to be desirable and just. Yet this claim is controversial in relation to the perpetrators of the Holocaust.

use' whereas adults who would anticipate their deaths were subjected to prolonged torture. The *jouissance* of cruelty requires reciprocal understanding between victim and perpetrator (Wieviorka 2009: 129).

Proximity and intimacy

Bauman regards proximity as engendering pity as opposed to the morally neutralizing effects of distance and anonymity. But evildoing *thrives* on proximity rather than distance. Bureaucracy dehumanizes but this is not a condition for this kind of mass brutality, where the victim *must* be recognized as human. The victims of the Holocaust were in a sense not anonymous but were also 'known' as a stigmatized racially Other – as degenerates and scheming enemies – and crucial to the perpetrator's logic was the belief that 'we know about these people'. Killing often involved close proximity. Goldhagen does not refer directly to Bauman (or Elias), but argues that 'to present mere clinical descriptions of killing operations is to misrepresent the phenomenology of killing, to eviscerate the emotional components of the acts'. Proper description must convey the horror and gruesomeness of events – 'blood, bone and brains flying about often landing on the killers. ... Cries and wails of people awaiting their imminent slaughter', including thousands of children (1997: 22; cf. Matthäus 1996). Goldhagen describes the mass shooting of the Jews of Józefów (southern Poland) by Police Battalion 101 of the Order Police in 1942, where the soldiers (who had been given the choice by their commanding officer of being excused from the detail) marched their victims into the wood. Some of them had children walking beside them. He imagines the soldier and a small girl:

> In these moments, each killer had a personalized, face-to-face relationship to his victim, to his little girl. Did he see a little girl, and ask himself why he was about to kill this little, delicate human being who, if seen as a little girl by him, would normally have received his compassion, protection, and nurturance? Or did he see a Jew, a young one, but a Jew nonetheless? Did he wonder incredulously what could possibly justify his blowing a vulnerable little girl's brains out? Or did he understand the reasonableness of the order, the necessity of nipping the believed-in Jewish blight in the bud? The 'Jew-child', after all, was mother to the Jew. The killing itself was a gruesome affair. (Goldhagen 1997: 218)

Shootings involved a high degree of contact between executioner and victim and there were intense contacts with the local population, including Jews (Matthäus 1996). Again, the commandant of Sobibor and Treblinka, Franz Stangl, 'understood his victims were humans' and loathed Jews – so the killings were never as factory-like as Bauman suggests, a view that 'projects sociological categories onto reality' (Vetlesen 2005: 34).

In civil wars, ethnic violence and genocide, the body is the site of horrifying acts of what Appadurai (1998) calls 'vivisectionist violence'. Rather than see genocide as impersonal, it is better understood as *intimately* violent politics of the body. A community that has often shared social spaces and had habitual interactions with the majority for centuries becomes 'unimaginable', frequently following state-initiated segregation and exclusion. This is not only physical segregation, but also a symbolic division of purity (a particular obsession of the Nazis) and deception. The stigmatized group is accused in state propaganda of treachery, betrayal, secrecy and conspiratorial cabals with the enemy, which were typical antisemitic myths. As Bauman and others have noted, in a context of increasing assimilation in the later nineteenth century, where one no longer necessarily 'knew' who the Jews were, racist antisemitism attempted to identify the Jews through embodied 'racial characteristics'. These were illustrated in the Nazis' cranial and facial measurements to determine who was really 'Aryan' and who was not. Appadurai (1998) suggests that brutality perpetrated by ordinary persons is culturally formed as the body becomes a 'necrographic map' of intimate brutality. 'Fake identities', he says, 'seem to demand the brutal creation of real persons through violence'. The restoration of purity involves not just killing, but symbolic opening of the body, hence his description of the violence as 'vivisection'. For example, the ethnic violence in Burundi against Hutus in 1972 involved 'nightmarish cruelty', including women killed with sharp bamboo sticks inserted in the vagina, anus and head (Appadurai 1998).[12] The frequent use of rape as a weapon of war is a further example, in which the penis is an instrument of degradation, of 'grotesque intimacy' and the enactment of ethno-patriarchal power. Victims are often beaten and physically mutilated and gruesome acts are often carried out in front of other family members. There have also been many instances of brutal rape among those who are pregnant which mostly end in miscarriages (Clifford 2008).

Jan Gross's study (2002) of the Jedwabne massacre is an example of ritualized extreme violence perpetrated by 'neighbours'. On 23 June 1941 the Germans entered Jedwabne (in north-west Poland) which had previously been under Soviet occupation. In the first attack on the local Jewish population on 25 June, local residents, in a band playing flutes, walked from house to house killing several Jewish residents. This was done with brutality. 'Krawiecki they knifed and then plucked his eyes and cut off his tongue. He suffered terribly for 12 hours before he gave up his soul' (2002: 3). The full assault occurred on 10 July when, following a meeting with the Gestapo, local Poles armed with axes and nail-studied clubs rounded up most of the remaining Jewish population of around 1,600 people. They were forced to dig pits for mass graves, perform

---

[12]This ethnic violence perpetrated by Tutsi militias was part of the context for the subsequent Rwandan genocide of Tutsis by Hutus in 1994.

ridiculous gymnastics and were then killed with knives and clubs (2002: 60ff). Prior to extremely brutal deaths there were rituals of humiliation, such as forcing a group led by the Rabbi to demolish and carry round the town a statue of Lenin. Violence continued to be done to the bodies after death. But 1,600 could not be killed quickly and those Jedwabne Jews still alive at the end of the day were then locked in a barn and burned alive.

Gross disputes the 'modernity' of the Holocaust, arguing that 'while it is clear that to kill millions of people an efficient bureaucracy is needed along with advanced technology' (2002: 80–1), it was also archaic. The residents of Jedwabne had not had time to soak up Nazi propaganda and used primitive, ancient methods and murder weapons – stones, wooden clubs, iron bars and fire and water. His account further illustrates the complexity of distinctions between 'perpetrators-victims-bystanders' since 'each episode of mass killing had its own situational dynamics' (Gross 2001: 12–13). This was more akin to the Rwanda genocide in that the killing was proximate and legitimated by supposed revenge. Invoking the myth of the *Żydokomuna* (Jewish Bolshevik) as the main force behind Communism, the Jedwabne Jews were accused of having collaborated with the Soviet occupation. The belief that Jews were 'behind' the Communists was itself a part of modern antisemitism.[13] But Zylinska (2007: 288) suggests that the Jedwabne murders were a ritualized 'semireligious ceremony' – a kind of sacrificial offering to the Germans guided by a desire for pacification, a view which has resonance with Girard's 'sacred violence' (Girard 1977). Having been murdered, the scapegoat becomes a holy healing agent, while the fact of the murder is repressed, as it was for a long time.[14] There are again echoes of Katz's 'righteous slaughter' – that is, murder committed between people who know each other where the perpetrator displays 'transcendent rage' expressive of their conviction of moral superiority and the worthlessness of their victims.

This phenomenon was replicated in the social order of the camps. Bauman (1999: 142–9) finds further evidence of 'rationality' in the system's ability to recruit the cooperation of its victims in the ghetto *Judenrät* (Jewish councils), whom he regards as motivated by rational self-preservation. He might have added that in the camps there were the *Kapos* (prisoners who worked in

---

[13]This long predates the development of twentieth-century socialism, appearing first in Julian Ursyn Niemcewicz's 1819 dystopic fantasy *Rok 3333* [The Year 3333], in which a future socialist society is run by Jews.

[14]Gross's *Neighbors* (2002) and later *Fear* (2006), which documented how Jewish survivors returning to Polish hometowns after the war experienced widespread violence, including murder, at the hands of their neighbours, provoked major controversies in Poland over history, memory and guilt. See, for example, Glowacka and Zylinska (2007) and Polonsky and Michlic (2003).

administrative positions) and the *Sonderkommandos* (special units of prisoners forced to remove and process bodies from the gas chambers). However, for Primo Levi (1988: 22–51), within this 'grey zone' the lines of guilt and responsibility were unclear and prisoners who took these positions had various motives – self-preservation certainly, but also sadism, social elevation and imitation of the victors. Levi also says the camps were an 'indecipherable world of ritual humiliation' that began with arrival, when inmates would be screamed at, stripped naked, shaved, dressed in rags, beaten and then inserted within a world that reproduced the ritual hierarchical order of the totalitarian state. It would be superficial to reduce actions in this context to 'rational self-interest'.

Social bonds

Goldhagen's thesis is important but is open to many criticisms. His thesis is not as original as he suggests and it was already known that many 'ordinary' Germans were 'willing' and cruel 'executioners'. It assumes that a disposition to act (eliminationist antisemitism) was necessarily followed by action (genocide). But Goldhagen (1997: 70) acknowledges that there were possible functional equivalents to elimination – 'total assimilation', 'verbal assault', 'legal restraints', 'physical assault', 'physical separation in ghettos', 'forcible and violent expulsion'. The racist disposition alone, then, cannot explain the genocidal outcome. Whatever 'ordinary Germans' knew, the Holocaust was kept secret or referred to in euphemisms and as Germany faced defeat the SS attempted to conceal it by sending prisoners on death marches and destroying gas chambers. Antisemitism was not the sole source of their actions, since they also killed millions of Russian prisoners of war, Slavs, Gypsies and homosexuals (Browning 1998; Fine and Turner 2000; Kamber 2000). Evidence of the biographies of known perpetrators questions the idea of the 'ordinariness' of many perpetrators. Mann analysed the careers of 1,581 convicted war criminals and found some typical features. High percentages were ethnic Germans from the 'lost territories', such as Sudetenland, rather than Germany itself. The career of Höss, the Commandant of Auschwitz, was typical. He went from teenage volunteer in the First World War to Freikorps action in the Baltics, joined the Nazi Party in 1922 and the SS in 1934. It is difficult to picture him as an 'ordinary manager' (Mann 2000). Intentionality and motives are complex and any general precondition – whether 'modernity' or 'antisemitism' – does not, as Healy (1997) says, distinguish those who *might* from those who *did*. People's actions and moral choices reproduce wider systems which in turn structure subsequent choices. Kamber (2000) says (and this was also noted in the last chapter) that racist motivation might be a *consequence* as much as a cause of involvement in racist organizations and, likewise, cruelty is a way of *producing* degeneration.

The visibly degraded victim might stimulate an even more fervent conviction among persecutors of their degeneracy, so that, similar to domestic violence perhaps, the cruelty becomes more intense the 'weaker' and more submissive is the victim.

The dynamics of genocide, then, are more complex than in Goldhagen's account, although antisemitism was crucial and underpinned social bonds, authorizing perpetrators to commit extreme acts of violence to restore 'purity' to the social body. There is evidence that genocidal killers can be united in a blood bond of murder which must be kept secret. In his review of literature on the Rwanda genocide, Dudai (2006) describes a 'carnivality of evil' and quotes perpetrators who talked of killers as 'marching choirs' and that the 'blast of music never stopped'. After each day's 'cutting', they ate, drank as much as they wanted and celebrated while becoming crueller with increased practice in killing. There was 'unity and comradeship' among the *genocidairs*, who said 'we helped our patriotic brothers', so if one did not feel up to the killing others would take over until 'his bravery returned'. Similarly, in Police Battalion 101, many claimed that had they excused themselves from the shooting they would have 'lost face' and let down their comrades (Browning 1998: 72–3). By contrast with Goldhagen, the post-war interrogations that form the basis of Browning's study do not reveal overt expressions of antisemitism. Rather, Browning notes that the Battalion members' standing among comrades overrode any empathy with their victims, whom they had accepted were 'the enemy' and 'stood outside their circle of human obligation and responsibility' (1998: 73). This was underlined by the commanding officer, Major Trapp, who though expressing distaste for the Józefóv killing, claimed that the Jews were assisting local partisans (1998: 2). Further, Alford (1997) suggests that violating a taboo may be experienced as thrilling, a transgression of the most sacred boundaries, especially when the taboo runs deep, not just against the murder of individuals but the extermination of a people.[15] In the brutal intimacy of comradeship there was also a narcissistic bond of victimhood. Reference to the *Judenaktion* was taboo among the policemen, but 'repression could not stop the nightmares' (Browning 1998: 69). Then the perpetrators came to view themselves as victims ('how awful it is for us to have had to do these things') who, like the addressees of Himmler's Poznań speech, reassured themselves that they remained 'decent

---

[15]Alford (1997) also offers a different interpretation of the Milgram experiment and asks what if the subjects *enjoyed* giving shocks, for which the experiment had given them permission. 'If you look at the films [of the experiment] long enough you will be struck by … the grotesque laughter, the giggling fits at the shock generator'. This is speculative and these could equally be shame cues or symptoms of acute stress. It is still likely, though, that for some, *permission* to engage in mass murder allowed expression of sadistic 'guilty pleasure'.

fellows'. This self-image was enhanced by occasional acts of 'mercy', such as one 10 year-old girl whom Trapp allowed to live (Browning 1998: 69).

Conclusion

The Holocaust was extremely complex and multifaceted and the different accounts here reflect this. Bauman's thesis was based largely on the 'factory-like' mass killing in the camps and the detachment of bureaucratic 'desk murderers', while Goldhagen and Browning, focus on mass shooting, albeit with different conclusions. Even so, I have argued that the modernity thesis is flawed in several ways. In particular, it is based on a one-sided understanding of 'modernity' and instrumentality and generalizes from the specific conditions of a decivilizational process in Germany, to a condition of (heavy) modernity *per se*. Modernity is anyway an abstraction and does not 'do' anything. The central issue here is to attempt to understand the social conditions for genocide, which, I have argued, Bauman does not do adequately. His notion of moral neutralization through bureaucratic distance simplifies the much more complex dynamics of intention, ritual, denial and normativity, including the moral ambiguities of what Levi calls 'the grey zone'. Genocide in the Holocaust and again more recently is not remote but rather involves proximity and a grotesque intimacy, along with the passionate intensity of Katz's righteous slaughter. This was not only the case (as it clearly was) in Józefów and Jedwabne, but the mass murder in the camps also involved many forms of direct contact with the damned and the dead – the *Sonderkommandos*, after all, dealt intimately with the victims' bodies.

Most of the discussion of violence in this book has focused on interpersonal violence, which has been framed largely through a macro social-theoretical analysis. At several points, including the discussion of hate crime in the last chapter, I drew attention to two dominant understandings of violence. On the one hand, institutional anomie theory emphasizes the importance of the strain between cultural values and institutional means, particularly with reference to market-driven social dislocation. This is what Vetlesen (2005: 105) calls the 'falling away from the good', where violence enters the spaces vacated by institutional governance, legality, civic trust and legitimate power. On the other hand, I argued in relation to hate groups that violence can be embedded in and solidify social bonds. In the present context, the two are compatible since while genocide occurs in what could be described as conditions of 'social strain', the transgression of deep taboos can also solidify social bonds. As Elias argues, a decivilizing process re-establishes the habitus of the warrior ethos but, further, in response to social crisis this spills over into ritual sacrifice. As Girard (1977) suggests, the surrogate victim is the carrier of all the 'subversive' elements in society – so Jews embodied 'threats' of communism, international capitalism, social decay, conspiracies, wild sexuality and so on. The victims satisfied two conditions for the scapegoat – they must be unable to take revenge and must be silenced, since, if heard, they might evoke sympathy (Praeg 2007: 43). The killings attempted to abolish violence and chaos and purify the social bond. This is in some ways unsettling for both Bauman and Elias since, for each, mass violence involves disidentification with the victim. For Bauman this is an outcome of civilization, but for Elias of decivilization. Genocide, on the contrary, involves a grotesque identification with the victim and pursuit of solidarity.

CONCLUSION

Violence is ubiquitous in human societies and lies deep in human history. This has prompted debate over many centuries as to whether violence, or at least aggression, is innate in the human condition. Hobbes famously formulated the view that, in a natural state, life was nasty, brutish and short, while other philosophers, on the contrary, viewed humans as naturally social and solidaristic. This debate has continued into the contemporary social and natural sciences. Some archaeological anthropologists and evolutionary psychologists argue that a predilection for violence has been selected into human social development and has its origins in the hunting practices and survival needs of pre-human hominids. Their conclusion is not that we should be complacent about aggression and violence in modern social life but that we need to recognize its deep roots in human evolution. On the other hand, and not denying that signs of violence lie deep in the archaeological record, a different view of the role of violence in human societies can be derived from prehistory. There is evidence for a disjuncture between pre-human uses of violence and its emergence within more recent post-Neolithic and state societies that suggests a close link between social distance, violence and hierarchy. According to this view, evidence of violence in early societies increases with the shift from relatively egalitarian non-state societies to complex hierarchically organized social systems. Further, the claim that there is a continuous link between pre-human and human life does not pay sufficient attention to the importance of symbolic communication, multiple role taking and the complex role of emotions in human social organization. Developing social and psychological inhibitions to aggression was probably critical to the survival of early humans, which required the capacity for complex cooperation in a highly precarious environment. Randall Collins (2008) has persuasively argued that 'violence is difficult' and humans are 'hard wired for solidarity' so the sociological problem is to understand the situational dynamics in which these inhibitions are overcome. Further, like all other human behaviour, violence takes place within systems of power and meaning, and to see violence as the product of biology ignores its social and cultural significance. Rather than see violence as an outlet of primal desire, it is better understood as innovative behaviour in which the capacities for human development of ritual cruelty (such as the Roman Arena) reflect a particularly human capacity for innovation. Violence has a symbolic and ritual character that, as Bowman (2001: 25) says, 'not only manifests itself in the destruction of boundaries but as well in their creation'.

However, the innate/socially learned polarity that has structured much debate about violence is too simple and does not pay enough attention to the ways in which violence is complexly related to social organization. The discussion here has developed a dialogue with Elias, who stands out as the social theorist for whom violence (or its pacification really) occupies a central place in an historical conception of social development. Elias's work is important here, first and foremost, in historicizing the social processes that give rise to a habitus of constraint and the formation of the state, whose control over the means of violence established spaces of 'pacification'. His thesis is also important because in mainstream social theory, which has focused on social formation *within* pacified spaces, there has been widespread avoidance of theorizing violence. Elias weaves together an account of the intersection of historical social development and interpersonal psychosocial formation in a way rarely equalled in social theory. His work avoids ahistorical and timeless comparisons between violence in very different societies, while the civilizing thesis opens up ways of thinking about violence and its macrosocial historical context. However, this is not in the end sufficiently focused or nuanced, at least not for the purposes of this analysis, and actually says relatively little about violence in itself. While there is evidence for a long-term trend towards a reduction in interpersonal violence that accompanied the modernization process (although this is hardly true of inter-state violence), there are also many counter-cyclical trends that can occur both over time and simultaneously. While he (and then his followers) have developed the concept of 'decivilization' to account for reversals in the civilizing process, a concept that certainly has value, this does not necessarily grasp the multifaceted complexities of these processes. This is in part because of the spatial distribution of violence, such that violence does not occur in 'society in general' but is highly socially differentiated by geographical space. As we saw in the analysis of homicide, the overall rates at a societal level are highly polarized into a few urban areas where there are high levels of lethal violence as opposed to many areas where there are not. This is true of many other types of violent crime too. While according to crime surveys, overall rates of crime, and especially violent crime, have been falling in many developed societies over the past two decades, homicides have followed different trends – rising in the UK though falling in the USA, for example. These manifold trends and patterns require more differentiated modes of analysis than the dichotomy civilizing/decivilizing allows, and accounts here of specific topics, such as violent crime, domestic violence and hate crime, have attempted to develop multilayered theoretical models. In other words, Elias enables us to pose some questions about violence and macrosocial historical processes, but does not offer a theory that might account for specific differences in patterns and trends, nor was this necessarily his intention.

This leads to a further limitation of Elias, which is his relative neglect of political economy. Although Elias has a concept of the spatial organization of cultural and economic interdependencies (figurations), this theory does not take account of the potentially decivilizational consequences of the spatial organization of capital. The discussions of the spaces of violence (Chapter 4), of domestic violence (Chapter 6) and homicides (Chapter 7) showed that patterns of known violent crime correspond to locations of high deprivation and inequality. These in turn coincide with the 1980–90s spatial restructuring of global capital and its aftermath in the 2000s. As Bourdieu (1998) argues, there is a relationship between this kind of structural violence and major acts of everyday violence in spaces of neoliberal abandonment. The analysis here suggests that space is a crucial site where socioeconomic processes are realized and structured. Certain spaces constitute complex patterns of social relationships that persist over time, in which violence is more likely to occur than elsewhere. Even so, while the relationship between deprivation and violent crime is well established in an extensive literature, we cannot simply read off the behaviour and meanings of actors from objective data such as unemployment and deprivation. The relationships between these factors are highly mediated by degrees of social cohesion (such as 'neighbouring') and the way in which social space is used, as routine activities theory suggests. But this still does not really explain the particular motivational patterns of violent actors. I have argued that a theory of violence needs, in addition, to understand the dynamics of the humiliation of class segmentation in a context where everyone has access to cultural ideals of a good life of high consumption.

This, in turn, relates to another theme in this book. There is evidence for the central role of shame in human psychosocial development. Elias too pointed to the importance of shame in the changing concepts of the body and the divisions of public and private that underpinned increasingly mannered norms of social interaction. But shame is double-edged. Shame both constrains behaviour that violates norms (in anticipation of the negative judgements of significant others), but the experience of shame is also a source of humiliation. Paradoxically, the very emotions that ferment social bonds might also underpin violent behaviour because of the way we repress humiliation, and as Scheff (2000b: 107) puts it, would rather 'turn the world upside down than turn [ourselves] inside out'. This metaphor might also illuminate 'vivisectionist violence', outlined in Chapter 9, where the body of the victim is opened in a symbolic purification of the social bond. There is a large amount of research from within the shame paradigm. This has the advantage again of focusing on the intersection of large-scale processes and transformations and the ways in which these enter the everyday life experiences of actors. However, this process needs to be further theoretically elaborated in terms of the relationships between hierarchy, formality and honour.

It has been argued here that modernization involved a transition from societies with formal, hierarchical cultures of honour to more anonymous legal and rights-based regulation that allowed increasing informalization and egalitarianism. One important condition for this is the legitimacy of the state across the class system, since (following Cooney, 1997) where the law is unavailable to disputants, because its agents are either too high or too low in social status, then feuding, brawling, seizing and killing as ways of resolving conflicts are likely to be common. However, this contrast can be found both diachronically (as Elias and Cooney suggest) and synchronically, within the same society. This is partly because equality of aspirations, weakening class and other hierarchies and cultural informalization can also increase the potential for resentment of social difference. Moreover, informality increases the risk of status competition, as Gould (2003) suggested, since informality can reduce shame thresholds and thereby increase the potential for shame-based conflict, especially in locations of dispossession and marginalization. Hence, in otherwise 'pacified' societies, one finds enclaves of cultures of honour and retribution with high levels of violence, including honour killing, gang murders and drug wars, beyond the reach of the legal state. Where spatial structuring of inequalities is further manifest in visible and ascribed characteristics, notably of race, as Messner (1989) argued, the potential for violence is further exacerbated. In this way, we can begin to develop a view of how the complex dynamics of social differentiation and inequality can impact on the availability of violence as a resource in everyday life.

Further, I have suggested that theories of violence, especially those that focus on interpersonal violence, are characterized by two dominant understandings. On the one hand, institutional anomie theory emphasizes the importance of strain between cultural values and institutional means, with reference particularly to market-driven social dislocation. This is not specifically a theory of violence, but predicts that in conditions of 'strain', combined with high commodification and weak social welfare, serious interpersonal violence will be higher than in conditions of 'cooperative individualism' (Thome 2007). Then violence enters the spaces vacated by institutional governance, legality, civic trust and legitimate power. On the other hand, and especially in relation to collective violence, it is possible to see violence as embedded in and solidifying social bonds. The latter view further resonates with Girard's (1977) theory of the scapegoat mechanism and the way (in his view) all original social order was based on the resolution of violent chaos through killing the scapegoat, whose murder is then re-enacted in sacred rituals. One does not have to accept this thesis in its entirety (or the Christian theological dimension that became central in Girard's later work) to recognize that violence against those who become symbolic substitutes for a community's inner and unacknowledged humiliation and conflict is a medium of social bonding. One can see this happening at the level of families, small groups and whole societies especially, again as Girard suggests, at points of crisis. In these terms, violence does not come from 'outside' necessarily but, as Bowman (2001) argues, is fundamental to forming boundaries and identities. Further, the enacting of violence in the very act of breaking taboos, which elevates perpetrators from everyday morality, can further establish exclusive social bonds. In Chapter 8 on racist and hate crime, it was suggested that racist and other difference-based violence summons up deeply embedded notions of the 'normal body' and its placing in space, which are linked to socioeconomic structures of masculinity and locality. The two points of view – violence as a falling away from the good through social dislocation and violence as a medium of cementing the social bond – are not of course incompatible. The structural processes of strain and dislocation have effects on patterns of cultural identification and, as Katz (1988) and others argue, extreme violence is often on both individual and collective levels an act of morality, of the righteous defence of 'the good'. Again in relation to racist crime, it was argued that offenders act within complex determinants and the risk of offending is high in conditions of deprivation and residential segregation, combined with street cultures of unfulfilled masculine expectations. It was seen that prejudices held by peer groups will underpin violence in combination with disinhibiting factors such as a perception of community 'under threat'. The goal of 'peace' in this context, that is pursuit of 'the good', can invoke an imaginary community from which degenerate or traitorous elements must be expelled, which is the script for ethno-national violence and genocide.

These processes were illustrated in a number of substantive discussions in which several different levels intersect. The social construction and performance of masculinities are central to understanding violence. The theory of hegemonic masculinities has shown how gender is performative, but in ways structured by class, social position and age. In Chapter 5, I argued that there is not *a* hegemonic masculinity, but rather multiple articulations of oppositional and embodied masculinities. These have been shaped by global economic restructuring and its interaction with local cultures of work and masculinity, which in combination with biographical and situational factors underlie transgressive thrill and risk seeking. This of course can take the form of both legitimate and illicit thrills. So sport can be both a medium for legitimate thrills (as Elias agued) but also a focus for violent posturing that deploys cultural resources for gendered and racialized identities. In this context, there is debate as to whether contemporary male youth violence is the result of a general decivilizational process (as Dunning (1999) suggests), although I argued that this is an outcome of reasserting a 'hyper-masculine' status, a context of social marginalization in which there are few routes into legitimate society.

Masculinities are central to understanding the performance of violence, while intimate partner violence (IPV) goes to the essence of interpersonal violence.

The increasing self-regulation of conduct in public has a reverse side – the increasing relative occurrence of violence in intimate life. The argument in Chapter 6 addressed the role of gendered inequality on several dimensions – the relative economic powerlessness of women in many locations, the way hegemonic masculinities provide legitimation for the exercise of power and control in intimate relations, and the 'right' to exercise violence. However, rather than view IPV only as an outcome of male power, this model attempts to bridge another literature and addresses the intra-psychic dynamics of trauma and shame in forming violence-prone personalities. It further locates domestic violence within a wider context of structural-spatial inequalities and tentatively proposes a nested ecological model of intimate violence on which there is again a need for further analysis. Patriarchal terroristic violence might partly be a response to the erosion of patriarchal power through informalization and det-raditionalization of the family, but this too is socially patterned. While IPV, as many point out, is prevalent in all social locations, its *risk*, as with other forms of violence, has a distinct pattern of spatial and social-class distribution. The distribution of domestic violence might best be approached though a spatial model that mediates among factors of personality, social context, socioeconomic location, and wider cultures. Again, this analysis aims to integrate cultural and economic with socio-spatial and structural explanations.

The intimacy of violence is its essence. Violence involves multiple violations of the body, privacy, normality, trust and social reciprocity. But in so doing it violates the impersonality of modern life, which Goffman (1983) called 'civic dissatention'. That is, in public places we disengage from other anonymous people who are in one's shared space. But Goffman (1983) added that so doing 'presupposes the benign intent of the other's appearance and manner', and that normalcy is a fragile façade, which the assailant threatens to shatter. Thus, there 'are enablements and risks inherent in co-bodily presence', which include physical assault, sexual molestation, robbery and obstruction of movement, and breaches of psychic reserves. These risks and vulnerabilities, he adds, are structured on lines of gender and race. This further enables us to see violence not as impersonal (even where perpetrator and victim are unknown to one another) but as intimate, a violation of the body and social distance.

The final discussion of the Holocaust (Chapter 9) took a different turn from earlier analysis and focused on Bauman's modernity thesis. Apart from being a (somewhat covert) critique of the civilizational thesis, Bauman raised the critical question of the relationship between genocide and modernity and in what circumstances 'ordinary people' might perform extraordinarily horrific acts. Bauman's thesis was criticized on several counts, not least because his claim that 'factory-like' mass killing involved bureaucratic moral detachment simplifies the much more complex dynamics of responsibility, ritual violence and purification of the social. In particular, he understood mass murder as 'faceless' and impersonal. But, on the contrary, genocide is intimacy, a grotesque intimacy that is at the core of violence. It is never 'impersonal'. Genocide is not remote, but rather involves proximity along with the passionate intensity of Katz's righteous slaughter. The Holocaust aimed to abolish violence and chaos, for which Jews were scapegoats, and purify the social bond. A similar logic can be identified in the Rwanda genocide. As I suggest at the end of Chapter 9, this is in some ways unsettling for both Bauman and Elias since they both regard mass violence as involving an absence of identification with the victim. For Bauman, this arises as an outcome of bureaucratic civilization, while for Elias it is a consequence of a decivilizational downswing. But genocide involves intimate dealings with the body – mutilation (often genital), rape, writing on the body (tattoos, for example), the visceral experience of blood and brains – and knowledge and pleasure in the victims' suffering.

Against a background of optimism following the end of the Cold War, the journalist Robert Kaplan warned that the emerging world order would not be one of peaceful development but rather of failing nation states, regional wars, terrorism, worldwide demographic, environmental, and societal stress, in which criminal anarchy and wars over water, cropland, forests, and food create a 'jagged-glass pattern of city-states, shanty-states, nebulous and anarchic regionalisms' (Kaplan 1994). The military stand-off of the Cold War had ensured that the effects of regional conflicts were contained, but in the absence of this restraint the world would become even more violent and insecure. One might find confirmation for his prediction in events such as the Rwandan genocide, the Yugoslavian civil wars, 9/11 and the consequent rise in global conflict, along with persistent intractable regional conflicts such as Israel/Palestine. But this warning was exaggerated since the two decades following the end of the Cold War were marked by fewer armed conflicts and generally declining rates of violent crime in many parts of the world. Further, there is continuing evidence of rising thresholds of repugnance towards violence – governments do not necessarily gain public support for involvement in regional wars, many forms of institutionalized violence, such as corporal and capital punishment, have been abolished in Europe, the everyday violences in families are increasingly placed under public scrutiny and intervention, and there is increased awareness of and compassion towards the suffering of strangers. Even so, a theme in this book has been how violence is spatially differentiated and linked to multiple inequalities both within nations and globally. The effects of current global crises and governmental responses to them will intensify these inequalities and increase the prospects of realizing Kaplan's prophecy. The alternative is to better understand the sources of human violence and struggle for a less unjust society.

BIBLIOGRAPHY

Abbink, J. (2000) 'Preface: violation and violence as a cultural phenomenon', in G. Aijmer and J. Abbink (eds), *Meanings of Violence: A Cross-Cultural Perspective*. Oxford: Berg, pp. xi–xvii.

Adorno, T.W. (1974) *Minima Moralia*. London: Verso.

Adorno, T.W. and Horkheimer, M. (1973) *Dialectic of Enlightenment*. London: New Left Books. (First published 1944.)

Adorno, T.W., Frenkel-Brunswik, E., Levinson, D.J. and Sanford, R.N. (1950) *The Authoritarian Personality*. New York: Harper & Row.

Aijmer, G. (2000) 'Introduction: the idiom of violence in imagery and discourse', in G. Aijmer and J. Abbink (eds), *Meanings of Violence: A Cross-Cultural Perspective*. Oxford: Berg, pp. 1–22.

Alder, C. (1991) 'Explaining violence: socioeconomics and masculinity', in D. Chappell, P. Grabosky and H. Strang (eds), *Australian Violence: Contemporary Perspectives*. Canberra: Australian Institute of Criminology.

Alford, C. F. (1997) 'Hitler's willing executioners: what does "willing" mean?', *Theory and Society*, 26: 719–38.

Alford, C.F. (1998) 'Freud and violence', in A. Elliott (ed.), *Freud 2000*. Cambridge: Polity Press, pp. 61–87.

Anahita, S. (2006) 'Blogging the border: virtual skinheads, hypermasculinity, and heteronormativity', *Journal of Political and Military Sociology*, 34 (1): 144–64.

Anderson, E. (2008) '"I used to think women were weak": orthodox masculinity, gender segregation, and sport', *Sociological Forum*, 23 (2): 257–80.

Anderson, K. and Umberson, D. (2001) 'Gendering violence: masculinity and power in men's accounts of domestic violence', *Gender and Society*, 15: 358–80.

Andrejevic, M. (2003) *Reality TV: The Work of Being Watched*. Lanham, MD: Rowman & Littlefield.

Appadurai, A. (1998) 'Dead certainty: ethnic violence in the era of globalization', *Public Culture*, 10 (2): 225–47.

Araghi, F.A. (2000) 'The great global enclosure of our times', in F. Magdoff, B. Foster and F. Buttel (eds), *Hungry for Profit: The Agribusiness Threat to Farmers, Food, and the Environment*. New York: Monthly Review Press, pp. 145–59.

Arendt, H. (1963) *Eichmann in Jerusalem* (revised edition). New York: Viking.

Arendt, H. (1970) *On Violence*. London: Allen Lane.

Arens, W. (1979) *The Man-Eating Myth: Anthropology and Anthropophagy*. Oxford: Oxford University Press.

Arnason, J.P. (1993) *The Future that Failed: Origins and Destinies of the Soviet Model*. London: Routledge.

Auyero, J. (2000) 'Hyper-shantytown: neo-liberal violence(s) in the Argentine slum', *Ethnography*, 1 (1): 93–116.

Bacciagaluppi, M. (2004) 'Violence: innate or acquired? A survey and some opinions', *Journal of the American Academy of Psychoanalysis and Dynamic Psychiatry*, 32 (3): 469–81.

Bäck, A. (2004) 'Thinking clearly about violence', *Philosophical Studies*, 117: 219–30.

Back, L. (2002) 'Aryans reading Adorno: cyber-culture and twenty-first century racism', *Ethnic and Racial Studies*, 25 (4): 628–51.

Bairner, A. (1999) 'Soccer, masculinity, and violence in Northern Ireland', *Men and Masculinities*, 1 (3): 284–301.

Balch, R. (2006) 'The rise and fall of Aryan nations: a resource mobilization perspective', *Journal of Political and Military Sociology*, 34 (1): 81–113.

Bandura, A. (1977) *Social Learning Theory*. New York: General Learning Press.

Barker, V. (2007) 'The politics of pain: a political institutionalist analysis of crime victims' moral protests', *Law & Society Review*, 41 (3): 619–64.

Bartov, O. (2000) *Mirrors of Destruction: War Genocide and Modern Identity*. Oxford: Oxford University Press.

Basson, S. (2006) '"Oh Comrade, what times those were!" History, capital punishment and the urban square', *Urban Studies*, 43 (7): 1147–58.

Batchelor, S. (2001) 'The myth of girl gangs', *Criminal Justice Matters*, 43: 26–7.

Batchelor, S. (2005) '"Prove me the bam!": victimization and agency in the lives of young women who commit violent offences', *Probation Journal*, 52 (4): 358–75.

Batchelor, S. (2009) 'Girls, gangs and violence: assessing the evidence', *Probation Journal*, 56 (4): 399–414.

Bauman, Z. (1979) 'The phenomenon of Norbert Elias', *Sociology*, 13 (1): 117–25.

Bauman, Z. (1991) *Modernity and Ambivalence*. Oxford: Polity Press.

Bauman, Z. (1992) *Intimations of Postmodernity*. London: Routledge.

Bauman, Z. (1999) *Modernity and the Holocaust*. Cambridge: Polity Press.

Bauman, Z. (2000) *Liquid Modernity*. Cambridge: Polity Press.

Beck, A. (2000) *Prisoners of Hate: The Cognitive Basis of Anger, Hostility and Violence*. New York: HarperCollins.

Ben-Itto, H. (2005) *The Lie That Wouldn't Die: The Protocols of the Elders of Zion*. London: Valentine Mitchell.

Bergen, D. (2009) *War and Genocide*. Lanham: Rowman & Littlefield.

Bjørgo, T. (1994) 'Terrorist violence against immigrants and refugees in Scandinavia: patterns and motives', in T. Bjørgo and R. Witte (eds), *Racist Violence in Europe*. London: St Martin's Press, pp. 29–45.

Black, D (1993) *The Social Structure of Right and Wrong*. San Diego, CA: Academic Press.

Blee, K.M. (2007) 'The microdynamics of hate violence: interpretive analysis and implications for responses', *American Behavioral Scientist*, 51 (2): 258–70.

Boesch, C., Crockford, C., Herbinger, I., Wittig, R., Moebius, Y. and Normand, E. (2008) 'Intergroup conflicts among chimpanzees in Tai National Park: lethal violence and the female perspective', *American Journal of Primatology*, 70: 519–32.

Bourdieu, P. (1998) *Acts of Resistance: Against the Tyranny of the Market*, trans. Richard Nice. New York: The New Press and Polity Press.

Bourgois, P. (2003) *In Search of Respect*. Cambridge: Cambridge University Press.

Bowling, B. (1999) 'The rise and fall of New York murder', *British Journal of Criminology*, 39 (4): 531–54.

Bowling, B. and Phillips, C. (2002) *Racism, Crime and Justice*. London: Longman.

Bowman, G. (2001) 'Violence and identity', in B.E. Schmidt and I.W. Schröder (eds), *Anthropology of Violence and Conflict*. London: Routledge, pp. 25–46.

Braithwaite, J. (1993) 'Shame and modernity', *British Journal of Criminology*, 33 (1): 1–18.

Brayne, H., Sargeant, L. and Brayne, C. (1998) 'Could boxing be banned?', *British Medical Journal*, 316: 1813–15.

Browning, C. (1998) *Ordinary Men: Reserve Police Battalion 101 and the Final Solution*. New York: Harper Perennial.

Bufacchi, V. (2005) 'Two concepts of violence', *Political Studies Association*, 3: 193–204.

Bundesamt für Verfassungsschutz (2003) *Annual Report of the Office for the Protection of the Constitution: 2002*. Berlin: Bundesministerium des Innern.

Burney, E. and Rose, G., with Joseph, S. and Newby, R. (2002) *Racist Offences: How is the Law Working?* Home Office Research Study 244. London: Home Office. Available at: www.homeoffice.gov.uk/rds/pdfs2/hors244.pdf.

Carter, C. and Weaver, C.K. (2003) *Violence and the Media*. Buckingham: Open University Press.

Castells, E. (1998) *End of Millennium. The Information Age: Economy, Society and Culture* (Vol. III). Oxford: Blackwell.

Chancer, L.S. (2004) 'Rethinking domestic violence in theory and practice', *Deviant Behavior*, 25: 255–75.

Clarke, J.W. (1998) 'Without fear or shame: lynching, capital punishment and the subculture of violence in the American South', *British Journal of Political Science*, 28: 269–89.

Clastres, P. (1994) *Archaeology of Violence*. New York: Semiotext.

Cleaver, E. (1968) *Soul on Ice*. London: Jonathan Cape.

Clifford, C. (2008) 'Rape as a weapon of war and its long-term effects on victims and society', Seventh Global Conference on Violence and the Contexts of Hostility, Budapest. Available at: www.inter-disciplinary.net/ptb/hhv/vcce/vch7/Clifford%20paper.pdf.

Cloward, L.E. and Ohlin, R.A. (1960) *Delinquency and Opportunity: A Theory of Delinquent Gangs*. Glencoe, IL: Free Press.

Cohen, A. (1955) *Deviance and Control*. London: Prentice Hall.

Cohen, D. and Nisbett, R.E. (1997) 'Field experiments examining the culture of honor: the role of institutions perpetuating norms about violence', *Personality and Social Psychology Bulletin*, 23 (11): 1188–99.

Cohen, L.E. and Felson, M. (1979) 'Social change and crime rate trends: a routine activity approach', *American Sociological Review*, 44: 588–608.

Collins, R. (1974) 'Three faces of cruelty: towards a comparative sociology of violence', *Theory and Society*, 1 (4): 415–40.

Collins, R. (2008) *Violence: A Micro-sociological Theory*. Princeton, NJ: Princeton University Press.

Collins, R. (2009) 'Micro and macro causes of violence', *International Journal of Conflict and Violence*, 3 (1): 9–22.

Committee on the Administration of Justice (2003) Response to the '*Race Crime and Sectarian Crime Legislation in Northern Ireland*' Northern Ireland Office consultation paper. London : HMSO.

Connell, R.W. (1987) *Gender and Power: Society, the Person and Sexual Politics*. Stanford, CA: Stanford University Press.

Connell, R.W. (1995) *Masculinities*. Berkeley, CA: University of California Press.

Connell, R.W. and Messerschmidt, J. (2005) 'Hegemonic masculinity – rethinking the concept', *Gender and Society*, 19 (6): 829–59.

Cooney, M. (1997) 'The decline of elite homicide', *Criminology*, 35: 3814.

Cooney, M. (2003) 'Privatization of violence', *Criminology*, 41 (4): 1337–406.

Cotula, L., Vermeulen, S., Leonard, R. and Keeley, J. (2009) *Land Grab or Development Opportunity? Agricultural Investment and International Land Deals in Africa*. London: FAO, IIED and IFAD. Available at: www.reliefweb.int/rw/RWFiles2009.nsf/FilesByRWDocUnidFilename/KHII-7SE4R4-full_report.pdf/$File/full_report.pdf.

CPS (Crown Prosecution Service) (2007a) *Reasonable Chastisement Research Report*. London: CPS. Available at: www.cps.gov.uk/Publications/research/chastisement.html#content.

CPS (Crown Prosecution Service) (2007b) *Racist Incident Annual Monitoring Report 2006–2007*. London: CPS.

CPS (Crown Prosecution Service) (2009a) *CPS Policy for Prosecuting Cases of Domestic Violence*. London: CPS. Available at: www.cps.gov.uk/publications/docs/domesticviolencepolicy.pdf.

CPS (Crown Prosecution Service) (2009b) *Hate Crime Report 2008–2009*. London: CPS. Available at: www.cps.gov.uk/publications/docs/CPS_hate_crime_report_2009.pdf.

Craig, K.M. (2003) 'Examining hate-motivated aggression', in B. Perry (ed.), *Hate and Bias Crime: A Reader*. London: Routledge, pp. 117–30.

Crawford, A. (2006) 'Networked governance and the post-regulatory state? Steering, rowing and anchoring the provision of policing and security', *Theoretical Criminology*, 10: 449–79.

CSIR (Centre for the Study of Violence and Reconciliation) (1998) *Into the Heart of Darkness: Journeys of the Amagents in Crime, Violence and Death*. South Africa CSIR. Available at: www.csvr.org.za/wits/papers/papcsir.htm.

Daly, M., Wilson, M. and Vasdev, S. (2001) 'Income inequality and homicide rates in Canada', *Canadian Journal of Criminology*, 43: 219–36.

Davis, M. (2004) 'Planet of slums', *New Left Review*, 26 (March–April): 5–34.

Day, K., Stump, C. and Carreon, D. (2003) 'Confrontation and loss of control: masculinity and men's fear in public space', *Journal of Environmental Psychology*, 23: 311–22.

De Swaan, A. (2001) 'Dyscivilization, mass extermination and the state', *Theory Culture & Society*, 18 (2–3): 265–76.

De Zeit (1964) "Ich habe das Gute gewollt" [I Wanted the Good] *Zeit Online*. Available at: http://www.zeit.de/1964/09/Ich-habe-das-Gute-gewollt.

Deane, S. (2008) 'Crime corrupting credibility: the problem of shifting from paramilitaries to parliamentarians', *Civil Wars*, 10 (4): 431–50.

Decety, J., Michalska, K.J., Akitsuki, Y. and Lahey, B.B. (2009) 'Atypical empathic responses in adolescents with aggressive conduct disorder: a functional MRI investigation', *Biological Psychology*, 80 (2): 203–11.

Delanty, G. (2001) 'Cosmopolitanism and violence: the limits of global civil society', *European Journal of Social Theory*, 4 (1): 41–52.

Demetriou, D.Z. (2001) 'Connell's concept of hegemonic masculinity: a critique', *Theory and Society*, 30: 337–61.

Dobash, R.E. and Dobash, R.P. (1992) *Women, Violence and Social Change*. London: Routledge.

Dobash, R.E. and Dobash, R.P. (eds) (1998) *Rethinking Violence Against Women*. London: Sage.

Dudai, R. (2006) 'Understanding perpetrators in genocides and mass atrocities', *British Journal of Sociology*, 57 (4): 699–707.

Duerr, H.-P. (1988) *Nacktheit und Scham*. Frankfurt: Suhrkamp.

DuGay, P. (1999) 'Is Bauman's bureau Weber's bureau? A comment', *British Journal of Sociology*, 50 (4): 575–87.

Dunning, E. (1999) *Sport Matters: Sociological Studies of Sport, Violence and Civilization*. London: Routledge.

Dunning, E. and Mennell, S. (1998) 'Elias on Germany, Nazism and the Holocaust: on the balance between "civilizing" and "decivilizing" trends in the social development of Western Europe', *British Journal of Sociology*, 49 (3): 339–57.

Dunning, E., Murphy, P. and Williams, J. (1987) *The Roots of Football Hooliganism*. London: Routledge.

Durkheim, E. (1933) *Divsion of Labor in Society*. Glencoe, IL: Free Press.

Durkheim, E. (1969) 'La prohibition de l'inceste et ses origines', *Journal Sociologique*, edited and introduced by J. Duvignaud. Paris: Presses Univesitaries de France, pp. 37–101.

Durkheim, E. (1970) *Suicide*. London: Routledge.

Durkheim, E. (2001) *The Elementary Forms of Religious Life*. Oxford: Oxford University Press.

Durkheim, E. (2003) *Professional Ethics and Civic Morals*. London: Routledge.

Dutton, D.G. (1999) 'Traumatic origins of intimate rage', *Aggression and Violent Behavior*, 4 (4): 431–47.

Dutton, D.G. and Corvo, K. (2006) 'Transforming a flawed policy: a call to revive psychology and science in domestic violence research and practice', *Aggression and Violent Behavior*, 11: 457–83.

Dutton, D.G. and Nicholls, T.L. (2005) 'The gender paradigm in domestic violence research and theory: Part 1 – The conflict of theory and data', *Aggression and Violent Behavior*, 10: 680–714.

Eck, J.E., Chainey, S., Cameron, J.G., Leitner, M. and Wilson, R.E. (2005) *Mapping Crime: Understanding Hot Spots*. Washington, DC: US Department of Justice Office of Justice Programs, National Institute of Justice.

Ehrensaft, M.K. (2008) 'Intimate partner violence: persistence of myths and implications for intervention', *Children and Youth Services Review*, 30: 276–86.

Eisner, M. (2001) 'Modernization, self-control and lethal violence: the long-term dynamics of European homicide rates in theoretical perspective', *British Journal of Criminology*, 41 (4): 618–38.

Elias, N. (with Dunning, E.) (1986) *Quest for Excitement. Sport and Leisure in the Civilizing Process*. Oxford: Blackwell

Elias, N. (1987) 'The retreat of sociologists into the present', *Theory, Culture & Society*, 4 (2): 223–47.

Elias, N. (1991) *The Symbol Theory*. London: Sage.

Elias, N. (1994) *The Civilizing Process* (revised ed.) Oxford: Blackwell.

Elias, N. (1996) *The Germans* (with a Preface by E. Dunning and S. Mennell). New York: University of Colombia Press.

Elias, N. (1997) 'Informalization and the civilizing process', in J. Goudsblom and S. Mennell (eds), *The Norbert Elias Reader*. Oxford: Blackwell, pp. 235–45.

Elias, N. (2001) *Society of Individuals*. London: Continuum.

Elliott, C. and Ellingworth, D. (1997) 'Assessing the representativeness of the 1992 British Crime Survey: the impact of sampling error and response biases', *Sociological Research Online*, 2 (4). Available at: www.socresonline.org.uk/socresonline/2/4/3.html.

Ellsberg, M. et al. (2000) 'Candies in hell: women's experiences of violence in Nicaragua', *Social Science and Medicine*, 51: 1595–610.

Ellul, J. (1976) *Ethics of Freedom*. Grand Rapids, MI: Eerdmans.

Ember, C. and Ember, M. (1997) *Cultural Anthropology*. London: Pearson.

Englander, E.K. (2007a) 'Is bullying a junior hate crime? Implications for interventions', *American Behavioral Scientist*, 51: 205–17.

Englander, E.K. (2007b) *Understanding Violence*. London: Taylor Francis.

Engels F (1884/1968) 'Origin of family private property and the state' in K. Marx and F. Engels *Selected Works*. London: Lawrence and Wishart, pp. 468–595.

Fackenheim, E. (1994) *To Mend the World: Foundations of Post-Holocaust Jewish Thought*. Bloomington, IN: Indiana University Press.

Fagan, J. (1995) *The Criminalization of Domestic Violence: Promises and Limits*. Washington, DC: US Department of Justice Office of Justice Programs, National Institute of Justice.

Faludi, S. (2000) *Stiffed: The Betrayal of the American Man*. New York: Harper Perennial.

Farrell, G. and Pease, K. (1993) *Once Bitten, Twice Bitten: Repeat Victimisation and its Implications for Crime Prevention*. Police Research Group Crime Prevention Unit Series, Paper No. 46. London: Home Office Police Department.

FBI (2009) *Uniform Crime Report*. Available at: www.fbi.gov/ucr/prelimsem2009/.

Felson, R.B. (2009) 'Violence, crime and violent crime', *International Journal of Conflict and Violence*, 3 (1): 23–39. Also available at: www.ijcv.org/.

Ferber, A.L. (1998) *White Man Falling: Race, Gender, and White Supremacy*. Lanham, MD: Rowman & Littlefield.

Ferber, A.L. (2000) 'Racial warriors and weekend warriors: the construction of masculinity in mythopoetic and white supremacist discourse', *Men and Masculinities*, 3 (1): 30–56.

Ferrell, J., Hayward, K. and Young, J. (2008) *Cultural Criminology: An Invitation*. London: Sage.

Fine, B. and Turner, C. (2000) *Social Theory after the Holocaust*. Liverpool: Liverpool University Press.

Finney, A. (2006) *Domestic Violence, Sexual Assault and Stalking: Findings from the British Crime Survey*. Home Office Online Report 12/06. Available at: www.homeoffice.gov.uk/rds/pdfs06/rdsolr1206.pdf.

FitzGerald, M. (2010) *Crime, Sentencing and Justice – An Overview of the Issues*, with J. Lowthian and James Riches. London: NACRO.

Fletcher, J. (1997) *Violence and Civilization: An Introduction to the Work of Norbert Elias*. Cambridge: Polity Press.

Foucault, M. (1976) *Discipline and Punish*. London: Allen Lane.

Foucault, M. (1979) *Power/Knowledge*. Brighton: Harvester.

Foucault, M. (1988) 'Technologies of the self', in L.H. Martin, H. Gutman and P.H. Hutton (eds), *Technologies of the Self*. Amherst, MA: University of Massachusetts Press.

Foucault, M. (1991) *The Foucault Reader* (ed. P. Rabinow). London: Penguin.

Fox, G.L. and Benson, M.L. (2006) 'Household and neighborhood contexts of intimate partner violence', *Public Health Reports*, 121 (4): 419–27.

Franklin, K. (2002) 'Good intentions: the enforcement of hate crime penalty-enhancement statutes, *American Behavioral Scientist*, 46 (1): 154–72.

Fraser, J.G. (2000) *The Golden Bough*. New York: Bartleby.com. Available at: www.bartleby.com/196/

Frayer, D.W. (1997) 'Ofnet: evidence for a mesolithic massacre', in D.L. Martin and D.W. Frayer (eds), *Violence and Warfare in the Past*. Amsterdam: Gordon and Breach, pp. 181–216.

Freeman, M. (1995) 'Genocide, civilization and modernity', *British Journal of Sociology*, 46 (2): 207–23.

Freud, S. (1913/1950) *Totem and Taboo*. London: Routledge & Kegan Paul.

Freud, S. (1930/1961) *Civilization and its Discontents*. New York: W.W. Norton.

Fromm, E. (1974) *Anatomy of Human Destructiveness*. New York: Holt, Rinehart & Winston.

Frye, V., Haviland, M. and Rajah, V. (2007) 'Dual arrest and other intended consequences of mandatory arrest in New York City: a brief report', *Journal of Family Violence*, 22: 397–405.

Frymer, B. (2009) 'The media spectacle of Columbine: alienated youth as an object of fear', *American Behavioral Scientist*, 52 (10): 1387–404.

Furet, F. (1999) *The Passing of an Illusion: The Idea of Communism in the Twentieth Century*. Chicago: University of Chicago Press.

Gadd, D. (2002) 'Masculinities and violence against female partners', *Social & Legal Studies*, 11: 61–80.

Galtung, J. (1969) 'Violence, peace and peace research', *Journal of Peace Research*, 6 (3): 167–91.

Garland, D. (1991) *Punishment and Modern Society*. Oxford: Clarendon Press.

Garland, D. (2001) *The Culture of Control: Crime and Social Order in Contemporary Society*. Oxford: Oxford University Press.

Gates, H.L., Griffin, A.P., Lively, D.E., Post, R.C., Rubenstein, R. and Strossen, N. (1999) *Speaking of Race, Speaking of Sex*. Albany, NY and London: New York University Press.

Gelles, R.J. (1997) *Intimate Violence in Families*. London: Sage.

Giddens, A. (1993) *The Transformation of Intimacy*. Cambridge: Polity Press.

Giddens, A. (1996) *Nation State and Violence*. Cambridge: Polity Press.

Gilligan, J. (2000) *Violence: Reflections on our Deadliest Epidemic*. London: Jessica Kingsley.

Gilligan, J. (2004) 'Shame, guilt and violence', *Social Research*, 70 (4): 1149–80.

Girard, R. (1977) *Violence and the Sacred*. Baltimore, MD: Johns Hopkins University Press.

Giroux, H.A. (2005) 'The terror of neoliberalism: rethinking the significance of cultural politics', *College Literature*, 32 (1): 1–19.

Glasser, M. (1998) 'On violence: a preliminary communication', *International Journal of Psycho-Analysis*, 79 (5): 887–902.

Glowacka, D. and Zylinska, J. (eds) (2007) *Imaginary Neighbors: Mediating Polish–Jewish Relations after the Holocaust*. Lincoln, NB: University of Nebraska Press.

Goffman, E. (1961) *Stigma: Notes on the Management of Spoiled Identity*. Englefield Cliffs, NJ and London: Prentice-Hall.

Goffman, E. (1983) 'The interaction order', *American Sociological Review*, 48: 1–17.

Goldhagen, D.J. (1997) *Hitler's Willing Executioners*. London: Abacus.

Goldhagen, D.J., Browning, C.R. and Wieseltier, L. (2001) 'The "Willing Executioners": the "ordinary men" debate'. Available at: www.ushmm.org/research/center/publications/occasional/1996-01/paper.pdf.

Goldman, L.R. (1999) 'From pot to polemic: uses and abuses of cannibalism', in L.R. Goldman (ed.), *The Anthropology of Cannibalism*. London: Bergin & Garvey, pp. 2–26.

Gondolf, E.W. (2007) 'Theoretical and research support for the Duluth model: a reply to Dutton and Corvo', *Aggression and Violent Behavior*, 12: 644–57.

Gottfredson, M.R. and Hirschi, T. (1990) *A General Theory of Crime*. Stanford, CA: Stanford University Press.

Gould, R. (2003) *Collision of Wills*. Chicago: Chicago University Press.

Graham, E.T. (2007) 'The danger of Durkheim: ambiguity in the theory of social effervescence', *Religion*, 37 (1): 26–38.

Grattet, R. and Jenness, V. (2003) 'Examining the boundaries of hate crime law: disabilities and the "dilemma of difference"', in B. Perry (ed.), *Hate and Bias Crime: A Reader*. London: Routledge, pp. 281–93.

Green, D.P., McFalls, L.H. and Smith, J.K. (2001) 'Hate crime: an emergent research agenda', *Annual Review of Sociology*, 27: 479–504.

Green, R. (2001) '(Serious) sadomasochism: a protected right of privacy?', *Archives of Sexual Behavior*, 30 (5): 543–50.

Gross, J. (2002) *Neighbors*. London: Penguin.

Gross, J. (2006) *Fear Anti-Semitism in Poland after Auschwitz: An Essay in Historical Interpretation*. Princeton and Oxford: Princeton University Press.

Guilaine, J. and Zammit, J. (2001) *The Origins of War: Violence in Prehistory*. Oxford: Blackwell.

Gurr, T.R. (1981) 'Historical trends in violent crime: a critical review of the evidence', *Crime and Justice*, 3: 295–350.

Habermas, J. (1975) *Legitimation Crisis*. London: Heinemann.

Habermas, J. (1979) *Communication and the Evolution of Society*. London: Heinemann.

Habermas, J. (1984) *Reason and the Rationalization of Society*. Vol. 1: *The Theory of Communicative Action*. Boston, MA: Beacon Press.

Habermas, J. and Rehg, W. (2001) 'Constitutional democracy: a paradoxical union of contradictory principles?', *Political Theory*, 29 (6): 766–81.

Hall, S. (2002) 'Daubing the drudges of fury: men, violence and the piety of the "hegemonic masculinity" thesis', *Theoretical Criminology*, 6 (1): 35–61.

Hall, S. (2007) 'The emergence and breakdown of the pseudo-pacification process', in K.D. Watson (ed.), *Assaulting the Past: Violence and Civilization in Historical Context*. Cambridge: Cambridge Scholars Publishing, pp. 77–103.

Hall, S. and McLean, C. (2009) 'A tale of two capitalisms: preliminary spatial and historical comparisons of homicide rates in Western Europe and the USA', *Theoretical Criminology*, 13 (3): 313–39.

Hamm, M.S. (1994) *American Skinheads: The Criminology and Control of Hate Crime*. Westport, CT: Praeger.

Hankiss, E. (1990) *East European Alternatives: Are There Any?* Oxford: Clarendon Press.

Hanmer, J. (2000) 'Domestic violence and gender relations: contexts and connections', in J. Hanmer and C. Itzin (eds), *Home Truths about Domestic Violence*. London: Routledge, pp. 9–23.

Hargreaves, J. (1992) 'Sex, gender and the body in sport: has there been a civilizing process?', in E. Dunning and P. Rock (eds), *Sport and Leisure in the Civilizing Process: Critique and Counter-Critique*. London: Macmillan.

Hatty, S.E. (2000) *Masculinities, Violence and Culture*. London: Sage.

Hayward, K. (2004) *City Limits: Crime, Consumer Culture and the Urban Experience*. London: Glass House Press.

Healy, M. (1997) 'The Holocaust, modernity and the Enlightenment', *Res Publica*, 3 (1): 35–59.

Hearn, J. (1998) *The Violences of Men*. London: Sage.

Hebdige, D. (1987) *Subculture: The Meaning of Style*. London: Methuen.

Heise, L.L. (1998) 'Violence against women: an integrated ecological framework', *Violence Against Women*, 4: 262–90.

Heitmeyer, W. (1994) 'Hostility and violence towards foreigners in Germany', in T. Bjørgo and R. Witte (eds), *Racist Violence in Europe*. London: St Martin's Press, pp. 17–28.

Henning, K., Renauer, B. and Holdford, R. (2006) 'Victim or offender? Heterogeneity among women arrested for intimate partner violence', *Journal of Family Violence*, 21: 351–68.

Hester, M., Kelly, L. and Radford, J. (eds) (1996) *Women, Violence and Male Power: Feminist Activism, Research and Practice*. Buckingham: Open University Press.

Hester, M., Westmarland, N., Pearce J. and Williamson E. (2008) *Early Evaluation of the Domestic Violence, Crime and Victims Act 2004*. Ministry of Justice Research Series 14/08. London: Crown Copyright.

Hipp, J., Tita, G. and Boggess, L. (2009) 'Inter- and intra-group violence: is violent crime an expression of group conflict or social disorganization?', *Criminology*, 47 (2): 521–64.

Hirschi, T. (1969) *Causes of Delinquency*. Berkeley, CA: University of California Press.

Hirschi, T. and Gottfredson, M. (2000) 'In defense of self-control', *Theoretical Criminology*, 4: 55–69.

Hobbes, T. (1651/1994) *Leviathan*. London: Everyman.

Hoffman, S. (2006) 'A note on Sartre and violence', *Journal of Romance Studies*, 6 (1&2): 61–5.

Home Office (2001) *Working Group on Football Disorder Report and Recommendations* (chaired by Lord Bassam). London: Home Office.

Home Office (2002) *A Report of the Independent Review Team Chaired by Ted Cantle*. London: Home Office. Available at: www.homeoffice.gov.uk/reu/community_cohesion.pdf.

Home Office (2004) *Defining and Measuring Anti-social Behaviour*. London: Home Office. Available at: www.homeoffice.gov.uk/rds/pdfs04/dpr26.pdf.

Home Office (2005a) *Domestic Violence: A National Report*. London: Home Office. Available at: www.crimereduction.homeoffice.gov.uk/domesticviolence/domesticviolence51.pdf.

Home Office (2005b) *Crime in England and Wales 2003/2004: Supplementary Volume 1: Homicide and Gun Crime*. London: Home Office. Available at: www.rds.homeoffice.gov.uk/rds/pdfs05/hosb0205.pdf.

Home Office (2006) *Crime Statistics: An Independent Review*. London: Home Office. Available at: www.homeoffice.gov.uk/rds/pdfs06/crime-statistics-independent-review-06.pdf.

Home Office (2009) *Crime in England and Wales 2008/09* (Vol. 1) (ed. A. Walker, J. Flatley, C. Kershaw and D. Moon). London: Home Office. Available at: www.homeoffice.gov.uk/rds/pdfs09/hosb1109vol1.pdf.

Home Office (2010) *Hate Crime: The Cross-Government Action Plan*. London: Home Office. Available at: www.homeoffice.gov.uk/documents/hate-crime-action-plan/hate-crime-action-plan.pdf?view=Binary.

Horkheimer, M. (1974) *Eclipse of Reason*. New York: Continuum.

Horvath, M. and Kelly, L. (2006) *Submission to the Equalities Review on Violence as a Cross-strand Theme for the Commission for Equality and Human Rights*. London: End Violence Against Women. Available at: http://www.endviolenceagainstwomen.org.uk

House of Commons Northern Ireland Affairs Committee (2005) *The Challenge of Diversity: Hate Crime in Northern Ireland*. London: House of Commons. Available at: www.parliament.the-stationery-office.co.uk/pa/cm200405/cmselect/cmniaf/548/548i.pdf.

Human Security Brief (2006) Human Security Report Project (HSRP), Simon Fraser University, Vancouver, Canada. Available at: www.humansecuritybrief.info/2006/index.html.

Hutchins, B. and Mikosza, J. (1998) 'Australian rugby league and violence 1970 to 1995: a case study in the maintenance of masculine hegemony', *Journal of Sociology*, 34 (3): 246–63.

Iganski, P. (2001) 'Hate crimes hurt more', *American Behavioral Scientist*, 45 (4): 626–38.

Iganski, P. (2008) *Hate Crime and the City*. Bristol: The Policy Press.

Ignatieff, M. (2000) 'Less race, please', in D.G. Green (ed.), *Institutional Racism and the Police: Fact or Fiction?* London: Institute for the Study of Civil Society, pp. 21–4.

IRR (Institute of Race Relations) (2010) 'Deaths with a (known or suspected) racial element 2000 onwards'. Available at: www.irr.org.uk/2002/november/ak000008.html.

Iyengar, R. (2009) 'Does the certainty of arrest reduce domestic violence? Evidence from the mandatory and recommended arrest laws', *Journal of Public Economics*, 93 (1): 85–93.

Jackman, M. (2002) 'Violence in social life', *Annual Review of Sociology*, 28: 387–415.

Jackson, R.L. (2006) *Scripting the Black Masculine Body: Identity, Discourse, and Racial Politics in Popular Media*. Albany, NY: University of New York Press.

Jacobs, J. (1993) 'Implementing hate crime legislation: symbolism and crime control', *Annual Survey of American Law 1992/3*, 4: 541–53.

Jacobs, J. (2002) 'The death and life of American cities', in Bridge, J. and Watson, S., (eds) *The Blackwell City Reader*. Oxford: Blackwell, pp. 351–56.

Jacobs, J. (2003) 'Policing hatred: police bias units and the construction of hate crimes', in B. Perry (ed.), *Hate and Bias Crime: A Reader*. London: Routledge, pp. 409–26.

James, O. (1995) *Juvenile Violence in a Winner–Loser Culture*. London: Free Association Books.

James, O. (1999) 'Can books be boys' toys?', *Times Educational Supplement*, 30 April.

Jenkins, H. (1999) 'Congressional testimony on media violence'. Available at: http://web.mit.edu/comm-forum/papers/jenkins_ct.html.

Jenness, V. and Broad, K. (1997) *Hate Crimes: New Social Movements and the Politics of Violence*. New York: Aldine de Gruyter.

John, M.D. (1999) 'Racialized bodies: the social construction of black identities in popular cinema', MA thesis for the Department of Sociology and Education in Equity Studies, Ontario Institute for Studies in Education of the University of Toronto. Available at: http://tspace.library.utoronto.ca/bitstream/1807/15098/1/MQ46178.pdf.

Johnson, M.P. (1995) 'Patriarchial terrorism and common couple violence: two forms of violence against women', *Journal of Marriage and Family*, 57 (2): 283–94.

Jurgensmeyer, M. (2003) *Terror in the Mind of God: The Global Rise of Religious Violence*. Berkeley and Los Angeles, CA: University of California Press.

Kamber, R. (2000) 'The logic of the Goldhagen debate', *Res Publica*, 6: 155–77.

Kantner, J. (1999) 'Anasazi mutilation and cannibalism in the American Southwest', in L.R. Goldman (ed.), *The Anthropology of Cannibalism*. London: Bergin & Garvey, pp. 75–104.

Kaplan, R. (1994) 'The coming anarchy', *Atlantic Monthly*, 273 (February): 44–76.

Kapralski, S. (1997) 'Identity building and the Holocaust: Roma political nationalism', *Nationalities Papers*, 25 (2): 269–84.

Karmen, A. (2000) *New York Murder Mystery: The True Story Behind the Crime Crash of the 1990s*. Albany, NY: New York University Press.

Katz, J. (1988) *Seductions of Crime: Moral and Sensual Attractions in Doing Evil*. New York: Basic Books.

Katz, J. (1996) 'The social psychology of Adam and Eve', *Theory and Society*, 25: 545–82.

Kawachi, I., Kennedy, B.P. and Wilkinson, R.G. (1999) 'Crime: social disorganization and relative deprivation', *Social Science & Medicine*, 48 (6): 719–31.

Kayle, D.G. (1998) *Spectacles of Death in Ancient Rome*. London: Routledge.

Keeley, L. (1997) *War before Civilization*. Oxford: Oxford University Press.

Kelly, L. (1996) 'When does the speaking profit us? Reflections on the challenges of developing feminist perspectives on abuse and violence by women', in M. Hester, L. Kelly and J. Radford (eds), *Women, Violence and Male Power: Feminist Activism, Research and Practice*. Buckingham: Open University Press, pp. 19–33.

Kelly, L. and Radford, J. (1998) 'Sexual violence against women and girls', in R.E. Dobash and R.P. Dobash (eds), *Rethinking Violence against Women*. London: Sage, pp. 53–76.

Kelly, R. C. (2005) 'The evolution of lethal intergroup violence', *Proceedings of the National Academy of Sciences*, 102 (43): 15294–98.

Kielinger, V. and Paterson, S. (2007) 'Policing hate crime in London', *American Behavioral Scientist*, 51 (2): 196–204.

Kiliminster, R. (2008) 'Narcissism or informalization? Christopher Lasch, Norbert Elias and social diagnosis', *Theory, Culture & Society*, 25 (3): 131–51.

Kimmel, M. (2002) 'Gender symmetry in domestic violence: a substantive and methodological research review', *Violence Against Women*, 8 (11): 1332–63.

Kimmel, M. and Mahler, M. (2003) 'Adolescent masculinity, homophobia and violence', *American Behavioral Scientist*, 46 (10): 1439–58.

King, A. (2001) 'Violent pasts: collective memory and football hooliganism', *Sociological Review*, 49: 568–85.

King, R.D., Messner, S.F. and Baller, R.D. (2009) 'Contemporary hate crimes, law enforcement, and the legacy of racial violence', *American Sociological Review*, 74: 291–315.

Kitchens, R. (2007) 'The informalization of the parent–child relationship: an investigation of parenting discourses produced in Australia in the inter–war years', *Journal of Family History*, 32 (4): 459–78.

Klein, J. (2005) 'Teaching her a lesson: media misses boy's rage relating to girls in school shootings', *Crime Media Culture*, 1 (90): 90–7.

Knauft, B.M. (1991) 'Violence and sociality in human evolution', *Current Anthropology*, 32 (4): 391–409.

Knüsel, C.J. and Outram, A.K. (2006) 'Fragmentation of the body: comestibles, compost, or customary rite?', in R. Gowland and C.J. Knüsel (eds), *The Social Archaeology of Funerary Remains*. Oxford: Oxbow Books, pp. 253–78.

Kohlberg, L. (1981) *The Philosophy of Moral Development: Moral Stages and the Idea of Justice*. New York: Harper & Row.

Kreager, D.A. (2007) 'Unnecessary roughness? School sports, peer networks, and male adolescent violence', *American Sociological Review*, 72 (5): 705–24.

Kreiken, R. van (1998) *Norbert Elias*. London: Routledge.

Kreiken, R. van (2005) 'Occidental self-understanding and the Elias–Duerr dispute: "thick" versus "thin" conceptions of human subjectivity and civilization', *Modern Greek Studies*, 13: 273–81.

Krell, G., Nicklas, H. and Ostermann, A. (1996) 'Immigration, asylum, and anti-foreigner violence in Germany', *Journal of Peace Research*, 33 (2): 153–70.

Krienert, J.L. (2003) 'Masculinity and crime: a quantitative exploration of Messerschmidt's hypothesis', *Electronic Journal of Sociology*, 7 (2). Available at: www.sociology.org/content/vol7.2/01_krienert.html.

Krivo, L.J., Peterson, R.D. and Karafin, D.L. (2006) 'Perceptions of neighborhood problems in racially and economically distinct neighborhoods', in R.D. Peterson, L.J. Krivo and J. Hagan (eds), *The Many Colors of Crime: Inequalities of Race, Ethnicity and Crime in America*. Albany, NY: New York University Press, pp. 237–55.

Krug, E.G., Dahlberg, L.L., Mercy, J.A., Zwi, A.B. and Lozano, A. (eds) (2002) *World Report on Violence and Health*. Geneva: World Health Organization.

Kudva, N. (2009) 'The everyday and the episodic: the spatial and political impacts of urban informality', *Environment and Planning*, 41 (7): 1614–28.

Kushner, T. (2003) 'Meaning nothing but good: ethic, history and asylum-seeker phobia in Britain', *Patterns of Prejudice*, 37 (3): 257–76.

Lasch, C. (1979) *Culture of Narcissis*. London: Abacus Press.

Lawrence, F. (1999) *Punishing Hate*. Cambridge, MA: Harvard University Press.

Lea, J. and Young, J. (1984). *What Is To Be Done About Law and Order – Crisis in the Eighties.* Harmondsworth: Penguin.

Lee, M.R. (2000) 'Concentrated poverty, race, and homicide', *The Sociological Quarterly*, 41 (2): 189–206.

Lee, M.R. and Shihadeh, E.S. (2009) 'The spatial concentration of Southern whites and argument-based violence', *Social Forces*, 87 (3): 1671–94.

Lefebvre, H. (1991) *The Production of Space*. Oxford: Blackwell.

Lemke, T. (2004) 'Disposition and determinism – genetic diagnostics in risk society', *The Sociological Review*, 52: 550–66.

Levi, M. and Maguire, M. (2004) 'Reducing and preventing organised crime: an evidence-based critique', *Crime, Law and Social Change*, 41: 397–469.

Levi, P. (1987) *If This is a Man: The Truce*. London: Abacus.

Levi, P. (1988) *The Drowned and the Saved*. London: Abacus.

Levin, J. (2002) *The Violence of Hate: Confronting Racism, Anti-Semitism, and Other Forms of Bigotry*. Boston, MA: Allyn & Bacon.

Lévi-Strauss, C. (1969) *The Elementary Structures of Kinship*. Boston, MA: Beacon Press.

Linklater, A. (2004) 'Norbert Elias, the 'civilizing process' and the sociology of international relations', *International Politics*, 41: 3–35.

Locke, J. (1980) *Second Treatise on Civil Government* (ed. C.B. Macpherson). Indianapolis, IN: Hackett (First published 1681–83.)

Lorenz, K. (1963) *On Aggression*. London: Methuen.

Loseke, D.R., Gelles, R.J. and Cavanaugh, M.M. (eds) (2005) *Current Controversies on Family Violence*. London: Sage.

Lyons, C. (2007) 'Community (dis)organization and racially motivated crime', *American Journal of Sociology*, 113 (3): 815–63.

Mac Ginty, R. (2001) 'Ethno-national conflict and hate crime', *American Behavioral Scientist*, 45 (4): 639–53.

MacInnes, J. (1998) *The End of Masculinity*. Buckingham: Open University Press.

Macmillan, R.I. and Gartner, R. (1999) 'When she brings home the bacon: labour force participation and spousal violence against women', *Journal of Marriage and the Family*, 61: 947–58.

Macpherson, W. (1999) *The Stephen Lawrence Inquiry: Report of an Inquiry by Sir William Macpherson of Cluny*. Cm 4262. London: The Stationery Office. Available at: www.archive.official-documents.co.uk/document/cm42/4262/sli-00.htm.

Malešević, S. (2010) *The Sociology of War and Violence*. Cambridge: Cambridge University Press.

Mann, M. (2000) 'Were the perpetrators of genocide "ordinary men" or "real Nazis"? Results from fifteen hundred biographies', *Holocaust and Genocide Studies*, 14 (3): 331–66.

Mares, D.M. (2009) 'Civilization, economic change, and trends in interpersonal violence in Western societies', *Theoretical Criminology*, 13 (4): 419–49.

Marquès-Boneta, T., Cáceresb, M., Bertranpetita, J., Preussc, T.M., Thomas, J.W. and Navarroa, A. (2004) 'Chromosomal rearrangements and the genomic distribution of gene-expression divergence in humans and chimpanzees', *Trends in Genetics*, 20 (11): 524–29.

Marsh, I. (ed.), with Melville, G., Morgan, K., Norris, G. and Walkington, Z. (2006) *Theories of Crime*. London: Routledge.

Martin, D.L. and Frayer, D.W. (eds) (1997) *Violence and Warfare in the Past*. Amsterdam: Gordon and Breach.

Martin, S. (1995) 'A cross-burning is not just an arson: police social construction of hate crimes in Baltimore County', *Criminology*, 33: 303–26.

Marvin, C. and Ingle, D. (1999) *Blood Sacrifice and the Nation: Totem Rituals and the American Flag*. Cambridge: Cambridge University Press.

Marx, K. (1972) *Ethnological Notebooks*, L. Krader (ed.). Assen Netherlands: Van Gorcum.

Mason, G. (2005) 'Hate crime and the image of the stranger', *British Journal of Criminology*, 45: 837–59.

Massey, D.S. and Fischer, M.J. (2000) 'How segregation concentrates poverty', *Ethnic and Racial Studies*, 23 (4): 670–91.

Matthäus, J. (1996) 'What about the "ordinary men"?: The German Order Police and the Holocaust in occupied Soviet Union', *Holocaust and Genocide Studies*, 10 (2): 134–50.

Matza, D. (1964) *Delinquency and Drift*. London: John Wiley.

McCall, G.S. and Shields, N. (2008) 'Examining the evidence from small-scale societies and early prehistory and implications for modern societies of aggression and violence', *Aggression and Violent Behavior*, 13: 1–9.

McCormack, M.P. (2008) 'Human–animal interdependence in the civilizing process', PhD thesis, University of Kent, UK.

McDevitt, J., Levin, J. and Bennett, S. (2002) 'Hate crime offenders: an expanded typology', *Journal of Social Issues*, 58: 303–17.

Melton, H.C. and Belknap, J. (2003) 'He hits, she hits – assessing gender differences and similarities in officially reported intimate partner violence', *Criminal Justice and Behaviour*, 30 (3): 328–48.

Mennell, S. (1992) *Norbert Elias: An Introduction*. Oxford: Blackwell.

Mennell, S. (2009) 'An exceptional civilizing process?', *Journal of Classical Sociology*, 9 (1): 97–115.

Merton, R. (1938) 'Social structure and anomie', *American Sociological Review*, 3: 672–82.

Messerschmidt, J.W. (1993) *Masculinities and Crime: Critique and Reconceptuatlization of Theory*. Lanham, MD: Rowman & Littlefield.

Messerschmidt, J.W. (1997) *Crime as Structured Action: Gender, Race, Class and Crime in the Making*. Thousand Oaks, CA: Sage.

Messerschmidt, J.W. (2002) 'On gang girls, gender and a structured action theory: Reply to Miller, *Theoretical Criminology*, 6 (4): 641–75.

Messerschmidt, J.W. (2008) 'Goodbye to the sex–gender distinction, hello to embodied gender: on masculinities, bodies, and violence', in A. Ferber, K. Holcomb and T. Wentling (eds), *Sex, Gender, and Sexuality: The New Basics*. New York: Oxford University Press, pp. 71–88.

Messner, S.F. (1989) 'Economic distribution and homicide rates: further evidence on the cost of inequality', *American Sociological Review*, 54 (4): 597–612.

Messner, S.F., McHugh, S. and Felson, R.B. (2004) 'Distinctive characteristics of assaults motivated by bias', *Criminology*, 42: 585–618.

Messner, S.F., Thome, H. and Rosenfeld, R. (2008) 'Institutions, anomie, and violent crime: clarifying and elaborating institutional-anomie theory', *International Journal of Conflict and Violence*, 2 (2): 163–81.

Mezey, G., Bacchus, L., Bewley, S. and Haworth, A. (2002) *An Exploration of the Prevalence, Nature and Effects of Domestic Violence in Pregnancy*. Violence Research Programme. London: Economic and Social Research Council. Available at: www.rhbnc.ac.uk/socio political-science/vrp/Findings/rfmezey.pdf.

Mihalic, S.W. and Elliott, D. (1997) 'A social learning model of marital violence', *Journal of Family Violence*, 12 (1): 21–47.

Miles-Doan, R. (1998) 'Violence between spouses and intimates: does neighborhood context matter?', *Social Forces*, 77 (2): 623–45.

Milgram, S. (1974) *Obedience to Authority*. London: Tavistock.

Miller, J. (1990) 'Carnivals of atrocity: Foucault, Nietzsche, cruelty', *Political Theory*, 18 (3): 470–91.

Miller, J. (2002) 'The strengths and limits of "doing gender" for understanding street crime', *Theoretical Criminology*, 6 (4): 433–60.

Mirrlees-Black, C. (1999) *Domestic Violence: Findings from a New BCS Self-Completion Questionnaire*. London: Home Office, RDS.

Misztal, B. (2000) *Informality*. London: Routledge.

Monkkonen, E. (2007) 'Homicide: explaining America's exceptionalism', *The American Historical Review*, 111 (1). Available at: www.historycooperative.org/journals/ahr/111.1/monkkonen.html.

Mooney, J. (2000) *Gender, Violence and the Social Order*. Basingstoke: Macmillan.

Moran, L. and Skeggs, B. (2004) *Sexuality and the Politics of Violence and Safety*. London: Routledge.

Morgan, L. H. (1877/2000) *Ancient Society*. New Brunswick: Transaction.

Moses, J. A. (1999) 'Review of Elias', *H-Net Reviews*. Available at: www.h-net.org/reviews/showpdf.php?id=2826.

Motz, A. (2001) *The Psychology of Female Violence: Crimes Against the Body*. Hove: Brunner-Routledge.

MPS (Metropolitan Police Service) (2001) *A Domestic Violence Strategy*. London: MPS. Available at: www.met.police.uk/dv/files/strategy.pdf.

MPS (2003) *Findings from the Multi-Agency Domestic Violence Murder Reviews in* London. Prepared for the ACPO Homicide Working Group. London: MPS. Available at: www.met.police.uk/csu/pdfs/MurderreportACPO.pdf.

Muir, K. B. and Seitz (2004) 'Machismo, misogyny and homophobia in a male athletic subculture: a participant observation study of deviant rituals in collegiate rugby', *Deviant Behavior*, 25 (4): 303–27.

Mukherjee, S. R. (2010) 'Introduction – On violence as the negativity of the Durkheimian: between anomie, sacrifice, and effervescence', in S. R. Mukherjee (ed.), *Durkheim and Violence*. Oxford: Wiley-Blackwell, pp. 5–39.

Nayak, A. (1999) '"Pale warriors": skinhead culture and the embodiment of white masculinities', in A. Brah, M. Hickman and M. Mac an Ghaill (eds), *Thinking Identities*. London: Macmillan, pp. 71–99.

Neustatter, A. (2008) 'Blood sisters', *The Guardian*, 4 July. Available at: www.guardian.co.uk/lifeandstyle/2008/jul/04/women.ukcrime.

New York Times (2010) 'Murder: New York City' [A map showing yearly and cumulative homicides 2003–09], *New York Times*. Available at: http://projects.nytimes.com/crime/homicides/map.

Newburn, T. and Stanko, E.A. (eds) (1995) *Just Boys Doing Business? Men, Masculinities and Crime*. London: Routledge.

Newman, K.S., with Fox, C., Harding, D., Mehta, J. and Roth, W. (2004) *Rampage: The Social Roots of School Shootings*. New York: Basic Books.

O'Brien, M. (2000) 'The Macpherson report and institutional racism', in D.G. Green (ed.), *Institutional Racism and the Police: Fact or Fiction?* London: Institute for the Study of Civil Society, pp. 25–36.

O'Brien, M. and Yar, M. (2008) *Criminology: The Key Concepts*. London: Routledge.

O'Kane, R.H.T. (1997) 'Modernity, the Holocaust and politics', *Economy and Society*, 26 (1): 43–61.

Oldham Council (2008) *Saddleworth North Ward Profile*. Available at: www.oldham.gov.uk/ward_profile_saddleworth_north_2008.pdf.

Oldham Primary Care Trust (2008) *Oldham's Joint Strategic Needs Assessment of Health and Wellbeing*. Available at: www.oldham.gov.uk/oldhams_joint_strategic_needs_assessment.pdf.

Ouimet, M. (2004) 'Explaining the American and Canadian crime drop in the 1990s', *Champ Penal/Penal Field*, 1 (1): 2–11.

Outhwaite, W. and Ray, L.J. (2005) *Social Theory and Postcommunism*. Oxford: Blackwell.

Oxfam America (2007) *Río Blanco: History of a Mismatch in Peru*. Available at: www. oxfamamerica.org/articles/rio-blanco-history-of-a-mismatch-in-peru.

Pahl, J., Hasanbegovic, C. and Yu, M.-K. (2004) 'Globalisation and family violence', in V. George and R. Page (eds), *Global Social Problems and Global Social Policy*. Cambridge: Polity Press, pp. 142–59.

Parker, K.F. (2008) *Unequal Crime Decline*. Albany, NY: New York University Press.

Parsons, T. (1966) *Structure of Social Action*. New York: McGraw-Hill.

Patton, C. (1999) 'Hate crime', *The Body*. Available at: www.thebody.com/content/art31237.html.

Pavelka, M. (1995) 'Sexual nature – what can we learn from a cross-species perspective?', in P.R. Abramson and S.D. Pinkerton (eds), *Sexual Nature, Sexual Culture*. London: University of Chicago Press, pp. 17–36.

Perrons, D. (2004) *Globalization and Social Change*. London: Routledge.

Perry, B. (2001) *In the Name of Hate*. London: Routledge.

Perry, B. (2002a) 'Defending the color line – racially and ethnically motivated hate crime', *American Behavioral Scientist*, 46 (1): 72–92.

Perry, B. (ed.) (2003) *Hate and Bias Crime: A Reader*. London: Routledge.

Phillips, C. (2003) 'Who's who in the pecking order? Aggression and "normal violence" in the lives of girls and boys', *British Journal of Criminology*, 43: 710–28.

Pinker, S. (2004) 'Why nature and nurture won't go away', *Dædalus*, Fall: 1–13.

Pinker, S. (2007) 'A history of violence', *The New Republic*, 9 March. Available at: www. edge.org/3rd_culture/pinker07/pinker07_index.html.

Polonsky, A. and Michlic, J. (2003) *The Neighbors Respond*. Princeton, NJ: Princeton University Press.

Praeg, L. (2007) *The Geometry of Violence: Africa, Girard, Modernity*. Stellenbosch, SA: Sun Press.

Presdee, M. (2000) *The Carnival of Crime*. London: Routledge.

Pridemore, W.A. (2005) 'Social structure and homicide in post-Soviet Russia', *Social Science Research*, 34: 732–56.

Pridemore, W.A. (2008) 'A methodological addition to the cross-national empirical literature on social structure and homicide: a first test of the poverty–homicide thesis', *Criminology*, 46 (1): 133–54.

Procter, R. (1988) *Racial Hygiene: Medicine Under the Nazis*. Cambridge, MA: Harvard University Press.

PSNI (Police Service of Northern Ireland) (2009) *Annual Statistical Report No. 3: Hate Incidents and Crimes 1 April 2008 – 31 March 2009*. Belfast: PSNI.

Radford, J. and Stanko, E. A. (1996) 'Violence against women and children: the contradictions of crime control under patriarchy', in M. Hester, L. Kelly and J. Radford (eds), *Women, Violence and Male Power: Feminist Activism, Research and Practice*. Buckingham: Open University Press, pp. 65–80.

Radford, J., Kelly, L. and Hester, M. (1996) 'Introduction', in M. Hester, L. Kelly and J. Radford (eds), *Women, Violence and Male Power: Feminist Activism, Research and Practice*. Buckingham: Open University Press, pp. 1–18.

Raghavan, C., Mennerich, A., Sexton, E. and James, S.E. (2006) 'Community violence and its direct, indirect, and mediating effects on intimate partner violence', *Violence Against Women*, 12 (12): 1132–49.

Ray, L.J. (2007a) 'From postmodernity to liquid modernity: what's in a metaphor?', in A. Elliott (ed.), *The Contemporary Bauman*. London: Routledge, pp. 63–80.

Ray, L.J. (2007b) *Globalization and Everyday Life*. London: Routledge.

Ray, L.J. and Smith, D. (2004) 'Racist offending, policing and community conflict' *Sociology*, 38 (3): 681–99.

Ray, L.J., Smith, D. and Wastell, E. (2003) 'Understanding racist violence', in E.A. Stanko (ed.), *The Meanings of Violence*. London: Routledge, pp. 112–29.

Ray, L.J., Smith, D. and Wastell, E. (2004) 'Shame, rage and racist violence', *British Journal of Criminology*, 44: 350–68.

Robb, J. (1997) 'Violence and gender in early Italy', in D.L. Martin and D.W. Frayer (eds), *Violence and Warfare in the Past*. Amsterdam: Gordon and Breach, pp. 111–44.

Rock, P. (2002) 'On becoming a victim', in C. Hoyle and R. Wilson (eds) *New Visions of Crime Victims*. Hart Publishing: Oxford, pp. 1–22.

Roscoe, P. (2007) 'Intelligence, coalitional killing and the antecedents of war', *American Anthropologist*, 109 (3): 485–95.

Rosen, A. (2003) *The Transformation of British Life, 1950–2000: A Social History*. Manchester: Manchester University Press.

Rousseau, E. (1968) *The Social Contract*. Harmondsworth: Penguin. (First published 1762.)

Sahlins, M. (1974) *Stone Age Economics*. London: Tavistock.

Sampson, R.J. and Raudenbush, S. (1999) 'Systematic social observation of public spaces: a new look at disorder in urban neighborhoods', *American Journal of Sociology*, 105: 603–51.

Sanderson, S. (1995) *Social Transformations*. Oxford: Blackwell.

Sassen, S. (2002) 'Globalization and its discontents', in J. Bridge and S. Watson (eds), *The Blackwell City Reader*. Oxford: Blackwell, pp. 161–70.

Savolainen, J. (2000) 'Inequality, welfare state, and homicide: further support for the institutional anomie theory', *Criminology*, 38 (4): 1021–42.

Saw, A. (2002) 'Violence as a reclamation of masculinity in the postmodern moment'. Available at: http://xroads.virginia.edu/~MA02/freed/fightclub/masviol.html.

Schatz, T. (2004) 'Introduction', in S.J. Schneider (ed.), *New Holywood Violence*. Manchester: Manchester University Press, pp. 1–10.

Scheff, T.J. (1997) *Emotions, the Social Bond, and Human Reality*. Cambridge: Cambridge University Press.

Scheff, T. J. (2000a) 'Shame and the social bond: a sociological theory', *Sociological Theory*, 18 (1): 84–99.

Scheff, T.J. (2000b) *Bloody Revenge: Emotions, Nationalism and War*. Lincoln, NE: Authors' Guild.

Scheff, T.J. (2001) 'Shame and community: social components in depression', *Psychiatry: Interpersonal & Biological Processes*, 64 (3): 212–24.

Scheff, T.J. (2006) 'Hypermasculinity and violence as a social system'. Available at: www.uni.edu/universitas/fall06/pdf/art_scheff.pdf.

Scheff, T.J. and Retzinger, S.M. (2001) *Emotions and Violence: Shame and Rage in Destructive Conflicts*. Lexington, MA: Lexington Books.

Schinkel, W. (2004) 'The will to violence', *Theoretical Criminology*, 8 (5): 5–31.

Schinkel, W. (2010) *Aspects of Violence: A Critical Theory*. London: Macmillan.

Schneider, D.J. (2005) 'The psychology of violence', Scientia Lecture. Available at: http://webcast.rice.edu/index.php?action=details&event=400.

Schrock, D.P. and Padavic, I. (2007) 'Negotiating hegemonic masculinity in a batterer intervention program', *Gender and Society*, 21 (5): 625–49.

Schwerhoff, G. (2002) 'Criminalized violence and the process of civilisation: a reappraisal', *Crime, Histoire & Sociétés/Crime, History & Societies*. Available at: http://chs.revues.org/index418.html.

Segal, L. (1990) *Slow Motion: Changing Masculinities, Changing Men*. New Brunswick, NJ: Rutgers University Press.

Shaw, C.R. and McKay, H.D. (1969) *Juvenile Delinquency and Urban Areas*. Chicago: University of Chicago Press.

Shaw, M. (2002) *War and Genocide: Organized Killing in Modern Society*. Oxford: Polity Press.

Shaw, M., Tunstall, H. and Dorling, D. (2005) 'Increasing inequalities in the risk of murder in Britain: trends in the demographic and spatial distribution of murder, 1981–2000', *Health Place*, 11 (1): 45–54.

Sherman, L.W. (1995) 'Hot spots of crime and criminal careers of places', in J. Eck and D. Weisburd (eds), *Crime and Place*. Crime Prevention Studies 4. New York: Willow Tree Press, pp. 35–52.

Sherman, L.W., Gartin, P.R. and Buerger, M.E. (1989) 'Hot spots of predatory crime: routine activities and the criminology of place', *Criminology*, 27 (1): 27–55.

Shilling, C. (2005) *The Body and Social Theory*. London: Sage.

Sibbitt, R. (1997) *The Perpetrators of Racial Harassment and Racial Violence*. London: Home Office.

Siebel, W. and Wehrheim, J. (2006) 'Security and the urban public sphere', *German Policy Studies*, 3 (1): 19–46.

Simon, B. (2005) 'The return of panopticisism: supervision, subjection and the new surveillance', *Surveillance and Society*, 3 (1): 1–20.

Slaughter, P. (2003) 'Of crowds, crimes and carnivals', in R. Matthews and J. Young (eds), *The New Politics of Crime and Punishment*. Collompton: Willan Publishing, pp. 178–98.

Slocum, J.D. (2005) 'Cinema and the civilizing process: rethinking violence in the World War II combat film', *Cinema Journal*, 44 (3): 35–63.

Smith, D. (1999) 'The civilizing process and the history of sexuality: comparing Norbert Elias and Michel Foucault', *Theory and Society*, 28: 79–100.

Smith, D., McVie, S., Woodward, R., Shute, J., Flint, J. and McAra, L. (2001) *The Edinburgh Study of Youth Transitions and Crime: Key Findings at Ages 12 and 13*. Edinburgh: University of Edinburgh, Centre for Law and Society. Available at: www.law.ed.ac.uk/cls/esytc/findings/findreport/chapter1.pdf.

Snider, L. (1998) 'Towards safer societies: punishment, masculinities and violence against women', *The British Journal of Criminology*, 38 (1): 1–39.

Soja, E.W. (2000) *Postmetropolis: Critical Studies of Cities and Regions*. Oxford: Blackwell.

Sowell, T. (1990) *Preferential Policies: An International Perspective*. New York: William Morrow.

Spaaij, R. (2008) 'Men like us, boys like them: violence, masculinity, and collective identity in football hooliganism', *Journal of Sport and Social Issues*, 32 (4): 369–92.

Spierenburg, P. (1994) 'Faces of violence: homicide trends and cultural meanings: Amsterdam, 1431–1816', *Journal of Social History*, 27 (4): 701–16.

Spierenburg, P. (2004) 'Punishment, power, and history: Foucault and Elias', *Social Science History*, 28 (4): 607–36.

Spierenburg, P. (2006) 'Democracy came too early: a tentative explanation for the problem of American homicide', *American Historical Review*, 111 (1): 104–14.

Stanko, E.A. (2001) 'Violence', in E. McLaughton and J. Munie (eds), *The Sage Dicitionary of Criminology*. London: Sage.

Steffensmeier, D., Schwartz, J., Zhong, H. and Ackerman, J. (2005) 'An assessment of recent trends in girls' violence using diverse longitudinal sources: is the gender gap closing?', *Criminology*, 43 (2): 355–406.

Stewart, J. and Strathern, A. (2002) *Violence: Theory and Ethnography*. New York and London: Continuum Publishing for Athlone Press.

Straus, M.A. and Gelles, R.J. (1990) *Physical Violence in American Families*. New Brunswick, NJ: Transaction Publications.

Stretesky, P.B., Schuck, A.M. and Hogan, M.J. (2004) 'Space matters: an analysis of poverty, poverty clustering, and violent crime', *Justice Quarterly*, 21: 817–41.

Sussman, R.W. (1999) 'The myth of man the hunter, man the killer and the evolution of human morality', *Zygon*, 32 (3): 453–71.

Sutherland, E., Cressey, D. R. and Luckenbill, D. (1939/1992) *Principles of Criminology*. Lanham, MD: Rowman Alta Mira.

Sznaider, N. (2000) *The Compassionate Temperament: Care and Cruelty in Modern Society*. Lanham, MD and Oxford: Rowman & Littlefield.

Taylor, I., Walton, P. and Young, J. (1975) *Critical Criminology*. London: Routledge & Kegan Paul.

Terry, P.C. and Jackson, J.J. (1985) 'The determinants and control of violence in sport', *Quest*, 37 (1): 27–37.

Thome, H. (2001) 'Explaining long-term trends in violent crime', *European Journal of Sociology*, 5 (2): 69–86.

Thome, H. (2007) 'Explaining the long-term trend in violent crime: a heuristic scheme and some methodological considerations', *International Journal of Conflict and Violence*, 1 (2): 185–202.

Tita, G. (2008) 'Mapping gang rivalries: exploring the spatial distribution of gang violence'. Available at: http://geodacenter.asu.edu/talks/tita.

Tittle, C. R. (2000) 'Theoretical developments in criminology', *Criminal Justice*, 1: 51–101.

Tombs, S. (2007) 'Violence, safety crimes and criminology', *British Journal of Criminology*, 47: 531–55.

Tomsen, S. (2001) 'Hate crimes and masculinity: new crimes, new responses and some familiar patterns'. Paper presented to the 4th Outlook Symposium on Crime in Australia at the Australian Institute of Criminology, Canberra. Available at: www.aic.gov.au/conferences/outlook4/Tomsen.pdf.

Tonso, K.L. (2009) 'Violent masculinities as tropes for school shooters: the Montreal massacre, the Colombine attack and rethinking schools', *American Behavioral Scientist*, 52 (9): 1227–45.

Topalli, V. (2006) 'The seductive nature of autotelic crime: how neutralization theory serves as boundary condition for understanding hardcore street offending', *Sociological Inquiry*, 76 (4): 475–501.

Turk, A.T. (1991) 'Review: seductions of criminology: Katz on magical meanness and other distractions', *Law & Social Inquiry*, 16 (1): 181–94.

Turner, B.S. (2003) 'Warrior charisma and the spiritualization of violence', *Body & Society*, 9 (4): 93–108.

Turner, J.H. (2007) 'Self, emotions and extreme violence: extending the symbolic interactionist theorizing', *Symbolic Interaction*, 30 (3): 501–30.

Vaughan, B. (2000) 'The civilizing process and the Janus-face of modern punishment', *Theoretical Criminology*, 4 (1): 71–91.

Vetlesen, A.J. (2005) *Evil and Human Agency*. Cambridge: Cambridge University Press.

Wacquant, L. (1998) 'Inside the zone: the social art of the hustler in the black American ghetto', *Theory, Culture and Society*, 15 (2): 1–36.

Wacquant, L. (2004) 'Decivilizing and demonizing: the weakening of the black American ghetto', in S. Loyal and S. Quilley (eds), *The Sociology of Norbert Elias*. Cambridge: Cambridge University Press, pp. 95–121.

Walby, S. and Allen, J. (2004) *Domestic Violence, Sexual Assault and Stalking: Findings from the British Crime Survey*. Home Office Research Study 276. London: Home Office, Research Development and Statistics Directorate. Available at: www.rds.homeoffice.gov.uk/rds/pdfs04/hors276.pdf.

Walker, P. (2001) 'A bioarchaeological perspective on the history of violence', *Annual Review of Anthropology*, 30: 573–96.

Walklate, S. (ed.) (2007) *Handbook of Victims and Victimology*. Cullompton: Willan Publishing.

Walks, R.A. (2001) 'The social ecology of the post-Fordist/global city? Economic restructuring and socio-spatial polarization in the Toronto urban region', *Urban Studies*, 38 (3): 407–47.

Warrington, M. (2001) '"I must get out": the geographies of domestic violence', *Transactions of the Institute of British Geographers*, 26: 365–82.

Weber, M. (1974) *Protestant Ethic and the Spirit of Capitalism*. London: Allen & Unwin.

Weber, M. (1978) *Economy and Society* (2 vols) (ed. G. Roth and C. Wittich). Berkeley, CA: University of California Press.

Weisburd, D., Lum, C. and Yang, S.-M. (2004) *Criminal Careers of Places: A Longitudinal Study*. Research report submitted to the U.S. Department of Justice. Available at: www.ncjrs.gov/pdffiles1/nij/grants/207824.pdf.

Wieviorka, M. (1995) *The Arena of Racism*. London: Sage.

Wieviorka, M. (2009) *Violence: A New Approach*. London: Sage.

Wilcox, P., Quisenberry, N., Cabrera, D.T. and Jones, S. (2004) 'Busy places and broken windows? Toward defining the role of physical structure and process in community crime models', *Sociological Quarterly*, 45 (2): 185–207.

Wilkinson, I. (2005) *Suffering: A Sociological Introduction*. Oxford: Polity Press.

Wilkinson, R. and Pickett, K. (2009) *Spirit Level: Why More Equal Societies Almost Always Do Better*. Harmondsworth: Penguin.

Windrum, K. (2004) '*Fight Club* and the political (im)potence of consumer era revolt', in S.J. Schneider (ed.), *New Hollywood Violence*. Manchester: Manchester University Press, pp. 304–17.

Wirth, L. (1938) 'Urbanism as a way of life', *American Journal of Sociology*, 44 (1): 1–24.

Wistrich, R. (1992) *Antisemitism: The Longest Hatred*. London: Thames Mandarin.

Wolfe, T. (1976) 'Pornoviolence', in T. Wolfe, *Mauve Gloves & Madmen*. Place: New York: Clutter & Vine Farr, Straus and Giroux, pp. 164–172.

Wolfgang, M.E. and Ferracuti, F. (1967) *The Subculture of Violence: Towards an Integrated Theory in Criminology*. London: Tavistock.

Women's Aid (2009) 'Statistics: domestic violence'. Available at: www.womensaid.org.uk/ domestic_violence_topic.asp?section=0001000100220036&sectionTitle=Statistics.

Wooldredge, J. and Thistlethwaite, A. (2003) 'Neighborhood structure and race-specific rates of intimate assault', *Criminology*, 41 (2): 393–422.

World Factbook (2009) *The World Factbook 2009*. Washington, DC: Central Intelligence Agency, www.cia.gov/library/publications/the-world-factbook/index.html.

Wouters, C. (2007) *Informaliztion, Manners and Emotions since 1890*. London: Sage.

Wrangham, R. and Peterson, D. (1996) *Demonic Males: Apes and the Origins of Human Violence*. Boston, MA: Houghton Mifflin.

Young, J. (1975) 'Working class criminology', in I. Taylor, P. Walton and J. Young (eds), *Critical Criminology*. London: Routledge & Kegan Paul, pp. 63–94.

Young, J. (2003) 'Merton with energy, Katz with structure: the sociology of vindictiveness and the criminology of transgression', *Theoretical Criminology*, 7 (3): 389–414.

Youth Justice Board (2009) *Girls and Offending: Patterns, Perceptions and Interventions*. London: Youth Justice Board. Available at: www.yjb.gov.uk/publications/Resources/ Downloads/Girls_offending_fullreport.pdf

Zahn, M.A. and McCall, P. (1999) 'Trends and patterns of homicide in the 20th century United States', in M.D. Smith and M.A. Zahn (eds), *Homicide: A Sourcebook of Social Research*. Thousand Oaks, CA: Sage, pp. 9–23.

Zhang, H. and Peterson, P. (2007) 'A spatial analysis of neighborhood crime in Omaha, Nebraska using alternative measures of crime rates', *International Journal of Criminology*. Available at: www.internetjournalofcriminology.com/Zhang%20Peterson%20-%20A%20 SPATIAL%20ANALYSIS%20OF%20NEIGHBOURHOOD%20CRIME.pdf.

Zimring, F.E. and Hawkins, G. (1999) *Crime is not the Problem: Lethal Violence in America*. New York: Oxford University Press.

Žižek, S. (2008) *Violence*. London: Profile Books.

Zylinska, J. (2007) 'Who is my neighbour: ethics under duress', in D. Glowacka and J. Zylinska (eds), *Imaginary Neighbors: Mediating Polish–Jewish Relations after the Holocaust*. Lincoln, NB: University of Nebraska Press, pp. 275–300.

INDEX

Heavy type indicates main reference